US Strategy in Africa

This book critically examines the construction, interpretations and understanding of US strategy towards Africa in the early twenty-first century.

No single issue or event in the recent decades in Africa has provoked so much controversy, unified hostility and opposition as the announcement by former President George W. Bush of the establishment of the United States Africa Command – AFRICOM. The intensity and sheer scale of the unprecedented unity of opposition to AFRICOM across Africa surprised many experts and led them to ask why such a hostile reaction occurred.

This book explores the conception of AFRICOM and the subsequent reaction in two ways. First, the contributors critically engage with the creation and global imperatives for the establishment of AFRICOM and present an analytical outline of African security in relation to and within the context of the history of US foreign and security policy approaches to Africa. Second, the book has original chapter contributions by some of the key actors involved in the development and implementation of the AFRICOM project including Theresa Whelan, the former US Deputy Assistant Secretary for African Affairs. This is not only an attempt to contribute to the academic and policy-relevant debates based on the views of those who are intimately involved in the design and implementation of the AFRICOM project but also to show, in their own words, that 'America has no clandestine agenda for Africa', a view that does not seem to be shared by the majority of political leaders in Africa.

This book will be of interest to students of US foreign policy/national security, strategic studies, international security and African politics.

David J. Francis is Professorial Chair of African Peace and Conflict Studies in the Department of Peace Studies at the University of Bradford.

Routledge global security studies

Series editors: Aaron Karp, Regina Karp and Terry Terriff

US Strategy in Africa

AFRICOM, terrorism and security challenges

Edited by David J. Francis

Routledge
Taylor & Francis Group

LONDON AND NEW YORK

First published 2010
by Routledge
2 Park Square, Milton Park, Abingdon, Oxon OX14 4RN

Simultaneously published in the USA and Canada
by Routledge
711 Third Avenue, New York, NY 10017

Routledge is an imprint of the Taylor & Francis Group, an informa business

© First issued in paperback 2011

© 2010 Selection and editorial matter, David J. Francis; individual
chapters, the contributors

Typeset in Times by Wearset Ltd, Boldon, Tyne and Wear

All rights reserved. No part of this book may be reprinted or reproduced or
utilised in any form or by any electronic, mechanical, or other means, now
known or hereafter invented, including photocopying and recording, or in
any information storage or retrieval system, without permission in writing
from the publishers.

British Library Cataloguing in Publication Data
A catalogue record for this book is available from the British Library

Library of Congress Cataloging-in-Publication Data
US strategy in Africa: AFRICOM, terrorism, and security challenges/
edited by David J. Francis.
p. cm.
1. United States. Africa Command. 2. United States–Armed Forces–
Africa. 3. Terrorism–Africa–Prevention. 4. Insurgency–Africa–Prevention.
5. United States–Relations–Africa. 6. Africa–Relations–United States.
7. United States–Military policy. 8. Africa–Strategic aspects. I. Francis,
David J. II. Title: U.S. strategy in Africa.
UA855.U77 2010
355′.0310973096–dc22

2009038187

ISBN13: 978-0-415-48510-4 (hbk)
ISBN13: 978-0-203-85530-0 (ebk)
ISBN13: 978-0-415-51001-1 (pbk)

Contents

Illustrations

Abbreviations

ABC	Agencia Brasileira de Cooperação
ACBS	African Coastal and Border Security (programme)
ACOTA	African Contingency Operations Training and Assistance
ACRI	African Crisis Response Initiative
AFRICOM	Africa Command
AFSI	Africa Financial Sector Initiative
AGOA	African Growth and Opportunity Act
AMISON	African Union Mission in Somalia
AOR	area of responsibility
APS	African Partnership Station
APSA	African Peace and Security Architecture
AQIM	Al-Qaeda Organization in the Islamic Maghreb
ASA	Africa–South America Summit
ASACOF	Africa–South America Cooperative Forum
ASF	African Standby Force
ASMEA	Association for the Study of the Middle East and Africa
ATA	Anti-Terrorism Assistance (programme)
AU	African Union
AVTA	Add Value to Agriculture
BADC	Brazilian Agency for Development Cooperation
BMATT	British Military Advisory and Training Teams
CADSP	Common African Defence and Security Policy
CENTCOM	Central Command
CEWARN	Conflict Early Warning and Response Mechanism
CJTF-HOA	Combined Joint Task Force – Horn of Africa
CNOOC	China National Offshore Oil Corporation
CNT	Counter Narcotics and Terrorism
COCOMs	combatant commands
CVRD	Companhia Vale do Rio Doce
DCS	Direct Command Sales (programme)
DDR	disarmament, demobilisation and reintegration
DENCAPs	dental civic action programmes
DoD	Department of Defense

DRC	Democratic Republic of Congo
DRS	Direction des Renseignments et de la Securite
EAC	East African Community
EACTI	East African Counter-Terrorism Initiative
EASBRIG	East African Standby Brigade
EASWIO	East Africa and Southwest Indian Ocean
ECOMOG	ECOWAS Ceasefire Monitoring Group
ECOWAS	Economic Community of West African States
EDA	Excess Defence Articles (programme)
EUCOM	European Command
FAN	Forces Armées Nigériennes
FAO	Food and Agricultural Organisation
FAO	Foreign Area Officer
FAR	Forces Armées Rwandaises
FBI	Federal Bureau of Investigation
FDI	foreign direct investment
FDIC	Federal Deposit Insurance Corporation
FMF	Foreign Military Financing (programme)
FMS	Foreign Military Sales (programme)
FOCAC	Forum on China–Africa Cooperation
GDI	gross domestic income
GDP	gross domestic product
GFLS	Group of Frontline States
GPOI	Global Peace Operations Initiative
GPS	global positioning system
GWOT	Global War on Terror
HASC	House Armed Service Committee
HCA	Humanitarian Civic Assistance
HDI	Human Development Index
IADB	Inter-American Development Bank
IBSA	India, Brazil and South Africa
ICBC	Industrial and Commercial Bank of China
ICC	International Criminal Court
IEHA	Initiative to End Hunger in Africa
IGAD	Intergovernmental Authority on Development
IGADD	Intergovernmental Authority on Drought and Development
ILEA	International Law Enforcement Academy
ILO	International Labour Organisation
IMET	International Military Education and Training (programme)
INCLE	International Narcotics Control and Law Enforcement
JCET	Joint Combined Exchange Training
JCS	Joint Chief of Staff
JIC	Joint Intelligence Centre
JIOC	Joint Intelligence Operations Centre
JTFAS	Joint Task Force Aztec Silence

KAPU	Kenyan Anti-terrorism Police Unit
LANTCOM	Atlantic Command
LDCs	least developed countries
LEAP	Livelihood Empowerment against Poverty
LRA	Lord's Resistance Army
MCA	Millennium Challenge Account
MDGs	Millennium Development Goals
MEDCAPs	medical civic action programmes
MEND	Movement for the Emancipation of the Niger Delta
MNCs	multinational corporations
NAM	Non-Aligned Movement
NATO	North Atlantic Trade Organization
NEPAD	New Partnership in African Development
NEPD	National Energy Policy Development
NGO	non-governmental organization
OAU	Organization of African Unity
ODA	overseas development aid
OECD	Organization for Economic Cooperation and Development
OEF	Operation Enduring Freedom
OEF-TS	Operation Enduring Freedom-TransSahara
OHDACA	Overseas Humanitarian Disaster and Civic Aid
ONLF	Ogaden National Liberation Front
PACOM	Pacific Command
PDD	Presidential Decision Directive
PEPFAR	President's Emergency Plan for AIDS Relief
PMCs	private military companies
PNAC	Project for the New American Century
PPP	purchasing power parity
PRC	People's Republic of China
PSC	Peace and Security Council
PSI	Pan-Sahel Initiative
QDR	Quadrennial Defense Review
REDCOM	Readiness Command
RPA	Rwandan Patriotic Front/Army
SACEUR	Supreme Allied Command Europe
SADC	Southern African Development Community
SADCC	Southern African Development Coordination Conference
SOCEUR	Special Operations Command Europe
SPP	State Partnership Program
SSR	security sector reform
STRICOM	Strike Command
TIP	Terrorism Interdiction Programme
TSCTI	Trans-Sahara Counter-Terrorism Initiative
TSCTP	Trans-Sahara Counter-Terrorism Program
TSOC	Theatre Special Operations Command

UAE	United Arab Emirates
UBA	United Bank for Africa
UCP	Unified Command Plan
UNDP	United Nations Development Programme
UNHCR	United Nations High Commission for Refugees
UNITAF	Unified Task Force
UNSC	UN Security Council
USAID	United States Agency for International Development
VETCAPs	veterinary civic action programmes
VSAT	Very Small Aperture Terminal
WFP	World Food Programme
WMD	weapons of mass destruction
WTO	World Trade Organization

Contributors

David J. Francis is Professorial Chair of African Peace and Conflict Studies in the Department of Peace Studies at the University of Bradford.

Theresa Whelan is the Deputy Assistant Secretary of Defence for Homeland Defence Domains and Defence Support to Civil Authorities in the Government of the United States of America. Until May 2009, Ms Whelan was the Deputy Assistant Secretary of Defence for African Affairs.

Daniel Volman is Director of the African Security Research Project in Washington, DC.

J. Peter Pham is Director of the Nelson Institute for International and Public Affairs at James Madison University in Harrisonburg, Virginia and Associate Professor of Justice Studies, Political Science and Africana Studies.

M.A. Mohamed Salih is Professorial Chair of Politics of Development at the Institute of Social Studies at The Hague and at the Department of Political Science at the University of Leiden, the Netherlands.

Shannon Beebe is Senior Africa Analyst in the US Department of Army, Department of Defense.

Jeremy Keenan is Professorial Research Associate in the Department of Anthropology and Sociology, School of Oriental and African Studies (SOAS) at the University of London.

Thomas Kwasi Tieku is Head of the African Studies Program in the Department of Political Science at New College at the University of Toronto.

David Chuter is a consultant and a London-based policy analyst.

Josephine Osikena is Programme Director for Democracy and International Development at the London-based Foreign Policy Centre.

Part I

AFRICOM and US security policy in Africa

1   Introduction

AFRICOM – US strategic interests and African security

David J. Francis

No single issue or event in the recent decades in Africa has provoked so much controversy and unified hostility and opposition as the announcement by former President George W. Bush, on 7 February 2007, of the establishment of the United Stated Africa Command (AFRICOM). The intensity and sheer scale of the unprecedented unity of opposition to AFRICOM across Africa surprised even experienced experts and pundits on Africa. Why this hostility to AFRICOM? Is the real purpose and intention of AFRICOM simply misunderstood? Are criticisms of the latest efforts by the United States to develop a consistent and long-term structural engagement with Africa by creating a new unified geographic combatant command for Africa a broader manifestation of the growing anti-American sentiments dominant during the Bush presidency, and partly a product of the US-led wars in Afghanistan and Iraq, as well as its Global War on Terror (GWOT)? President Bush announced the establishment of AFRICOM thus:

> Today, I am pleased to announce my decision to create a Department of Defence Unified Combatant Command for Africa. I have directed the Secretary of Defence to stand up US Africa Command by the end of the fiscal year 2008. We will be consulting with African leaders to seek their thoughts on how Africa Command can respond to security challenges and opportunities in Africa. We will work closely with African partners to determine an appropriate location for the new command in Africa.[1]

The focus of the President's announcement of the stand up of a unified combatant command for Africa immediately sparked off a controversial debate and international media frenzy about two core issues: the perception of a lack of consultation and the location of the military command in Africa. Based on the President's announcement, it is generally assumed that AFRICOM was designed and established without consultation with African partners, hence the inevitable unified opposition and hostility across the continent. But this latest US approach to establish a unified geographic combatant command for Africa and then try to secure consultation with African partners is not different from other traditional US military and security projects developed and prescribed for the continent. In addition, introducing the issue of 'location' of the military command also inevitably overshadowed and detracted attention from the central debate about the purpose and objectives of AFRICOM, as well as its potential benefits for Africa.

To be clear, AFRICOM's core objectives and mission statement are at the heart of the critical challenges faced by post-Cold War Africa around the issues of peace, stability, security, development and governance. The four core objectives of AFRICOM include: bolstering security and stability in Africa; improving cooperative security and partnership between US and African states in the effort to address transnational terrorism; and developing and sustaining enduring efforts that contribute to African peace, security and unity by focusing on capacity building to prevent, rather than fight, wars. AFRICOM's mission statement states that

> United States Africa Command, in concert with other US government agencies and international partners, conducts sustained security engagement through military-to-military programs, military-sponsored activities, and other military operations as directed to promote a stable and secure African environment in support of US foreign policy.[2]

AFRICOM is thus oriented towards preventing conflicts and is designed as a new US approach to responding to security challenges in Africa and, according to Theresa Whelan, the former US Deputy Assistant Secretary of Defence for African Affairs, to 'prevent problems from becoming crises, and crises from becoming catastrophes' (see Chapter 2). In essence, AFRICOM focuses on both traditional military and security issues as well as non-traditional security sources of threats and challenges, but crucially facilitated and implemented through a military structure.

If this is the case, i.e. that AFRICOM is essentially about African security rather than US strategic interests in Africa, then why did the establishment of the unified combatant command for Africa generate such widespread and unified opposition across the continent? Most of the criticism and controversy surrounding the establishment and operations of AFRICOM have focused on the potential negative impact and implications of the unified command located in Africa, treating it as if it were a single and straightforward issue. Francois Furet aptly draws our attention to the fact that 'an event, if considered in isolation, is unintelligible.... For it to acquire significance, it must be integrated into the pattern of other events, in relation to which it will become meaningful.'[3] By all indications, AFRICOM raises fundamental and broader issues pertinent to international and African security, US foreign and security policy, the role of the United States as the dominant hegemonic power in a unipolar world challenged by an uncertain global security environment. If anything, explanatory variables such as history, strategic national interests, economics and geo-politics are at the core of the creation of AFRICOM as a foreign and security policy approach to Africa.

The establishment of AFRICOM represents a fundamental shift in the US policy approach to Africa because, for more than four decades, US relations and responsibility for the continent have been shared by three government departments including the Pentagon/Department of Defense (DoD), the State Department and US International Agency for Development (USAID), as well as three separate military commands, i.e. European Command (EUCOM), Central Command (CENTCOM) and Pacific Command (PACOM). AFRICOM therefore creates a single and unified command for US foreign and security relations with Africa. But the decision to establish AFRICOM and locate on the continent has provoked intense debate and speculations about the intentions, motivations and capabilities of the AFRICOM project in Africa. The popular opposition to the location of AFRICOM command in Africa has been led by civil society organisations, African regional economic and political organisations such as the Southern Africa Development Community (SADC), the African Union (AU) and leading African governments. In November 2007, President Shehu Musa Yaradua of Nigeria publicly stated that he will oppose the location of AFRICOM headquarters in West Africa, in direct opposition to the confirmation by President Helen Johnson-Sirleaf of Liberia, who had offered to host AFRICOM headquarters. The popular criticisms against AFRICOM and its location have primarily, and sometimes uncritically, focused on the perception that the unified command amounts to a militarisation of US foreign policy in Africa, that the command will be used as a Trojan horse to achieve US strategic interests and objectives on the continent – in particular, the possibility of using AFRICOM as an instrument to effect regime change and/or prop up brutal dictatorships and unpopular regimes amenable to US strategic interests in Africa. There are serious concerns amongst diverse actors and stakeholders in Africa that AFRICOM will be used to militarily dictate policies in pursuit of US strategic interests and to impose an American version of democracy on the continent.

It is therefore not surprising that President Bush's visit to Africa on 17–22 February 2007, just after announcing the stand up of AFRICOM, included three key West African states, demonstrating the growing strategic importance of the volatile sub-region and its threat to global security: Benin (maritime security and piracy issues); Ghana (the region's new oil producer and major political player); and Liberia (the only country that offered to host AFRICOM). A simple analysis of most of the criticisms about AFRICOM in African newspapers and other electronic media sources reveal that most of the concerns have to do with the perception that AFRICOM is simply an attempt to expand a new front of the War on Terror and to combat terrorism in Africa. AFRICOM is therefore seen as a new military command post for the 'American empire'. There is also the perception that it will inevitably set up Africa as a target for terrorists, citing the terrorist bombings of the US embassies in Kenya and Tanzania in 1998 as justification for this concern. According to one senior senator in Liberia, 'Terrorists follow America where ever they go.'[4] This view is further reinforced by the comments of a taxi driver in the West African state of Benin: 'Having the US here would help us but it could bring terrorists.'[5]

But it is important to put this in perspective. The US military has operated in the Gulf of Guinea and has a military base in Djibouti. These US military operations and base have not attracted the much-touted influx of terrorists. However, AFRICOM headquarters located on the continent, no doubt, are a symbol and icon of US power and dominant influence in Africa – a powerful attraction for terrorist activities. It is this concern about terrorist interest in Africa through the presence of AFRICOM that has agitated the majority of people on the continent.

Furthermore, media commentators, policy practitioners and academics argue that AFRICOM is an attempt to counter China's growing influence in Africa in that AFRICOM is a strategic military and diplomatic attempt to counter and contain China's growing interest in the region. Some observers perceive China's increasing role in the continent as a threat to US strategic interests, in particular, its energy security, based on the view that China's trade and commerce with Africa in 2006 alone was US$50 billion, and Africa now supplies one-third of China's crude oil imports. In effect, China has provided an alternative bilateral funding framework for cash-strapped African governments without the usual restrictions and conditions imposed by Western governments and global governance institutions such as the IMF and World Bank. The main concern is that this predatory capitalist competition between two major powers for African resources will not only negatively affect the continent, but will mark a return to the Cold War politics of confrontation and propping up 'friendly' regimes. In effect, this so-called 'battle of the giants' and the new scramble for the continent's natural resources is not in the interest of African security. The most critical voices have focused on the view that AFRICOM is a strategic attempt to protect the oil and energy security of the United States. According to Swart, 'West Africa is increasingly becoming important to the world's energy supplies even as the region remains under threat from lawlessness and piracy.'[6] West Africa and the Gulf of Guinea have emerged as major players in global energy security, exporting more oil to the United States than does the unstable Persian Gulf region. For example, Nigeria, a leading oil producer, supplies about 15 per cent of US oil, but violence (Niger Delta region) and political instability affects oil production. This unstable and volatile security situation has led to more investment by multinational corporations (MNCs) to increase oil production and US military presence to police the criminalised states in the region. Therefore, AFRICOM is perceived as the instrument to protect and secure US energy security.

Despite the international media hype about the unified criticisms against AFRICOM, it is easy to conjecture that the fundamental opposition to the creation of the unified command is primarily a reflection of the concerns about the history of the US government's role, predatory capitalist and geo-strategic activities in Africa, in particular the negative international perceptions about President Bush's wars in Afghanistan and Iraq. In effect, the history of the negative perception of US foreign and security policies and covert interventions to prop up brutal dictators and overthrow populist legitimate regimes in Africa (e.g. Patrice Lumumba of Congo) seems to have clouded the perceptions of the purpose and motivations of AFRICOM. But this negative perception fails to explain the estimated US$9 billion spent by the Bush administration on development, humanitarian relief and health issues in Africa, as against the US$250 million per annum spent on security and military issues on the continent. These figures show a significant financial commitment of the Bush administration to non-military issues in Africa in the pursuit of US foreign and security policy engagement with the continent.

Furthermore, the controversy generated by the creation of AFRICOM and its location on the continent has simply being cast in terms of African security versus pursuit of US strategic interests, i.e. how the perceptions of and the nature, dynamics and complexity of African security contradicts with US strategic national interests in Africa. Academics and intellectuals further cast the creation of AFRICOM as an imposition of a particular version of a liberal peace project to protect, or as in the service of the American empire, in that AFRICOM represents the construction and homogenisation of a particular version of security in Africa, i.e. military security (see Chapters 5, 6 and 8). According to this view, it is this hegemonic construction of security that has framed the debates on security in Africa in relation to the creation of AFRICOM, whereby African security is now defined and constructed according to Western (i.e. the United States') interests, values, norms, expectations and policy preferences which are embedded in the dominant economic, political, cultural and intellectual preferences and interests. The debate (largely conducted at conferences and universities, or in print media and policy circles) has primarily focused on the negative aspects of AFRICOM, with little effort to critically engage with the opportunities for understanding and addressing the underlying causes and drivers of insecurity in Africa, such as poverty, disease, corruption, political repression and widespread under-development.

In addition, the design and implementation of AFRICOM seem not to have taken into consideration existing proposals developed by the AU as part of its new continental architecture for peace and security, such as the African Standby Force (ASF) for peacekeeping and conflict management (see Chapter 8). The evolving peace and security framework of the AU has divided Africa into five combat-ready rapid deployment regional standby forces, including NASBRIG (North Africa); EASBRIG (East Africa); ECOBRIG (West Africa); FOMAC (Central Africa) and SADCBRIG (Southern Africa). Though the AFRICOM commander, General William Ward, and Theresa Whelan have confirmed the importance of partnership with African regional organisations in achieving its objectives and mandate and, in the words of Theresa Whelan, 'US intervention under AFRICOM would be in partnership with regional actors', it is clear that the development and operations of AFRICOM will not only potentially conflict with the mandate of the ASF, but also duplicate their operational activities.

Against the background of the unified opposition to the location of AFRICOM on the continent, and in an attempt to limit the damage to the image of the newly created unified combatant command for Africa, during his Africa tour on 18 February 2008, President Bush announced a major policy shift in that the AFRICOM headquarters will no longer be located in Africa, but will remain in Stuttgart, Germany, where the EUCOM headquarters is located.[7] The Pentagon centralisation @ the cost of militarisation?

has now settled for a 'distributed command', with five AFRICOM regional centres in Africa in an attempt to limit the visibility of AFRICOM on the continent. This was a rare 'victory' for Africa and a major challenge to the US stranglehold on the continent, demonstrating that Africa has come of age and could no longer be taken for granted in the post-Cold War era. A glimpse of the frustrations in US policy circles about the unified hostility to AFRICOM and its location in Africa could be seen in the statement of Theresa Whelan when she warned African states that 'If Africa does not accept AFRICOM then the United States will sever its military-to-military defence relations with the continent.'

Notwithstanding, not everyone in Africa has been hostile to the creation and location of AFRICOM on the continent, and public opinion has been divided across Africa about the motivations and capabilities of the unified command on the continent. Based on field research, there is some agreement amongst policy practitioners, militaries and governments on merits of the opportunities that AFRICOM will bring in building the capacity for African states to prevent wars and maintain security and stability, thereby creating an environment conducive to governance, foreign direct investments and long-term development. Those involved in development, humanitarian relief and conflict interventions in Africa are positive about AFRICOM, because it represents a framework for a joined-up government/inter-agency single coordination of US policy relations with the 53 states of Africa. According to this view, AFRICOM will centralise US government relations with Africa, hitherto shared by three departments and three military commands. This joined-up government approach will hopefully lead to a more focused, coherent, coordinated, consistent and predictable response to crisis situations in Africa. It is suggested that a single command will make it easier to respond to humanitarian crises in complex political emergencies in Africa. Though there has been the practice of joint inter-agency task forces based on necessity and improvisation, AFRICOM provides the unique opportunity for a more 'permanent and single' US agency for African military and security affairs. In addition, AFRICOM is perceived as an important opportunity to develop and strengthen peacekeeping capacity building of African armies and regional economic communities (RECs) such as ECOWAS and its military wing ECOMOG, SADC, IGAD and the AU's regional standby forces. Those involved in African and regional peacekeeping deployments and conflict management interventions perceive AFRICOM as potentially a support structure for 'African Solutions to African Problems', through provision of education, training, joint exercises, professionalism, equipment, logistical support and financial resources. There is a view amongst African militaries and regional organisations that AFRICOM will lead to the expansion of the State Department's African Contingency Operations Training and Assistance (ACOTA) programme within an interdepartmental framework of the US government. Additionally, that it will provide an opportunity for co-deployment peacekeeping between AFRICOM and African regional organisations such as ECOWAS and ECOMOG.

The private sector and, in particular, the economic and commercial actors and operatives have been the most vocal supporters for the location of AFRICOM on the continent because they equate American military presence in Africa with the provision of security and stability – the essential ingredients for business to thrive and attract foreign direct investments. The view is that the presence of foreign American military bases in different parts of the world has served as a guarantor in these countries for peace, security and stable political order, thereby making it possible for long-term economic development and social progress. In fact, the private economic sector in countries emerging from war and other transition states such as Liberia have supported the location of AFRICOM on the continent purely for the putative economic benefits and the potential neo-patrimonial resources AFRICOM will generate for the ruling and governing elites.

But is AFRICOM a paradigm shift in US foreign and security relations with Africa? Some analysts argue that though establishing a unified command for Africa is new, the focus, purpose, strategic motivations and operational activities are not fundamentally different from the traditional US foreign and security policy approach and engagement with Africa, in that the core objectives of AFRICOM are a mere expansion of the traditional military and non-military foreign and security policy priorities in Africa (see the arguments presented in the chapters by Daniel Volman, J. Peter Pham and Jeremy Keenan). Sceptics point to the fact that, historically, AFRICOM is nothing new because it has been in the making for nearly two decades. Rather than a paradigm shift in US foreign policy engagement with Africa, the unified command is simply a re-orientation of US strategic priorities as a strategy to cope with and respond to the ever-increasing global security threats and challenges such as energy security, pursing the GWOT and the stiff competition from China for access to and control over African natural resources. Therefore, Isike *et al.* posit that there is

> scepticism around the 'real' national security interests and strategic economic motives of the US in this latest foreign policy onslaught on Africa – especially in view of the dissonance between US strategic security concerns on the continent and the issues that constitute the African security predicament.[8]

However, some scholars and policy practitioners disagree and argue that AFRICOM represents a fundamental shift in US foreign policy approach and strategic engagement with Africa (see Chapter 2). This view is based on the fact that it is the first time the US government has established a unified command for Africa. As such, the strategic military and political relevance of this single act cannot be over-emphasised. It has therefore led to a fundamental internal structural re-organisation of the traditional government agencies responsible for Africa.[9] With the establishment of AFRICOM, US military and security interests in Africa are now coordinated and organised under one centralised administrative command, under the leadership of a four-star general, operating from the designated location and headquarters in Stuttgart. AFRICOM became fully operational on 1 October 2008, taking over all operational and administrative responsibilities previously undertaken by the three separate military commands and government departments.

The fundamental re-orientation of the US strategic approach to Africa is based on the fact that, according to Theresa Whelan, Africa remains 'an ever-increasing strategic significance in today's global security environment'. The sharing of responsibility for Africa by separate military commands and government agencies has historically led to problems and lack of a consistent US approach and engagement with Africa. As Theresa Whelan puts it, 'between 1971 and 1983 no specific command had any responsibility for paying attention to security issues in Africa' (Chapter 2). The sharing of responsibility for Africa amongst commands and departments created problems of coordination and harmonisation of US Africa engagement and inevitably led to a lack of consistent, coherent and sustained focus on Africa. All these problems and challenges inevitably led to the imperative to establish a geographic command for Africa. Therefore, AFRICOM was a 'logical next step on a course set more than a decade ago' (Chapter 2).

Strategic relevance of Africa: history of United States–Africa relations

But what does this say about the strategic relevance of Africa to the United States? In 2000 President Bush famously stated that 'While Africa may be important, it does not fit into the national strategic interests, as far as I can see them.'[10] After 9/11 and the threats to US energy security and the new scramble for Africa's strategic resources by China and the emerging economies in the global South, the Bush administration in 2007 regarded African oil resources as a 'strategic national interest'. But why this contradictory approach to Africa? Africa's importance to US strategic national interests has been a subject of much controversy. But there is general agreement that the relevance of Africa's strategic resources in the international division of labour and power is beyond question and, as such, America is forced to recognise the continent's strategic significance, though with varying degrees of policy focus and long-term engagement. In geo-strategic and demographic terms, Africa is the second largest continent, accounting for 22 per cent of the world's total land mass, with an estimated population of 690 million people – about 14 per cent of the world population. In economic terms, Africa is rich in strategic mineral resources and accounts for an estimated 8 per cent of the world's petroleum resources. The continent's membership of the UN General Assembly and US Security Council through its three African elected memberships gives the continent added political leverage and relevance in international affairs. Therefore, Africa has and will continue to be of strategic relevance to US national interests.

Historically, US foreign, security and military engagement with Africa has been through joint military exercises and training programmes with African militaries; covert military, security and counter-terrorism operations; peacekeeping and peace support operation deployments in Africa's complex political emergencies; and humanitarian relief operations. Therefore, according to Theresa Whelan 'despite this long history of engagement on the continent, the DoD has never focused on Africa with the same level of consistency with which it has focused on the other regions of the world' (Chapter 2). This view is reinforced by Robert Putman, who aptly states that 'Despite historic ties with the continent, US policy towards Africa has generally been marked by indifference and neglect.'[11] But why is this so? Putman's explanation is that US policies towards Africa since the end of the Second World War have been underpinned by the dominant themes of American exceptionalism, the foreign relations of a global hegemon, Cold War strategic interactions with periphery states, the American post-Cold War search for new foreign and security policy purpose and the imperatives of the post-9/11 GWOT.[12] To understand this historic pattern of US indifference and so-called neglect of Africa it is important to outline the context of United States–Africa relations.

The history of US relations with Africa has been marked by four different, but interrelated, phases. The first phase is marked by the Cold War approach, whereby Africa is perceived as a 'pawn' and a battleground to limit or contain USSR and communist/socialist influence and power on the continent by propping up illegal and authoritarian regimes, such as Samuel Doe of Liberia, Mobuto of Zaire and UNITA's Savimbi of Angola. This phase of US 'selective engagement' with Africa was informed by its new doctrine of national security that focused on external threats. This framed the US Cold War Africa policy.[13] In effect, it was not only an anti-communist doctrine of containment, but also a ruse for access to strategic mineral resources. The second phase marks the end of the Cold War and the emergence of the US-led new world order, framed by concerns about under-development and humanitarian issues such as wars and armed conflicts, failed and collapsed states, poverty, HIV/AIDS and environmental catastrophes such as drought and famine and their collective impact on US national security. President Bush Snr's new world order heralded a change in US policy towards Africa. This positive engagement was manifested by the willingness to work with the UN for humanitarian and peacekeeping deployments and the idea that the international community could work together to solve problems in Africa and guarantee freedom, peace and security and promote democracy. The US-led UN-authorised Unified Task Force (UNITAF) deployed in Somalia in 1992–3 was a demonstration of President Bush's new world order policy towards Africa. This in itself was a radical shift in the US Africa policy in the post-Cold War period. The third phase represents the Somalia Syndrome and the retreat from Africa. The US-led UN humanitarian intervention in the Somalia civil war and the death of American soldiers led to the withdrawal of the United States and the subsequent policy retreat from Africa under President Clinton, despite his policy of 'assertive multilateralism' through US–UN co-deployment for humanitarian activities. Presidential Decision Directive (PDD) 25 by President Clinton effectively 'outlawed' US participation in UN peacekeeping operations and unilateral deployments in Africa, except when regarded as being of direct national interest. The Somalia Syndrome had a considerable impact on the retreat of the United States from Africa. The fourth phase represents the post-9/11 security threats and the emergence of Africa as vital to US strategic national interests. The US Africa policy with the dawn of the twenty-first century is marked by a U-turn from retreat to full-scale engagement in that the US could no longer afford to treat the continent as a foreign and security policy 'back water'. The renewal of US strategic engagement with Africa started with the recognition of the international security threats posed by Africa to the US in terms of violent wars and armed conflicts, failed and collapsed states serving as terrorist havens, poverty, under-development and HIV/AIDS. This US Africa policy approach is manifested by programmes such as Clinton's African Growth and Opportunity Act (AGOA) and the African Crisis Response Initiative (ACRI). Both of these programmes and policy intervention approaches to Africa combine traditional military and security issues with humanitarian and development concerns. The small-scale US military deployment in August 2003 during the Liberian civil war marked a definitive break from the Somalia Syndrome. This fundamental shift in US policy towards Africa is based on the view of the 'securitisation of Africa', that is, the continent poses a threat to international peace and security as well as US strategic national interests. The administration of President Bush has therefore expanded the GWOT into Africa by creating counter-terrorism operations such as the Combined Joint Task Force – Horn of Africa (CJTF-HOA) and Pan-Sahel Initiative (PSI), all in an attempt to reduce and eliminate the ability of terrorist organisations to function or carry out activities detrimental to US national interests. These concerns and strategic interests set the context and frame the imperative for the establishment of AFRICOM – a product of the history of United States–Africa relations.

The above analysis shows that United States–Africa relations have not been defined by a single issue nor dominated by a singular approach and have not remained the same for the past six decades. If anything, United States–Africa relations have been marked by periods of selective engagement, neglect, retreat and contradictions. The nature and complexity of US strategic interests in Africa in the post-Cold War era is aptly captured by the report of the Centre for Strategic and International Studies Task Force on the Gulf of Guinea security, which states:

> An exceptional mix of US interests are at play in West Africa's Gulf of Guinea. The region starkly illustrates both the challenges and the promise of the efforts to foster democracy, respect for human rights, poverty alleviation, counterterrorism, regional conflict prevention and peacekeeping, and to curb HIV/AIDS and other infectious diseases, organised crime, corruption, and instability. Also at stake are rising US interests in the region's energy sector, already prominent and set to expand even further in the coming decade. At the same time, many countries in the region are vulnerable to instability and violence, stemming from vast internal disparities in wealth, poor governance, a lack of state capacity, and rising criminality.[14]

This view highlights the nature and complexity of the security threats posed by Africa and, in particular, the Gulf of Guinea region to international peace and security. According to the CSIS report,

> The Gulf of Guinea is a nexus of vital US foreign policy priorities. Every US foreign policy interest in Africa –democracy, respect for human rights, poverty alleviation, terrorism, HIV/AIDS, organised crime, energy security, strengthening regional peacekeeping capabilities and regional political integration – is significantly at play there.[15]

In simple terms, the US has very high stakes and vital strategic interests in Africa, especially the imperative to have access to and control the rich energy sector in the Gulf of Guinea and pursue the GWOT. For better or for worse, US national interests are now inextricably linked to Africa's security vulnerability and risks. As such, no relevant US policy practitioner can afford to ignore this unpalatable fact. The multiple US strategic interests in Africa, to a very large extent, reflect the wider US global foreign and security policy priorities.

But AFRICOM raises wider issues pertinent to the understanding of United States–Africa relations and its global foreign and security approach, as well as concerns central to the understanding of international relations and world politics. Some of these issues relate to the link between AFRICOM and the GWOT, the new scramble for Africa's strategic resources by the BRIC powers (Brazil, Russia, India and China), the expansion of the American empire and the security–development nexus debate. These issues are extensively and analytically discussed in the chapters of this book. This introductory chapter will therefore further examine the link between AFRICOM and the expansion of the American empire and how the core issues raised by AFRICOM reflect the security–development nexus debate, with a particular focus on African perceptions of security.

AFRICOM and the expansion of the American empire

Much has been said about the suggestion that AFRICOM is nothing more than a military outpost and front to expand and protect the so-called American empire in Africa, now that the continent is officially recognised as strategic to US national interests. But is this latest Pax Americana any different from that of Pax Romana or Pax Britannica?[16] The creation of a unified geographic command for Africa is generally perceived as an attempt to control and enforce the pursuit of US strategic national interests in Africa. Though AFRICOM programme activities and operational mandate are a combination of military and non-military activities, i.e. exercise of 'hard' and 'soft' power through cooperative security and partnerships with African governments and regional organisations, the fact still remains that AFRICOM is to protect US strategic national interests and foreign policy objectives in Africa, very much similar to what the Roman and British empires did by creating foreign military bases to control and enforce their rule. Therefore, the AFRICOM project is not different from what other empires have done before and, according to Arnold Toynbee, this was 'the principle method by which Rome established her political supremacy in her world'.[17] Britain ruled its vast colonial empire in the nineteenth century – an 'empire on which the sun never sets' – through an international system of foreign military bases supported by naval power and sea corridors in the Mediterranean through the Suez Canal to India, South Pacific, North America and the Caribbean, West Africa and the South Atlantic.

If this is the historic pattern of what great powers do, then the US action to establish AFRICOM is understandable because as the sole remaining superpower, in command of the capitalist world economy, this is what is expected of America as a world power, protecting its strategic national and global interests, irrespective of the considerable negative impact on other states, communities and peoples in different parts of the world. It is therefore not surprising that, with the end of the Second World War, the United States established 'the most extensive system of military bases that the world had ever seen', consisting of 'over thirty thousand installations located at two thousand base sites residing in around one hundred countries and bases, and stretching from the Arctic Circle to Antactica'.[18] The Truman doctrine on foreign military bases enunciated in 1945 was that 'We are going to maintain military bases necessary for the complete protection of our interests and of world peace.'[19] The US overseas basing structure has been refined over the decades, including substantial reductions of military bases in the aftermath of the Second World War, as well as the intensified acquisition of new bases during the Korean, Vietnam, Afghanistan and Iraq wars and the post-9/11 GWOT. While US military bases were justified during the Cold War to 'ring' and 'contain' communism and Soviet military threats, AFRICOM is now a means to access, protect and control US strategic national interests in Africa. AFRICOM is part and parcel of the US strategic defence initiative to meet the challenges of the changed international security environment, as well as to project US global power to intimidate and coerce rival powers in Africa, such as China. Therefore the editors of *Monthly Review* argue that:

> The projection of US military power into new regions through the establishment of US military bases should not of course be seen simply in terms of direct military ends. They are always used to promote the economic and political objectives of US capitalism. For example, US corporations and the US government have been eager for some time to build a secure corridor for US-controlled oil and natural gas pipelines from the Caspian Sea in Central Asia through Afghanistan and Pakistan to the Arabian Sea. The War in Afghanistan and the creation of US bases in Central Asia are viewed as a key opportunity to make such pipelines a reality.... Needless to say, without a strong US military presence in the region, through the establishment of bases as a result of war, the construction of such a pipeline would almost certainly have proven impracticable.[20]

The global reality is that the United States has emerged in the post-Cold War era as the dominant power in the world and in control of the democratic and capitalist world order, though with varying degrees of capabilities and obstacles. By all indications, the United States is a modern-day empire, though without formal conquest and acquisition of sovereign territories and control over subject peoples.[21] Therefore, John Ikenberry boldly asserts that 'The United States is today a global superpower without historical precedent.'[22] America's global dominance and unipolar power is not only acknowledged the world over, but also taken as given. As one former French Minister, Hubert Vedrine, put it in 1999,

> The United States of America today predominates on the economic level, the monetary level, on the technological level and in the cultural area in the broadest sense of the word. It is not comparable, in terms of power and influence, to anything known in modern history.[23]

There is a controversial debate on whether in fact the American empire is benign and benevolent or an exploitative, arrogant, coercive and predatory imperial power.[24] Irrespective of the debates generated by the notion of an American empire, it is important to recognise that

> The American order is built on power – at least at its core. The extended system of American-led security protection in Europe, the Middle East and Asia is an essential element of this order and it can only be sustained by dominant military capabilities, which in turn depends on continuing American economic and technological strength.[25]

From a realist perspective, AFRICOM is an attempt to further strengthen and control the political, economic and security order America has constructed and maintained to its advantage in the post-Second World War period. In effect, AFRICOM is the latest manifestation of what Harold Laski alluded to in 1947, stating that 'America bestrides the world like a colossus; neither Rome at the height of its powers nor Great Britain in the period of its economic supremacy enjoyed an influence so direct, so profound, so pervasive.'[26] Viewed from this perspective and given the global context of the exercise of US dominance and hegemonic power and, in particular, the enormity of the responsibility to protect and secure US global strategic and national interests, it is therefore not surprising and inevitable that the United States will establish a unified geographic command for Africa. The inevitable opposition and controversy generated by the creation of AFRICOM is hardly surprising and is, in fact, nothing new. As Fareed Zakaria bluntly puts it 'There is one ideology left standing, liberal democratic capitalism, and one institution with universal reach, the United States. If the past is any guide, America's primacy will provoke growing resistance.'[27] AFRICOM is an illustration of the view expressed by Jules Dufour, that the United States has divided the earth surface

> into five spatial units [AFRICOM now the sixth] and four unified combatant commands. Each unit is under the command of a General. The earth surface is being conceived as a battlefield which can be patrolled or steadfastly supervised from the Bases.[28]

That's kind of a crazy image: six generals overseeing the globe.

--- 24 Stars...

The continent-wide criticism and opposition to AFRICOM is therefore not surprising, fearing that it will not only make Africa a target for terrorists, but also pose a serious threat to the sovereignty of African states, as well as creating an 'open season' for American military and security intervention to effect regime change against governments and leaders labelled as recalcitrant and non-servile. This concern is historically justified by the report of the 1970 US sub-committee on Security Agreements and Commitments Abroad of the Senate Foreign Relations Committee which stated that 'Overseas bases, the presence of elements of United States armed forces, joint planning, joint exercises, or excessive military assistance programs ... all but guarantee some involvement by the United States in the internal affairs of the host government.'[29]

The concerns and opposition by African leaders and peoples are therefore not misplaced, but based on well-founded perceptions of the dangers of becoming entangled and embroiled in the activities of the American empire. From a global perspective, US foreign military bases have been subjected to social and anti-American protests due to the political, economic, social and environmental impact of these bases, often evoking perceptions of US colonialism and imperialism.[30]

AFRICOM and the security–development nexus policy and practice

AFRICOM represents the merging of traditional US military thinking and activities with that of humanitarian and development foreign policy concerns. According to President Bush, the 'new command will enhance our efforts to bring peace and security to the people of Africa and promote our common goals of development, health, education, democracy and economic growth in Africa'.[31] All the programmes and operational activities of AFRICOM geared towards achieving the foreign and security policy objectives of the US government illustrate the linking of security and development issues in that Africa is perceived as a threat to global peace and security, as well as US strategic national interests. The securitisation of Africa presents the view that disorder and anarchy exist in large and ungovernable areas of the continent due to extreme poverty and deprivation, violent wars and armed conflicts, failed and collapsed states, widespread insecurity and under-development, including depressing socio-developmental indicators such as the HIV/AIDS pandemic and environmental catastrophes. This perception of Africa as a threat to global peace and security is what *The Economist Magazine* in 2000 infamously described as 'the Hopeless Continent' and was reinforced by the former British Prime Minister, Tony Blair, who presented Africa as a 'scar on the conscience of the world'. Hence the political, development and moral responsibility of the international community to help 'sort out the mess' and to restore peace, security and stability on the continent. The post-9/11 security threats and the ensuing 'politics of fear' further reinforced the international policy and intervention practices of the security–development nexus.

The Blair–Bush Transatlantic axis succeeded in putting Africa at the top of the international political agenda in 2005.[32] AFRICOM, as represented by the DoD, State Department and USAID, is the embodiment of US strategic thinking and policy practice on the inextricable link between security and development in the context of Africa. To achieve the merging of military/security issues with development and humanitarian foreign policy goals, the AFRICOM framework has incorporated civilian agencies and capabilities needed to deliver the security–development nexus intervention programmes. AFRICOM, according to Theresa Whelan, is in several ways, a concrete manifestation of the security–development nexus in that 'African security issues could no longer be viewed as only a humanitarian concern. Cold hard "real-politik" dictated a US national interest in promoting a secure and stable African continent' and that 'If a secure and stable Africa is in US national interest, then the US would need to take a holistic approach to addressing the challenges.' Therefore, the new US approach to responding to security challenges in Africa, as provided by the AFRICOM framework, was to focus diplomatic, political and development efforts to 'prevent problems from becoming crises and crises from becoming catastrophes' (Chapter 2). This is what the US Secretary of State, Hilary Clinton, described as the exercise of 'smart power' and the focus on non-military dimensions of security such as development and humanitarian issues in an attempt to de-militarise US foreign policy in Africa.

Notably, the National Security Strategy of the US government in 2002 established the positive correlation between weak, failed and collapsed states, poverty, bad governance and the emergence of radical extremist groups or havens for terrorist networks and transnational criminal networks, such as drug trafficking and arms smuggling.[33] In addition to the threats posed by insurgency groups to US energy security in the Gulf of Guinea region of Africa, there is increasing evidence that al-Qaeda is shifting its terrorist operations into Africa because of the strategic advantages provided by the dysfunctional nature of large regions of the continent.[34] The most recent manifestation of the security threats posed by Africa to international peace and security is the phenomenon of Somali piracy and its threats to international maritime commerce and security. The collapsed state of Somalia has become not only a safe haven for al-Qaeda terrorists and networks, but also the new hub for modern-day piracy in the Gulf of Aden, which has disrupted international maritime activities and commerce. Maritime shipping activities and flow in the Gulf of Aden, off the coast of Somalia, have been increasingly threatened by Somali pirates, with more than 100 pirate attacks in 2008 alone, demanding millions of dollars in ransom. Piracy in Somalia is a thriving multi-million dollar business enterprise, operated by the informal sector through organised crime and with the alleged complicity of officers of the Puntland administration. According to BBC sources, 22,000 ships pass through the Gulf of Aden annually, to or from the Indian Ocean, carrying an estimated 8 per cent of the world's trade.[35] To prevent casualties and damage to the ships, owners have resorted to paying huge ransoms, thereby fuelling the escalation of pirate attacks in the Gulf of Aden. The increasing vulnerability of international shipping activities to Somali pirates has led to international naval patrols and foreign military vessels in the Gulf of Aden to police and deter pirates. One recent high-profile victim was an American cargo ship, Maersk Alabama, captured in April 2009 off the coast of Somalia by pirates who held the captain hostage. Although the captain was subsequently freed by US marines, it underscored the fact that failed and collapsed states, with conditions of extreme poverty and under-development, create the breeding ground for piracy and terrorist activities.

The presentation and perceptions of Africa as a threat to US national interests and global peace and security is nothing new. This approach builds on the traditional policy interventions and practices in Africa by the international community in the last two decades, which have led to the increasing securitisation of development issues on the continent. The emergence of a developmental approach to security and the policy practice of 'security as development' in the case of the United States, for example, have led to the spending of billions of dollars on development and humanitarian issues in Africa. This is what Tom Tieku describes (Chapter 8) as the 'Three Ds' approach to security, which links Defence, Diplomacy and Development. The appendix to this chapter gives a detailed and comprehensive outline of the scale and total value of US government spending on development and humanitarian issues in Africa, worth billions of dollars. But the United States is not unique in the securitisation of development approach to Africa. In the last decade, there has been increasing convergence and consensus between security and development policies of the international community, framed as part of the liberal peace discourse and policy practice in Africa.[36] In support of this international policy approach to Africa, the G8 Africa Action Plan perceives development issues as the new security concern, stating that 'Poverty, underdevelopment and fragile states create fertile conditions for violent conflict and the emergence of new security threats, including international crime and terrorism. There will be no lasting security without development and no effective development without security and stability.'[37] Therefore development is now considered as the insurance against security threats and instability and, according to the UN High-level Panel Report (2004), 'Development is the first line of defence for collective security system that takes prevention seriously.... Development makes everyone secure.' The increasing 'securitisation of development' and the 'developmentalisation of security' in Africa, according to Susan Willett, mean that the continent 'has become a laboratory for the liberal peace project'.[38]

This security–development nexus approach to Africa, as represented by AFRICOM, is the latest international policy approach to addressing endemic insecurities and under-development in Africa, and has several implications. David Chandler challenges not only the linking of security and development as if it were a new research and policy concern, but that the emerging policy convergence and consensus on the 'nexus' 'reflects a retreat from strategic policy-making and a more inward-looking approach to foreign policy, more concerned with self-image than the policy consequences in the areas concerned.'[39] While there is general consensus on the fact that insecurity affects development and under-development negatively impacts on security and stability, the security–development nexus approach has emerged in the last ten years as an all-embracing political, security and development paradigm within which all interventions by the international community in Africa are framed, especially in post-conflict and war-torn societies – what Chandler describes as 'a way of cohering national and international policymaking interventions in non-Western states'.[40] This international policy convergence on the nexus of security and development has created an international consensus and perception that internal disorder and chaos exist in Africa, and thus justifies external intervention to impose order and stability, hence the multiplicity of military and non-military interventions in Africa, often framed as forcible and non-forcible humanitarian interventions. In the process, this type of intervention approach has led to the creation of 'phantom states' in transition and post-conflict societies often propped up and controlled by the agencies of the liberal peace project. It is therefore not surprising that the security–development nexus policy approach and intervention practices have led to the promotion and implementation of two contrasting sets of policies by the international community in that the mainstream security community is increasingly preoccupied by the securitisation of development while the development community is now engaged with 'developmentalising security'.[41] In addition, this type of security and development intervention approach has led to the increasing neglect of African traditional approaches, societal agencies and indigenous resources in post-war peace building and reconstruction of collapsed states. Little wonder, then, the widespread opposition to AFRICOM for its lack of consultation with Africa and its neglect of core African security imperatives.

Perceptions of African security

If AFRICOM is a manifestation of the security–development nexus debate and policy practice, how is this linked to the understanding of security in the context of Africa? How do Africans perceive security? What are the security threats and challenges facing Africans and Africa, irrespective of the heterogeneity of the continent? In other words, how do we understand and appreciate the security risks, vulnerabilities and challenges faced by Africans (peoples) and Africa (continent)? How are they different from the traditional Western explanations and dominant interpretations of African security challenges and predicaments? How does the African-centred perception of security fit into the US and AFRICOM interpretation of security in Africa? There is no simple or essentialist definition of what is and what constitutes African security. The contested nature of security in Africa not only exists because of its complex, multi-faceted and multi-layered dimensions, but also the fact that Africa is not a homogenous continent or a 'single country', hence there exists different and diverse forms of local, national, regional, human and societal security threats or sources of threats to security. Despite this, there are some commonalities and general characteristics across the continent that constitute generic perceptions of African security. Security in

Africa is embedded in a relational context and, according to Caroline Thomas, it is about 'the whole range of a state's dimensions … nation building, the search for secure systems of food, health, money and trade'.[42]

The dominant and traditional explanations of security in Africa have largely been state-centric and military, both in terms of policy and practice. Across Africa, the state (the imposed Westphalian state system) has been accepted as the primary provider of security and as the referent object of security. The security of the state has been paramount and thus it resorts to the threat or the use of force to provide and maintain national security. The Cold War period perpetuated the dominance of the traditional notions and practices of security in Africa, i.e. security primarily perceived in terms of state/national security and military/ use of force. The African regional organisations, like the states and the ruling and governing elites on the continent, have all pursued the dominant military conception of security.[43] In effect, leaders in Africa have privileged the state and national security issues and regime survival and protection over considerations for human and societal security.

But this rather narrow and restrictive explanation of security in the context of Africa has not only been limited in several respects, but is also at odds with the genuine perceptions and appreciation of security threats and vulnerabilities in Africa. To start with, the state itself has been a source of threat to the security and survival of peoples and societies in Africa, whereby the ruling and governing elites subvert and informalise the official state institutions and agencies to serve their vested patrimonial interests and to coerce consent and legitimacy from the people, or to ensure regime protection and survival.[44] This traditional interpretation of security in Africa and the use to which it was put by both internal and external actors eroded and undermined all notions of human and societal security and led to the persistent neglect of basic human needs by the state and ruling elites, whereby state resources were diverted to military security issues, for regime protection and wasteful prestige projects such as President Mobuto of Zaire's US$1 million missile project in the 1980s – at a time when more than 60 per cent of the population were living on less than US$2 per day.

African peoples and communities across the continent, faced with extreme survival conditions of under-development, insecurity and permanent 'red line' poverty and deprivation, and in some situations, compounded by seemingly unending wars and armed conflicts, already know what their security threats and vulnerabilities are. Therefore, even before the academic and policy debate about the need to broaden and deepen the conception and understanding of security, away from the narrow militaristic and state-centric preoccupation of security in the 1980s, ordinary peoples and societies across Africa were already ahead in terms of their understanding and appreciation of the broader notions of security and how it impacted on their daily conditions of survival, i.e. the impact and relevance of non-military sources of threat to human and societal security. In effect, when the UNDP Human Development Report of 1994 brought about international focus and preoccupation with human security, it was only to confirm and internationally legitimise in the academic discourse and policy practice what the majority of Africans across the continent and other non-Western developing societies already live on a daily basis in terms of conditions of survival – often depicted with the crude statistic of living on less than US$1 per day. Importantly, the UNDP 1994 report identified seven key areas of sources of threat to human existence, including community security, economic security, environmental security, food security, health security, personal security and political security.[45] While almost all of these security threats in Western and global North societies are often taken for granted in terms of the ability of peoples, societies and states to protect or create the conditions to mitigate the worst forms of the impact of these security threats, this is not the case in many parts of Africa. As Mohamed Salih's chapter emphasises, Africa and Africans face multiple security threats and challenges that are very different from, though in some cases inextricably linked to, the traditional militaristic conception of security. These include non-military sources of threat such as health issues, in particular the HIV/AIDS pandemic, malaria and other largely preventable diseases. According to the UN Climate Change Report (2008), the continent of Africa is predicted to be the region of the world worst affected by global warming in the coming decades. In addition, extreme poverty, under-development and bad governance, coupled with the harsh impact of external factors such as the global financial crisis and the policies of the global governance institutions, have perpetually aggravated the conditions of survival of African peoples, as well as eroding the attainment of human and societal security.

Though perceptions of African security have been dominated by the traditional and dominant military discourses of threats to security or hard-edge conceptions of security, the preoccupation with the non-military sources of security or the soft-edge dimensions of security has been historic and pervasive across the continent. In other words, notions and perceptions of African security in terms of the conditions of survival are inextricably linked with human security in all its forms, societal security and environmental security. As stressed by Mohammed Salih and Shannon Beebe in Chapters 5 and 6, African perceptions of security are fundamentally different from the traditional military and dominant Western-based conceptions of security foisted on Africa. African security is largely and primarily about critical conditions of survival on a daily basis, and hence the preoccupation with human and societal security issues or sources of threat and vulnerability. It is primarily a human and people-centred perception of security that embraces issues of basic human needs (income poverty and quantitative dimensions of the conditions of human existence), elimination of sources of direct, structural and cultural violence, empowerment, dignity and participation in the decisions that affect their daily lives (human poverty and the qualitative dimensions of the conditions of human existence).[46] However, it is important to emphasise that this African perception of security is not new and the antecedents include slavery and its legacies on the continent; colonialism and neo-colonialism and the devastating negative impact; the negative effects thereof of global systemic forces (e.g. the global financial crisis and credit crunch); and the manner in which Africa has been incorporated into the international systems on terms disadvantageous to the continent, whereby Africa is consigned to the peripheral status of producer of raw materials. This situation is compounded by the fact that the majority of the states in Africa have limited capacity to respond, on a long-term basis, to the diverse non-military and soft-edge sources of threat to security faced by the peoples and societies. In addition, non-military sources of threat to security often provide the drivers for grievances and instigation of wars and armed conflicts, terrorism (state-sponsored and non-state actors) and criminal violence. These, in turn, aggravate the problems and conditions of survival relating to poverty, food insecurity, economy and health, environmental, personal and political insecurities. Therefore, in the context of Africa, both military and non-military sources of threats to security are inextricably linked and mutually reinforcing.

Based on the above, is the US conception of security as represented by AFRICOM diametrically different from the African perceptions of security and how they could be secured? Shannon Beebe's chapter gives an insightful illustration of the difference in perceptions of security between the US/Western understanding of security and the African notions of security based on non-traditional sources of threat to security. Security in Africa is therefore not simply about defence and protection of states and peoples from domestic and external military sources of threats. As Beebe aptly argues, 'To maintain relevance in the eyes of Africans, the West will have to shift from imposing what we see as the right definition of security for Africa to what Africans see as a relevant definition for their own security.'

Outline of the book

This book has benefited from the Royal United States Institute (RUSI) conference, 'AFRICOM and US-Africa Relations' on 18 February 2008 in London. The high-profile conference brought together key US military and policy figures such as General William Ward, the AFRICOM Commander and Theresa Whelan, the former Deputy Assistant Secretary of Defence for African Affairs, as well as African, American and British academics, policy practitioners, research and policy think-tanks and advocacy groups. The book is divided into two parts. Part I examines the historical context of US engagement with Africa; the conceptual issues and theoretical debates pertinent to the understanding of African security and perceptions of security in Africa; the strategic thinking that underpins the creation of AFRICOM and the establishment of a unified US geographic command for Africa; and the dominant US foreign and security policy approach towards Africa as part of the wider US response to security threats and challenges to global peace and security in the post-Cold War period. Part II focuses on a critical overview of the diverse African responses to AFRICOM in terms of threats and opportunities and the nature, dynamics and complexity of international partnerships in the provision of African security and how AFRICOM fits into the debate on the security–development nexus international policy and practice.

After the critical outline of the main thematic issues pertinent to the understanding of US strategic relations with Africa, focusing on AFRICOM, terrorism and African security, Theresa Whelan (Chapter 2) examines the strategic relevance of Africa to the United States, mapping out the history of neglect of the continent and the increasing strategic significance of Africa to both US strategic national interests and the global security environment. She argues that AFRICOM is part of the shift and the change in paradigm in US foreign and security policy in the post-Cold War period and thus the unified geographic command for Africa is not only about facilitating greater consistency of focus on Africa and harmonisation of the activities of the different government departments and military commands with responsibility for the continent, but also to make Africa more secure for the attainment of long-term peace, stability, durable security and sustainable development in strategic partnership with African states, peoples and regional institutions.

In Chapter 3, Daniel Volman presents a detailed examination of the history and formation of AFRICOM, its mission statement, the rationale for its creation and its operational activities within the wider purview of the US foreign and security policy approach to Africa, driven by the imperative of the post-Cold War and post-9/11 security and military considerations. Volman explains that AFRICOM will assume operational responsibility and implementation of a range of military, security cooperation and security assistance programmes funded through the State Department and the DoD. They include bilateral and multilateral joint training programmes and military exercises, such as Flintlock 2005 and 2007 (Joint Combined Exchange Training (JCET)), the Trans-Saharan Counter-Terrorism Partnership (TSCTP), the East Africa Counter-Terrorism Initiative (EACTI), the ACOTA, the International Military Education and Training Programme (IMET), the CJTF-HOA, the Joint Task Force Aztec Silence (JTFAS), the Naval Operations in the Gulf of Guinea and the base access agreements for cooperative security locations and forward operating sites.

J. Peter Pham, in Chapter 4, analytically argues that AFRICOM is not merely a post-Cold War experiment to respond to the security challenges of the twenty-first century, but also a much-needed updating of the internal structural framework that has long handicapped efforts by the US military to build bilateral and multilateral partnerships and engagement with Africa, given the increasing strategic significance of the continent to US national security and the global security environment. Pham posits that though historically US relations and engagement in Africa have been driven by selective strategic interests and moral impulses around humanitarian consequences of poverty, wars and natural disaster, Africa's increasing relevance for the US is motivated by three major factors including the pursuit of the GWOT; Africa's abundant natural resources and the strategic significance of the continent's vast oil resources to the energy security of the US; and humanitarian issues and consequences in Africa such as HIV/AIDS, poverty, war, armed conflicts and natural disasters. Pham therefore focuses on a critical assessment of the issue of terrorism and security threats in Africa and the US pursuit of the GWOT in Africa, and how this provides a unique opportunity for America to pursue other strategic national interests, as well as wider foreign and security policy considerations and whether AFRICOM will help achieve these core objectives.

In Chapter 5, Mohamed Salih engages with the contested notion of security in the context of Africa and how the imposition of the dominant and traditional preoccupation of security with state, military and national security in the continent has led to the neglect of human and societal security considerations. Salih argues that security and the perceptions of security in the context of Africa are not driven by the logic of military security or hard security, but rather by human security considerations or soft-edged perceptions of security around poverty, marginalisation, basic human needs, lack of human dignity, empowerment and participation. In explaining the retreat of African regional and sub-regional organisations from development issues to militarised security considerations, and why Africa needs a different perspective on security, Salih offers a human security framework as a strategy to respond to and interrogate the conditions of survival on the continent. He critically outlines the human security challenges and problems facing Africans and the continent, and why the traditional military and security preoccupations of African regional organisations and AFRICOM will potentially reinforce the militarisation of human security in Africa.

In Chapter 6, Shannon Beebe focuses on the imperative for the US defence and military establishment to develop a human security approach, because the national security strategy does not fully capture or take into serious consideration other strategic security threats, and as such 'we must therefore look to twenty-first century solutions to twenty-first century problems'. Beebe argues that the traditional security thinking and approaches to Africa are of limited relevance to the diverse and multi-faceted human security challenges facing Africa in the twenty-first century. With the end of the Cold War, US security engagement has been largely reactive and further aggravated by the GWOT. In offering a human security paradigm to frame the policy and practice of the US defence and security approach to Africa, Beebe contends that non-traditional security threats such as HIV/AIDS, poverty, environmental degradation, failed cities and slum growth do not specifically inform and frame the US security approach to Africa. He concludes that AFRICOM provides the opportunity for a proactive US engagement in conflict prevention and response to human security issues which primarily recognises that without jobs, food and health, security will not be sustained.

In Chapter 7, Jeremy Keenan argues that AFRICOM is primarily about the attempt by the DoD to expand the GWOT and how this explains America's foreign and security policy approach to post–Cold War Africa. In charting the historical development of the thinking for a unified geographic command for Africa, Keenan alludes to the role played by global security challenges in the post-Cold War era and the post-9/11 period, the increasing strategic significance of Africa to the energy security of America, the influence of the neo-Conservatives in the administration of President Bush and, in particular, the intellectual force of the 'Project for the New American Century' and the competition created by major economies like China in the new scramble for Africa's natural resources. In Keenan's view, AFRICOM is a security/military structure to take the GWOT into Africa and the operational activities of the unified geographic command are masked by propaganda and 'information war'. His conclusion is that AFRICOM has little prospect of providing long-term peace, security and sustainable development in Africa, and that the unified command is but an instrument to achieve America's strategic interests on the continent, as well as facilitate its broader foreign and the security policy objectives – hence the unified opposition to AFRICOM in Africa.

In Chapter 8, Tom Teiku critically examines how the international media hype and controversy generated by the establishment of AFRICOM have obscured the important issues relating to the understanding of security in the context of Africa, and in particular what relationships exist between AFRICOM and the AU peace and security architecture. To address these core issues, Teiku conceptualises the AFRICOM–AU–Africa security relations through the framework of what he calls 'hard' (i.e. coercive military and economic instruments); 'soft' (i.e. cultural values and ideological tools and resources) and 'smart' (i.e. combination of hard and soft powers in ways that are mutually reinforcing) activities that underpin both AFRICOM and AU security architecture. The central argument is that while AFRICOM and the AU security institutions may appear to be contradictory in some areas of hard and soft activities, the potential synergy of AFRICOM and its impact on winning the hearts and minds of stakeholders in Africa lies in the joint development and implementation of sustainable partnerships in the areas of 'smart' activities by AFRICOM and the AU in peace, security and development cooperation in Africa.

David Chuter, in Chapter 9, deconstructs the dominant Western-centric approach to African security. He states that Africa is the only region in the world that has no control over or ownership of the interpretations and representations of its own history and security predicament because of Western dominance on the continent and their disproportionate economic, political and intellectual power. This strategic advantage and dominance have been used to force on Africa a set of ill-suited interpretations, prescriptions and policies, of which the latest version is the AFRICOM project. Chuter therefore argues that the history and approach of the West, telling Africa what its security problems are, undermines indigenous solutions and local development approaches to problems. In Chuter's view, this situation is further complicated by the competing foreign and Western agendas foisted on the continent, sometimes failing to grasp the realities of the African context and conditions.

In Chapter 10, Josephine Osikena situates the development of AFRICOM against the background of the global security challenges in the post-Cold War era and the impact on America. These developments coincide with the increasing strategic relevance of Africa, not only to the major developed economies and political centres of the world, but also to the major emerging economies such as the BRIC countries. Osikena therefore argues that any analysis of AFRICOM has to take into account the impact of these global developments on America and how they inform and frame US security approaches to Africa – in particular the possible backlash against a US-promoted democracy agenda and its GWOT, and the assertive foreign and economic policies of the global South in the G20 major economies. Against this background, the emerging China–Africa, Brazil–Africa, India–Africa partnerships are redefining the traditional geo-politics of the continent, with a particular focus on South–South cooperation and collective solidarity.

Appendix: the United States and Africa – partnering for growth and development

The following fact sheet is provided by the Department of State's Bureau of Economic, Energy, and Business Affairs. Where appropriate, U.S. Africa Command coordinates military support of these U.S. government policies and initiatives through its theatre security cooperation programs and activities.

The United States and Africa: partnering for growth and development

Fact sheet – September 16, 2008

> We are treating African leaders as equal partners, asking them to set clear goals, and expecting them to produce measurable results. For their part, more African leaders are willing to be held to high standards. And together, we're pioneering a new era in development. The new era is rooted in a powerful truth: Africa's most valuable resource is not its oil, it's not its diamonds, it is the talent and creativity of its people. So we are partnering with African leaders to empower their people to lift up their nations and write a new chapter in their history.
>
> (President George W. Bush, February 14, 2008)

The United States is committed to fostering growth and development in Africa. At the 2005 G-8 Summit, world leaders renewed their commitment to support reform efforts in African countries and build on the progress of many African nations to create a strong, peaceful and prosperous continent. The U.S. has worked to keep this pledge by increasing investments in health and education, stimulating growth, improving the investment climate, and making trade work for Africa.

The U.S. record

- $5.7 billion in Official Development Assistance, including through multilateral institutions, to sub-Saharan Africa in fiscal year (FY) 2007.
- Led and contributed over $34 billion in debt relief under the Multilateral Debt Relief Initiative for 19 African countries.
- $4.6 billion in compact funding approved for 11 strongly performing African countries in the last four years by the Millennium Challenge Corporation.

- Approximately $200 million per year for the multi-year Presidential Initiative to End Hunger in Africa (IEHA) in 2006 and 2007.
- $575 million in trade-related assistance in 2007, a 66% increase over FY 2005.
- $18.8 billion to fight HIV/AIDS worldwide, including 12 African focus countries, since 2003 through the U.S. President's Emergency Plan for AIDS Relief. Reauthorization of up to an additional $48 billion for HIV/AIDS, tuberculosis and malaria for 2009–2013.

Elements of U.S. assistance in Africa

In advance of the 2005 G-8 Summit, President Bush announced that the United States would double its assistance to sub-Saharan Africa from 2004 to 2010. From a 2004 base of $4.3 billion, with planned increases in disbursements, the U.S. is on track to meet that pledge.

In 2007, total net U.S. Official Development Assistance (ODA) to sub-Saharan Africa was roughly $5.7 billion, of which $4.5 billion was contributed bilaterally and an estimated $1.2 billion was contributed through multilateral organizations. Bilateral assistance in 2007 was $1.1 billion less than in 2006 due to significant, one-time debt forgiveness of $1.4 billion in that year. Excluding debt forgiveness, U.S. bilateral assistance increased by $300 million from 2006 to 2007.

Debt relief

The United States has led international debt relief efforts that have eliminated over $87 billion in debt for 25 countries worldwide. To date, 19 African countries have benefited from the Multilateral Debt Relief Initiative, receiving about $34 billion in debt relief. Another 14 African countries are eligible to receive similar debt cancellation once they achieve the required standards. This debt cancellation is in addition to the nearly $58 billion in debt relief that the United States and international creditors have committed to 27 African countries under the Heavily Indebted Poor Countries (HIPC) initiative. The U.S. forgives 100 percent of all eligible bilateral debt for countries that reach the HIPC completion point.

Millennium Challenge Corporation

The Millennium Challenge Corporation (MCC) awards grants to countries that rule justly, invest in their people, and promote economic freedom. Through MCC compacts, partner countries identify development priorities and implement their own programs. Since its inception in 2004, the MCC has awarded eleven compacts to African countries totalling nearly $4.6 billion. African countries that have received compacts are: Benin, Burkina Faso, Cape Verde, Ghana, Lesotho, Madagascar, Mali, Morocco, Mozambique, Namibia, and Tanzania. Two other

African countries are eligible and developing their compacts. Eight African countries have MCC threshold programs to help them improve policies so that they might qualify for full compacts.

Agriculture and food security

The United States is the largest donor of humanitarian food aid to Africa, including through the United Nations World Food Program; in 2007, the U.S. provided $1.23 billion worth of food aid to Africa. The U.S. is also a global leader in addressing the root causes of food insecurity. The Presidential Initiative to End Hunger in Africa (IEHA), launched in 2002, provided approximately $200 million per year in 2006 and 2007 for food security and agricultural development in Africa. By fuelling agricultural growth, IEHA is helping to break the cycle of poverty and hunger in sub-Saharan Africa and fulfil the Millennium Development Goal of halving the number of hungry people in the world by 2015. IEHA activities focus on improving strategic planning, public and private institutions, and policies that facilitate private sector investment in the production, marketing, and trade of agricultural products, while integrating vulnerable populations into the development process. In June 2008, Congress approved an additional $770 million for food aid and agriculture development programs to help address global food insecurity issues. This includes $200 million in development assistance to address urgent agricultural reform and support local and regional procurement, including efforts to make this work for smallholder farmers in Africa.

Investment and finance

In May 2007, President Bush launched the Africa Financial Sector Initiative (AFSI) to provide technical assistance and mobilize capital to help African nations strengthen their financial markets. The United States, through the Overseas Private Investment Corporation (OPIC), has announced $750 million dollars of financing to support the creation of 11 new private equity funds that will marshal nearly $3 billion of additional investment in Africa; these funds will target a variety of sectors, including housing, water, healthcare, and small and medium enterprise development. Through the Department of the Treasury, the United States will strengthen country and regional debt markets by providing expert advisors to African governments between 2008 and 2010. The U.S. also provides training for banking regulators to improve the security and stability of the region's financial systems through the Federal Deposit Insurance Corporation (FDIC), the U.S. Securities and Exchange Commission is supporting development of capital markets, and the U.S. Agency for International Development (USAID) is helping African governments develop payment systems and credit bureaus to support retail and commercial banking. The African Mortgage Market Initiative, announced in 2003, is designed to increase wealth and welfare for households, deepen retail banking, and create local capital markets.

Trade

The United States is a leading provider of trade-related assistance, including physical infrastructure, to sub-Saharan Africa. In 2007, U.S. trade assistance to Africa reached $575 million, a 66 percent increase from FY 2005. The U.S. Trade and Development Agency (USTDA), for example, increased its activity in sub-Saharan Africa from 12 to 21 percent of its program budget over the past three years. Through its support of project preparation assistance and trade capacity building activities, USTDA helps to build physical infrastructure in the region by helping countries leverage international sources of project financing.

In 2005, President Bush launched the African Global Competitiveness Initiative (AGCI), a five-year, $200 million program through USAID to help boost African export competitiveness, focusing on investment climate, enterprise development, financial sector development, and infrastructure. The African Growth and Opportunity Act (AGOA), signed into law on May 18, 2000, is a program that rewards reforming African countries with U.S. trade preferences that have helped reduce barriers to trade, increase exports, create jobs, and expand business opportunities between the U.S. and eligible African economies. AGOA exports to the U.S. increased from $14 billion in 2003 to $51 billion in 2007.

Health

In 2003, President Bush launched the U.S. President's Emergency Plan for AIDS Relief (PEPFAR) to combat global HIV/AIDS, the largest commitment by any country to combat a single disease in history. By the end of FY 2008, PEPFAR will have invested $18.8 billion in the global fight against HIV/AIDS. On 30 July, President Bush signed into law a bill to reauthorize PEPFAR, authorizing up to $48 billion to combat HIV/AIDS, tuberculosis, and malaria for five additional years, from 2009 to 2013. When President Bush launched PEPFAR, approximately 50,000 people in sub-Saharan Africa were receiving antiretroviral treatment. Today, PEPFAR supports lifesaving treatment for over 1.7 million people worldwide, the vast majority of them in sub-Saharan Africa. Additionally, through PEPFAR, the U.S. government is the largest single contributor to the Global Fund to Fight HIV/AIDS, Tuberculosis, and Malaria, having provided over $2.5 billion since the launch of the Global Fund to Fight HIV/AIDS in 2002. The United States is also a leading donor towards efforts to combat other serious diseases in Africa. Launched in 2005, the President's Malaria Initiative is a five-year, $1.2 billion program that aims to cut the malaria mortality rate by 50 percent in 15 countries in sub-Saharan Africa. In February 2008, the President announced a five-year initiative that will provide $350 million for neglected tropical diseases worldwide, including in Africa. The United States also maintains strong support, including substantial funding, to the Global Polio Eradication Initiative (GPEI), which is working worldwide, including in Africa, to eradicate this disease.

Education

In May 2007, President Bush announced a commitment to provide an additional $525 million over five years for the Expanded Education of the World's Poorest Initiative, providing up to four million more children with access to quality basic education in six target countries, four of which are in Africa. In 2002, President Bush established the Africa Education Initiative (AEI), a multi-year $600 million initiative focused on increasing access to basic education in over 40 sub-Saharan African countries through scholarships, textbooks, and teacher training programs. By 2010, AEI will have trained nearly one million teachers, provided 550,000 scholarships for girls, and distributed 15 million textbooks.

Water and sanitation

President Bush signed the Senator Paul Simon Water for the Poor Act of 2005 into law December 1, 2005, which requires the Secretary of State, in consultation with USAID and other U.S. Government agencies, to develop a strategy to provide affordable and equitable access to safe water and sanitation in developing countries. In 2007, United States agencies such as USAID, Peace Corps, and the Centres for Disease Control and Prevention implemented new water and sanitation programs in 14 sub-Saharan African nations. In FY 2007, USAID alone provided nearly $104 million for drinking water, sanitation, and hygiene projects; these programs helped over 350,000 people gain improved access to water or sanitation.

Notes

1 White House Press Statement, February 2007. AFRICOM Factsheet, at: www.africom.mil.
2 AFRICOM Factsheet.
3 Furet 2001.
4 Interview in Monrovia, Liberia on 15 January 2008.
5 Interview in Cotonou, Benin, 20 January 2008.
6 *Wall Street Journal*, 29 June 2007.
7 Incidentally, while President Bush was announcing Stuttgart as the new location of AFRICOM, General Ward presented a different policy version to the audience attending the 18 February 2008 RUSI conference, 'AFRICOM and US–Africa Relations' in London, confirming that the location of AFRICOM in Africa was yet to be decided.
8 Isike *et al.* 2008, p. 22.
9 The US, in the Second War World, divided the world into military commands and this practice continued in the post-Second World War and post-Cold War eras. The practice led to designated military commands for specific regions of the world, with a Unified Command Plan (UCP) having responsibility for US military forces globally. The unified commands and geographic responsibilities include: USNORTHCOM (US Northern Command), USSOUTHCOM (US Southern Command), USPACOM (US Pacific Command), USEUCOM (US Europe Command) and USCENTCOM (US Central Command).
10 G. W. Bush interview by Jim Lehrer, NewsHours, PBS, 16 February 2000, at: www.pbs.org/newshour/bb/election/jan-june00/bush2–16.html

11 Putman 2008, p. 316.

12 Ibid.

13 Rothchild and Keller 2006, pp. 3–4; K. Magyar 2000; Schraeder 1994.

14 Goldwyn and Morrison 2005.

15 Ibid., p. 1. See also, Goldwyn and Morrison 2004.

16 Magdoff *et al.* 2002, p. 1.

17 Toynbee 1962, quoted in Magdoff *et al.* 2002.

18 Magdoff *et al.* 2002.

19 Magdoff *et al.* 2002.

20 Magdoff *et al.* 2002.

21 But this notion of the non-territorial perspective of the American empire is contested. The war and subsequent military occupation of Iraq, including the acquisition of foreign military bases, are used as justification to support the territorial dimension of the American empire.

22 Ikenberry 2001, p. 191.

23 Quoted in Ikenberry, 2001, p. 191.

24 See the following: Johnson 2000; Erlanger 2001; Bacevich 2002; Rodman 2000, pp. 33–41; Huntington 1999, pp. 35–49.

25 Ikenberry, 2001, p. 193.

26 Laski 1947, quoted in Ikenberry 2001.

27 Zakaria 1999, p. 99.

28 Dufour 2007.

29 Quoted in Magdoff *et al.* 2002.

30 For a critical examination of the large-scale political, socio-economic and environmental impact of US global military bases, see: Lutz 2008; Sweezy 1989, pp. 1–17.

31 Statement by President George Bush, 'President Bush Creates a Department of Defence Unified Combatant Command for Africa', The White House Office of the Press Secretary, 6 February 2007.

32 See Abrahamsen 2005, pp. 55–80.

33 White House 2002. See also Cabinet Office 2008, pp. 10–24.

34 See J. Peter Pham's chapter. Also see: Abraham 2006; Azzam al-Ansari 2007, pp. 27–30; Paz and Terdman 2006; Shay 2008.

35 *Somalia Piracy: Global Overview*, at http://news.bbc.co.uk.

36 Willett 2005, pp. 569–70.

37 G8 Africa Action Plan 2005.

38 Willett, 2005, p. 571.

39 Chandler 2007, p. 362. For critical discussion of the security–development nexus debate, see: Buur *et al.* 2007; Duffield 2008; Menkhaus 2004, pp. 150–65; Youngs 2007.

40 Chandler, 2007, p. 362.

41 Willett, 2005, p. 570.

42 Thomas 1987, p. 1.

43 For an outline of some of the dominant and traditional security approaches in Africa, see Howe 2001, pp. 70–5.

44 Ayoob 1995.

45 UNDP, *Human Development Report 1994*.

46 Thomas 2000.

2 Africa

A new strategic perspective

Theresa Whelan

Introduction

Former Deputy Assistant Secretary of Defense for African Affairs, James Woods, used to begin his annual presentation to U.S. Army Foreign Area Officers (FAOs) with a question: "Why is Africa important to the United States?" The answers would range from the practical (natural resources) to idealistic (people yearning to be free of dictators) to the altruistic (prevent disease and save lives from humanitarian disasters). According to Woods, while those were sound reasons, he wanted to draw the FAOs' thinking to the strategic level, so the answer was: "Because it's there."

That's a simplification, but Africa's place in the world cannot be overlooked. As the second-largest continent in the world – 11,700,000 square miles (22 percent of the world's total land area) with an estimated population of 690 million (roughly 14 percent of the world's population) – it is geographically and demographically important. It's economically important as well: by 2005 economic growth was averaging 5 percent, and there were tens of thousands of U.S. jobs tied to the African market; Africa possesses an estimated 8 percent of the world's petroleum; and it is a major source of critical minerals, precious metals, and food commodities. It is also politically important: of the ten elected members of the UN National Security Council, three are elected from the General Assembly by African nations.

Africa's strategic importance has been reflected historically in ways that have sometimes been less than a blessing for the continent. It sits astride millennia-old trade routes; the possession of its resources and even its people have been fought over by many nations, both ancient and modern – a "fight" that continues to this day, albeit in less stark terms than occurred during the so-called "scramble for Africa" of the nineteenth century. The legacies of such colonialism continue to haunt the international community. There is perhaps a magazine or newspaper article written somewhere in the world every week that draws a parallel between what happened during the "scramble" and the alleged maneuvering between modern powers for access to African natural resources, be they oil, minerals, timber, or fish.

Africa remains a rich, vibrant and diverse place, with an ever-increasing strategic significance in today's global security environment. Former President

Bush's 2007 decision to direct the reorganization of the Department of Defense's (DoD) unified command structure in order to add a new stand-alone unified command for Africa, AFRICOM, was a direct recognition of Africa's importance, as well as a clear signal that the United States understands the need to work more regularly and consistently on developing, building and expanding security partnerships with African states in order to help promote a more secure and stable global environment.

U.S. military engagement on the continent is not new. For many years the U.S. military has undertaken joint military exercises and training programs to assist African nations in the professional development of their military forces. The DoD has also had a long history of working in support of other U.S. government agencies and international relief organizations in delivering humanitarian assistance and medical care and coordinating disaster relief. However, despite this long history of engagement on the continent, the DoD has never focused on Africa with the same level of consistency with which it has focused on the other regions of the world. The intent of this new unified geographic command is to enable greater consistency of focus in a way that reflects post-Cold War and post-9/11 lessons learned. Those lessons learned highlighted the changing nature of the twenty-first-century threat environment, the consequent value of building security partnerships with like-minded nations throughout the world, and the importance of a holistic approach to security and stability issues.

The DoD's Unified Command Plan

To understand the concept behind a unified command, one must understand the Unified Command Plan (UCP), and how the DoD does business around the world. It is defined as:

> The document, approved by the President, which sets forth basic guidance to all unified combatant commanders; establishes their missions, responsibilities, and force structure; delineates the general geographical area of responsibility for geographic combatant commanders; and specifies functional responsibilities for functional combatant commanders.

The UCP is regularly reviewed and updated and this includes, when appropriate, modifications to areas of responsibility or command alignments or assignments. As of January 2007, there were nine unified commands, stated in law and the latest UCP. Five were regional responsibilities, and four have functional responsibilities. With the advent of AFRICOM, there will be six geographic combatant commands COCOMs.

The development of the UCP

Following World War II, the United States adopted a new system of defense organization under a single Secretary of Defense. The system established the U.S. Air Force, the Joint Chiefs of Staff and new commands composed of more than one military service. These new "unified commands" were intended to ensure that forces from the Army, Navy, Air Force and Marine Corps would all work together.

The most senior U.S. General or Navy Flag Officers were assigned to command the new multi-service unified commands, and their commands were differentiated by the assignment of either functional (e.g., transportation) or regional responsibilities and missions. The commanders are directly responsible to the National Command Authority (the President and the Secretary of Defense) for the performance of these missions and the preparedness of the command.

The present division of responsibility for African issues among three commands (European Command (EUCOM), Central Command (CENTCOM) and Pacific Command (PACOM)) was driven by historical, cultural, and geo-political factors. Responsibility for North African issues (Morocco, Algeria, Tunisia, and Libya) was assigned in 1952 to EUCOM, given those nations' European cultural linkages and their perceived relevance to the increasingly important Middle East. As the Cold War grew in complexity and the United States and the Soviet Union maneuvered for influence among the newly independent African states, the UCP was revised in 1960 to include sub-Saharan Africa under the area of responsibility (AOR) of Atlantic Command (LANTCOM). Shortly after, in 1962, a new command, Strike Command (STRICOM), was formed and assigned oversight of sub-Saharan Africa, the Middle East, and South Asian issues. This continued until 1971 when STRICOM became Readiness Command (REDCOM), with a revised AOR that did not include sub-Saharan Africa. Therefore, between 1971 and 1983 no specific command had any responsibility for paying attention to security issues in Africa.

In 1983, the UCP was again revised in order to recognize Africa's growing strategic importance to the both the United States and Europe in the context of the Cold War. EUCOM was assigned the responsibility of focusing on security-related issues in continental African nations, save Egypt, Sudan, Djibouti, Somalia, Kenya, and Ethiopia. These nations were seen as having closer ties to the Middle East, and issues there were deemed to be CENTCOM's responsibility. This left island nations off the eastern coast (Madagascar, Mauritius, Seychelles, and the Comoros) under PACOM; those off the western coast were assigned to LANTCOM. This division, as one might imagine, led to difficulties coordinating U.S. activities, and thus gave rise to the first thoughts of creating a single, unified Africa Command.

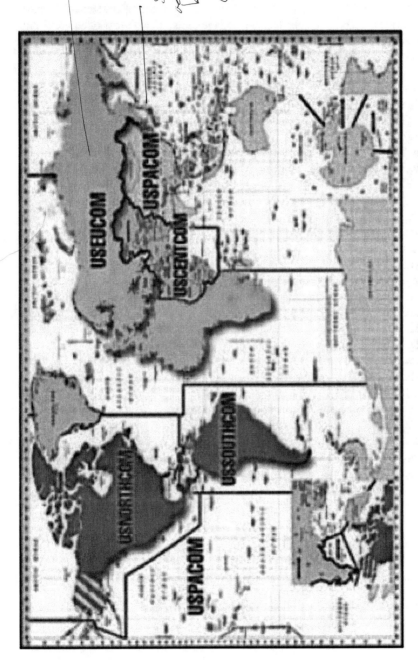

Figure 2.1 US Unified Command Plan (source: www.nau.usace.army.mil/where/areaop.php).

A not uncontestable reading of 9/11.
(a) Is it really – global security issue?
(b) Development = less terrorism?
(c) Security layers within the US failed to detect + prevent 9/11.

Changing paradigms

With the end of the Cold War the strategic paradigm the United States had used for nearly 50 years to understand and respond to the global security environment gradually became less and less relevant. No place was this more apparent than in Africa, where Africa's strategic importance to the United States had been defined almost entirely in relation to U.S. Cold War security objectives. In the absence of the Cold War, U.S. national security policymakers in the 1990s struggled to understand exactly where and how Africa fit in the security context. The initial answer was that Africa's security challenges manifested no direct threat to the United States, militarily or economically (given the assumption that the collapse of the bipolar division of the globe would now allow free market-based access to world commodities), and therefore were relevant to the United States primarily in a humanitarian context. However, the events of 9/11, combined with 20/20 hindsight, made clear that Africa was integral, not peripheral, to global security in general, and U.S. security in particular, in the post 9/11 world.

This was a world in which catastrophic threats to a nation-state's security were not simply confined to rival nation-states with the capacity to build large, sophisticated, conventional militaries with the means to deliver WMD. Rather, such threats could come from anywhere in the world, including from among the poorest, least developed, and least secure countries on the planet. If a small group of terrorists operating out of an undeveloped country in Central Asia could inflict more damage on the United States in a few hours than the entire Japanese Imperial Navy did at Pearl Harbor, the United States could no longer afford to prioritize its security concerns using traditional and conventional power-based criteria. To further complicate matters, it became clear that non-state actors could now be just as dangerous, if not more so, as an aggressive state-based power. In this post 9/11 world, African security issues could no longer be viewed as only a humanitarian concern. Cold, hard "real-politik" dictated a U.S. national interest in promoting a secure and stable African continent.

Security and stability in Africa, however, are not merely a case of developing competent military and police forces. Experiences in Africa and the Balkans in the 1990s and in Afghanistan and Iraq over the last five years have made clear that those tools only provide security and stability on a temporary basis. Sustainable security and stability are dependent on good governance, the rule of law, and economic opportunity. Those elements of security, in turn, have a symbiotic relationship with such things as health and education. If a secure and stable Africa is of U.S. national interest, then the United States would need to take a holistic approach to addressing the challenge. Additionally, in the new, more volatile, fluid and unpredictable global security environment, the old adage about an ounce of prevention being worth a pound of cure does not only make sense from a resource perspective, but also from a risk mitigation and management perspective.

The relevance of places like Africa to global security is highlighted by the problem of ungoverned or under-governed space and its impact on security in the twenty-first century. Under-governed space can be either physical or non-physical in nature. The common denominator is an area where there is an absence of state capacity or political will to exercise control. Africa is dominated by vast expanses of rugged and remote land, as well as large areas of ocean, lakes and rivers where central state-based governments have difficulty even establishing physical presence, let alone control.

This is hardly the least of the continent's problems, but it is the one category of ungoverned space that is most directly addressed by expanding the capacity of African countries to provide security along their borders and in their maritime zones. However, expanding a country's capacity to provide physical security addresses only part of the problem.

Beyond their inability to exercise control over physical space, numerous African governments still have difficulty exercising meaningful control over "governing" space. There are many cases in which African governments find themselves competing with outsiders for influence within their own country. Unable, or in some cases even unwilling, to exercise particular governing responsibilities, they cede authority to non-state or even outside elements. For example, lack of government support for education can ultimately default this "space" to potential exploitation by extremists who set-up madrassas that directly and indirectly spread religious intolerance and extremist hatred. This kind of "ungoverned space" can be as dangerous as the physical kind, but it does not necessarily lend itself to a security fix. African governments are also subject to the exploitation of weak legal systems and to their inability to monitor business and money transactions, as well as being hamstrung by their inability to control their ports and airports. While improvements in security capacity may address some aspects of these non-physical areas, they do not address all of them.

AFRICOM

It is in this context that the former Secretary of Defense, Donald Rumsfeld, asked his military and civilian staff to re-examine the merits and feasibility of establishing a stand-alone U.S. military unified command focused exclusively on security issues in Africa. Africa's direct relevance to U.S. national security demanded that the DoD re-think its Cold War-based organizational structure that artificially divided responsibility for U.S. security issues related to Africa among three different U.S. commands that were frequently distracted by responsibilities in their primary geographic regions. Keeping African issues divided among three commands would mean that, at best, Africa and its issues and challenges would remain a secondary and sometimes even tertiary concern for those commands. As such, neither the commands, nor the military services that supported them with personnel, would deem it a priority to develop a large body of personnel with knowledge and expertise on Africa. Yet the complexities and subtleties of the security challenges in Africa require regional expertise to navigate. Keeping the issues divided also meant that the bureaucratic barriers created by the "seams" between the commands would continue to present challenges to coherent and efficient action in the areas where the "seams" met. The fact that the "seams" ran through key areas of conflict and instability on the continent made them even more problematic. Additionally, the establishment of the African Union (AU) and its ambitious program for a continent-wide multilateral security architecture created further complications for the DoD's command seams, as EUCOM found itself working more and more in CENTCOM's backyard in Addis Ababa with the AU. Further, both CENTCOM and EUCOM struggled to engage and interact with emerging regional African standby brigade structures that cut across their respective areas of responsibility.

Beyond simply mandating a re-look at the way lines were drawn on the DoD map, the Secretary of Defense also directed that the effort involve members of the U.S. government across different agencies, in particular the State Department and USAID, and that the team consider innovative organizational constructs, as well as mission sets for a command dedicated solely to security issues in Africa. The former Secretary of Defense believed that if the DoD was going to establish a command focused on African security issues, it needed to be a twenty-first-century command, not a twentieth-century command, and it needed to be tailored to address the unique security challenges of the continent. Dealing with security challenges in Africa required not only an organizational restructuring in the DoD, but also new ways of doing business.

Secretary of Defense Gates subsequently embraced the effort, stressing that the command should "oversee security cooperation, building partnership capability, and defense support to non-military missions" while expressing the importance of moving away from an "outdated arrangement left over from the Cold War."

The result of the inter-agency study team's work was a proposal for a unified command focused on Africa that would concentrate its efforts on prevention rather than exclusively on reaction. Its primary objective would be to contribute the DoD's expertise in the security arena in support of U.S. diplomacy and development efforts to "prevent problems from becoming crises, and crises from becoming catastrophes." In that context the command would help build the capacity of African countries to reduce conflict, improve security, deny terrorists sanctuary, and support crisis response. In order to do this, the traditional military J-code organization structure designed for combat operations would need to be significantly changed to incorporate an integrated civilian–military architecture that would emphasize and facilitate non-kinetic missions such as military capacity building training, security sector reform, and military professionalization. It would also need to provide support for the humanitarian assistance, disaster relief and medical assistance efforts of other U.S. government agencies. The study team also recommended that the command not be developed in a U.S. vacuum, but rather that the specifics of its mission, design and even possible location be informed by consultation with international partners. Particular importance was placed on consultation with African partners to insure that it would be appropriate to the African context. On 7 February 2007, former President Bush publicly announced his direction to the DoD to develop and stand up a unified command focused on Africa by the end of September 2008, based on the principles outlined by the inter-agency study team.

AFRICOM myth vs. reality

This new single focal point for U.S. military engagement with Africa will enable greater responsiveness to Africa's quickly evolving continental and regional security architectures and African nations' increasing capacities to synergize efforts in both the governmental and non-governmental spheres to address security challenges all over the continent. Yet, despite the opportunities AFRICOM presents for U.S./African military cooperation, a certain level of skepticism regarding the nature of the command, as well as its purpose and intentions, has existed in some quarters.

The 600 pound gorilla?

The charge most frequently levied in the United States, early on, was that the creation of a DoD unified command focused on Africa would represent the militarization of U.S. foreign policy in Africa. This is hardly the case, particularly if one examines the facts. AFRICOM is merely the logical next step on a course set more than a decade ago as the United States began to increase its emphasis on supporting trade, development and health initiatives on the continent. The best measure of the focus and emphasis of U.S. engagement in Africa can be seen in its programs: U.S. health and development programs for Africa consistently dwarf U.S. security assistance programs. The former programs dollar figures run into the multi-billions on an annual basis, while the latter is a mere fraction of that at a few hundred million dollars annually. Despite newspaper headlines and uninformed rhetoric to the contrary, the facts and figures show that trade, health, development, and governance issues and programs, not military programs, dominate the landscape of U.S. policy toward Africa today, and will continue to do so in the future. The creation of a DoD command focused on African security issues has not to date, and will in no way in the future, "militarize" U.S. policy priorities in Africa.

Additionally, AFRICOM, just like EUCOM, CENTCOM and PACOM, is a supporting organization in the implementation of U.S. foreign policy as articulated by the Secretary of State. No one has been more articulate and forceful in arguing for the primacy of the State Department in the management and implementation of U.S. foreign policy than Secretary of Defense Robert Gates. Secretary Gates has also publicly called for greater funding and support for the civilian structures, such as the Department of State and USAID, which have the lead in diplomacy and development. The creation of a DoD command focused on African security issues is fully consistent with Secretary Gates' view of the necessary relationship between diplomacy, development, and defense. A single DoD point of contact for Africa will simply allow for the better synchronization and coordination of DoD efforts to help build security capacity in Africa in support of the Department of State and USAID efforts to improve governance and development capacity and opportunities. The inclusion of State Department, USAID, and other U.S. government inter-agency personnel in the command structure improves the command's capabilities by injecting knowledge and expertise into the organization, but not authority. The traditional lines of authority in these agencies and between these agencies and U.S. embassies in Africa has not changed, nor has the presence of inter-agency personnel in AFRICOM diluted or undermined the independence of their home agencies in executing their own missions.

Who's in charge?

Another concern/criticism that has been raised about the establishment of a DoD command focused on Africa is that it would attempt to usurp African leadership on the continent. In fact, the reality is just the opposite. The creation of this DoD command is actually a direct recognition of the relevance and increasing importance of African leadership on the continent, and the need to engage more effectively and productively with African nations and multilateral institutions. The DoD applauds the leadership role that individual African nations and multilateral African organizations are taking in promoting peace, security, and stability on the continent. This is exactly the type of initiative and leadership needed to address the diffuse and unpredictable global security challenges the world currently faces. The purpose of AFRICOM is to encourage and support such African leadership, not discourage and suppress it. U.S. security is enhanced by African nations being able to address and resolve emerging security issues in their countries, regions, and across the continent on their own. It would be counter-productive for the DoD to take actions that undermine that goal. AFRICOM is intended to compliment, not compete with, the AU. Its mission will be to facilitate the AU's efforts to develop the capabilities and mechanisms across the continent needed to promote and sustain peace and stability.

"It's about the oil ..."

Many pundits, both inside and outside Africa, have asserted that AFRICOM's primary purpose is to secure U.S. access to African oil. Much has been made of the fact that the United States currently receives roughly 15 percent of its oil from Africa, and that percentage is projected to grow over the next 5–10 years. That said, the United States is far from the only beneficiary of African oil. Given the nature of the global oil market, African oil production is important to all oil consuming nations. While Africa's growing importance as a global oil producer is certainly a factor in the continent's strategic significance, it was not the rationale for the creation of a DoD command focused on Africa. It would not, therefore, be AFRICOM's mission to provide security for African oil or, for that matter, any other African natural resource. Rather, AFRICOM will work to help *amounts to the same thing... getting oil to market*

African nations develop their own capacities to protect their natural resources to insure they are not illegally exploited and diverted, thereby undermining economic development potential while possibly fueling conflicts or even terrorism. If African nations have adequate capability to protect their own natural resources, then the global market system will be sufficient to insure international access to them as needed.

It's also important to note that oil is not the only natural resource worth protecting in Africa. The international press focus on African oil obscures the importance of other natural resources, particularly the more mundane, such as timber and fish, to African economic potential. For example, coastal African nations lose billions of dollars of resources annually to international illegal fishing. AFRICOM can help such nations develop maritime security capacities to protect their territorial waters, which could contribute to those countries' economic health, a key component of long-term stability.

Taking the "road not taken"

AFRICOM's mission statement succinctly articulates the tasks ahead:

> United States Africa Command, in concert with other U.S. Government agencies and international partners, conducts sustained security engagement through military-to-military programs, military-sponsored activities, and other military operations as directed to promote a stable and secure African environment in support of U.S. foreign policy.

Significantly, this mission statement places emphasis on what the February 2006 DoD Quadrennial Defense Review (QDR), refers to as "anticipatory measures." In other words, AFRICOM's primary objective will be, as the QDR put it, to "prevent problems from becoming crises and crises from becoming catastrophes." Given AFRICOM's mission emphasis on prevention versus reaction, one of the most significant organizational structure innovations that has been developed for the command is the creation of a Deputy for Civil/Military Activities. This dramatically elevates the role and importance of security cooperation and assistance activities in the command, making them equivalent to more traditional military operational functions. Further, for the first time, the DoD would have a non-DoD civilian as a senior official in AFRICOM's chain of command. A State Department Senior Foreign Service officer is the Deputy for Civil/Military Activities and serves as one of two deputies reporting directly to the AFRICOM commander.

Areas of focus include security capabilities (both land and maritime), medical skills, command, control and communications, disaster relief, and security sector reform/restructuring (such as is occurring in Sierra Leone, Liberia, and the Democratic Republic of Congo). In particular, AFRICOM leadership is working hard to interface with the AU on developing ways in which AFRICOM can provide effective training, advisory support, and technical support to the development of the African Standby Force (ASF). AFRICOM has already placed a senior US Army colonel in Addis Ababa to serve as liaison to the AU. The State Department's embedded personnel in AFRICOM will also enhance AFRICOM's ability to support such State Department-funded endeavors as the African Contingency Operations Training and Assistance (ACOTA) program, a mainstay of the U.S. effort to build peace support operations capacity in Africa. Additionally, the integrated approach AFRICOM facilitates allows the DoD's various military exercise programs in Africa – such as the African Endeavor communications exercise, Joint Combined Exchange Training (JCET) exercises, and MEDFLAG exercises – to be more effectively synchronized with ASF development goals.

A senior development advisor from USAID, along with USAID personnel embedded in the command, provide AFRICOM with the expertise and guidance it needs to manage more effectively its small humanitarian assistance and civic action projects, as well as HIV/AIDs prevention programs with other U.S. government agencies that have the lead in the development and health sectors. This type of coordination/cooperation has already proven effective in the Horn of Africa, where Combined Joint Task Force – Horn of Africa (CJTF-HOA) has worked closely with USAID and regional African governments, responding to flood emergencies and conducting civic action projects such as digging wells and building schools in places where development agencies have identified critical needs. AFRICOM will continue to build on this success.

The DoD, working through EUCOM, CENTCOM, and PACOM, currently has existing programs in many areas. AFRICOM will continue to execute those programs and, over time, seek to use its leverage as a stand-alone unified command to gain additional resources to strengthen and expand them, as well as develop new ones to address emerging African security needs.

Importantly, AFRICOM's sustained engagement in Africa is the means by which the DoD can more easily consult with friends on the continent, collaborate on important initiatives that promote security and stability, and learn from civilian and military African leaders about how they view their own challenges, opportunities, and remedies for helping the continent achieve its full potential.

Conclusion

As illustrated above, the United States presently enjoys thriving security, economic, and political relationships with most of the countries in Africa. In a sense, the creation of AFRICOM finally brings the DoD in line with the rest of the U.S. government and U.S. policy toward Africa. The DoD's development of a command focused on African issues to streamline its Cold War legacy organizational structures is a logical step in what has been, and will continue to be, a long journey for both the United States and Africa – a journey toward a more stable, peaceful and prosperous world. The security challenges of the twenty-first century demand that Africa be an integral, not peripheral, element of that world in a security context, as well as in political and economic contexts.

"Streamlining ... logical step ... bringing into line ..."

Consequently, African countries should be partners in the journey. The idea of partnership has characterized the U.S. approach to security challenges in other parts of the world, which is one reason why the United States has had geographically focused commands for those other regions for some time. In that context, some might argue a DoD unified command focused on Africa is long overdue. Whether it's overdue or right on time, AFRICOM is a concrete manifestation of the U.S. commitment to establish a serious long-term partnership with African nations to address the issues that present challenges to their mutual security interests in this new century.

3   AFRICOM

What is it for and what will it do?

Daniel Volman

On 6 February 2007, President Bush announced that the United States would create a new military command for Africa, to be known as Africa Command, or AFRICOM. Throughout the Cold War and for more than a decade afterwards, the United States did not have a military command for Africa; instead, US military activities on the African continent were conducted by three separate military commands: European Command (EUCOM), which had responsibility for most of the continent; Central Command (CENTCOM), which oversaw Egypt and the Horn of Africa region, along with the Middle East and Central Asia; and Pacific Command (PACOM), which administered military ties with Madagascar and other islands in the Indian Ocean.

Until the creation of AFRICOM, the administration of US–African military relations was conducted through these three different commands. All three were primarily concerned with other regions of the world that were of great importance to the United States on their own, and had only a few middle-rank staff members dedicated to Africa. This reflected the fact that Africa was chiefly viewed as a regional theater in the global Cold War, or as an adjunct to US–European relations, or – as in the immediate post-Cold War period – as a region of little concern to the United States. But when the Bush administration declared that access to Africa's oil supplies would henceforth be defined as a "strategic national interest" of the United States and proclaimed that America was engaged in a Global War on Terror (GWOT) following the 9/11 attack on the World Trade Center and the Pentagon, Africa's status in US national security policy and military affairs rose dramatically.

According to Theresa Whelan, Deputy Assistant Secretary of Defense for African Affairs – the highest ranking Defense Department official with principal responsibility for Africa at the Pentagon, who has supervised US military policy toward Africa for the Bush administration – AFRICOM attained the status of a sub-unified command under EUCOM on 1 October 2007, and is scheduled to be fully operational as a separate unified command no later than 1 October 2008. The process of creating the new command will be conducted by a special transition team – which will include officers from both the State Department and the Department of Defense (DoD) – that will carry out its work in Stuttgart, Germany in coordination with EUCOM.

What is AFRICOM?

AFRICOM will not look like traditional unified commands. In particular, there is no intention, at least at present, to assign the new command control over large military units. This is in line with ongoing efforts to reduce the presence of large numbers of American troops overseas in order to consolidate or eliminate expensive bases and bring as many troops as possible back to the United States, where they will be available for deployment anywhere in the world. Since there is no way to anticipate where troops will be sent, and the Pentagon has the ability to deploy sizable forces over long distances in a very short time, Washington plans to keep as many troops as possible in the United States and send them abroad only when it judges it necessary. This, however, was exactly the intention when the Clinton and Reagan administrations created CENTCOM and based it in Tampa, Florida; and now CENTCOM is running two major wars in Southwest Asia from its headquarters in Qatar.

AFRICOM will also be composed of both military and civilian personnel, including officers from the State Department and USAID. The commander of AFRICOM will have both a military and a civilian deputy. On 10 July 2007, Secretary of Defense Robert Gates announced that the President had nominated four-star General, William E. "Kip" Ward to be the commander of AFRICOM. General Ward, an African-American who was commissioned into the infantry in 1971, is currently serving as the deputy commander of EUCOM. Previously he served as the commander of the 2nd Brigade of the 10th Mountain Division (Light Infantry) in Mogadishu, Somalia during Operation Restore Hope in 1992–4; as commander of the NATO-led stabilization force in Bosnia during Operation Joint Forge in 2002–3; and as chief of the US Office of Military Cooperation at the American Embassy in Cairo, Egypt. The novel structure of the new command reflects the fact that AFRICOM will be charged with overseeing both traditional military activities and programs that are funded through the State Department budget.

What is AFRICOM's mission?

The Bush administration has emphasized the uniqueness of this hybrid structure as evidence that the new command has only benign purposes. In the words of Theresa Whelan, testifying before the Senate Foreign Relations Committee in August 2007, "[t]here are fears that AFRICOM represents a militarization of US foreign policy in Africa and that AFRICOM will somehow become the lead US government interlocutor with Africa. This fear is unfounded."[1] Therefore, Bush administration officials insist that the purpose of AFRICOM is misunderstood.

As Theresa Whelan put it in her congressional testimony,

> Some people believe that we are establishing AFRICOM solely to fight terrorism, or to secure oil resources, or to discourage China. This is not true. Violent extremism is cause for concern, and needs to be addressed, but this

is not AFRICOM's singular mission. Natural resources represent Africa's current and future wealth, but in a fair market environment, many benefit. Ironically, the US, China and other countries share a common interest – that of a secure environment. AFRICOM is about helping Africans build greater capacity to assure their own security.

DoD recognizes and applauds the leadership role that individual African countries and multilateral African organizations are taking in the promotion of peace, security and stability on the continent. For example, AFRICOM can provide effective training, advisory and technical support to the development of the African Standby Force. This is exactly the type of initiative and leadership needed to address the diverse and unpredictable global security challenges the world currently faces. The purpose of AFRICOM is to encourage and support such African leadership and initiative, not to compete with it or discourage it. US security is enhanced when African nations themselves endeavor to successfully address and resolve emergent security issues before they become so serious that they require considerable international resources and intervention to resolve.

On closer examination, however, the difference between AFRICOM and other commands – and the allegedly "unfounded" nature of its implications for the militarization of the continent – are not as real or genuine as the Bush administration officials would have us believe. *Of course* Washington has other interests in Africa besides making it another front in its GWOT, maintaining and extending access to energy supplies and other strategic raw materials, and competing with China and other rising economic powers for control over the continent's resources. These include helping Africa deal with the HIV/AIDS epidemic and other emerging diseases, strengthening and assisting peacekeeping and conflict resolution efforts, and responding to humanitarian disasters. But it is simply disingenuous to suggest that accomplishing the former three objectives is not the main reason that Washington is now devoting so much effort and attention to the continent.

Indeed, General Ward, his military deputy Vice Admiral Robert Moeller, and the other professional military officers who will actually run AFRICOM have made it clear in their public statements that they are under no illusion about the purpose of AFRICOM or about its primary missions. Thus, General Ward cited America's growing dependence on African oil as a priority issue for AFRICOM when he appeared before the House Armed Services Committee on 13 March 2008, and went on to proclaim that combating terrorism would be "AFRICOM's number one theater-wide goal."[2] He barely mentioned development, humanitarian aid, peacekeeping, or conflict resolution. And in a presentation by Vice Admiral Moeller at an AFRICOM conference held at Fort McNair on 18 February 2008, he declared that protecting "the free flow of natural resources from Africa to the global market" was one of AFRICOM's "guiding principles" and specifically cited "oil disruption," "terrorism," and the "growing influence" of China as major "challenges" to US interests in Africa.[3]

Washington would prefer that selected friendly regimes take the lead in meeting these objectives, so that the United States can avoid direct military involvement in Africa, particularly at a time when the US military is so deeply committed to the wars in Iraq and Afghanistan, and preparing for possible attacks on Iran. The hope that the Pentagon can build up African surrogates who can act on behalf of the United States is precisely why Washington is providing so much security assistance to these regimes and why it would like to provide even more in the future. Indeed, this is one of the main reasons that AFRICOM is being created at this time.

Why is AFRICOM being created now?

So, why is AFRICOM being created, and why now? First, the Bush administration would like to significantly expand its security assistance programs for regimes that are willing to act as surrogates. These assistance programs are aimed at friendly regimes – particularly in countries with abundant oil and natural gas supplies – and also go toward efforts to increase the United States' options for more direct military involvement in the future. However, the Bush administration has had some difficulty getting the US Congress and the Pentagon to provide the required funding or to devote the necessary attention and energy to accomplishing these tasks. Using a number of new security assistance channels – which are described in detail below – the Bush administration has increased the value of US arms deliveries and military training programs for Africa from about $100 million in 2001 to approximately $600–800 million in 2008. But the administration wants AFRICOM to spend far more money on security assistance in the coming years, including: US military exercises in Africa; the operations of the Combined Joint Task Force – Horn of Africa (CJTF-HOA), conducted from the US base in Djibouti – including continuing attacks on Somalia; base improvements at the US base in Djibouti and at local military facilities elsewhere on the continent; expanded naval operations, particularly off the Gulf of Guinea; and setting up the new AFRICOM headquarters in Stuttgart, Germany (including the creation of a Joint Intelligence Operations Center (JIOC), a Theater Special Operations Command (TSOC) for Africa, and regional AFRICOM offices in five African countries).

The creation of AFRICOM will allow the White House to go to the US Congress and argue that its establishment demonstrates the importance of Africa for US national security and the administration's commitment to give the continent the attention that it deserves. If Africa is so important and if the administration's actions show that it really wants to do all sorts of good things for Africa, it hopes that the next president will be in a much stronger position to make a convincing case that the legislature must appropriate substantially greater amounts of money to fund the new command's operations. The establishment of AFRICOM as a unified command under the authority of a high-ranking officer with direct access to the Secretary of Defense and the Joint Chiefs of Staff (JCS) will put the new command in a much stronger position to compete with other commands for resources, manpower, and influence over policymaking.

Second, key members of the Bush administration, a small, but growing and increasingly vocal group of legislators, and influential think-tanks have become more and more alarmed by the growing efforts of China to expand its access to energy supplies and other resources from Africa, and to enhance its political and economic influence throughout the continent. These "alarmists" point to the considerable resources that China is devoting to the achievement of these goals and to the engagement of Chinese officials at the highest level – including President Hu Jintao and Premier Wen Jiabao, both of whom have made tours of the continent and hosted high-level meetings in Beijing with African heads of state – as evidence of a "grand strategy" on the part of China, a strategy that jeopardizes US national security interests and is aimed, ultimately, at usurping the West's position on the continent. The creation of AFRICOM, therefore, should be seen as one element of a broad effort to develop a "grand strategy" on the part of the United States that will counter, and eventually defeat, China's efforts. It should also be understood as a measure that is intended to demonstrate to Beijing that Washington will match China's actions, thus serving as a warning to the Chinese leadership that they should restrain themselves or face possible consequences to their relationship with America, as well as to their interests in Africa.

What will AFRICOM do?

So what will AFRICOM actually do when it becomes fully operational? Basically, it will take over the implementation of a host of military, security cooperation, and security assistance programs, which are funded through either the State Department or the DoD.

Bilateral and multilateral joint training programs and military exercises

The United States provides military training to African military personnel through a wide variety of training and education programs. In addition, it conducts military exercises in Africa jointly with African troops and the troops of its European allies in order to provide training to others and also to train its own forces for possible deployment to Africa in the future. These include the following.

Flintlock 2005 and 2007

Flintlock 2005 and 2007 are Joint Combined Exchange Training (JCET) exercises conducted by units of the US Army Special Forces and the US Army Rangers, along with contingents from other units, to provide training experience both for American troops and for the troops of African countries. Small numbers of European troops are also involved in these exercises. Flintlock 2005 was held in June 2005, when more than 1,000 US personnel were sent to North and West Africa for counter-terrorism exercises in Algeria, Senegal, Mauritania, Mali,

Niger, and Chad, which involved more than 3,000 local service members. In April 2007, US Army Special Forces personnel went to Niger for the first part of Flintlock 2007, and in late August 2007 some 350 American troops arrived in Mali for three weeks of Flintlock 2007 exercises with forces from Algeria, Chad, Mali, Mauritania, Morocco, Niger, Nigeria, Senegal, Tunisia, Burkina Faso, France, the Netherlands, and the United Kingdom.

Trans-Saharan Counter-Terrorism Partnership (TSCTP)

Both Flintlock exercises were conducted as part of Operation Enduring Freedom. The Trans-Saharan Counter-Terrorism Partnership (TSCTP) now links the United States with nine African countries: Mali, Chad, Niger, Mauritania, Nigeria, Senegal, Tunisia, Morocco, and Algeria. In 2004, the TSCTP was created to replace the Pan-Sahel Counter-Terrorism Initiative, which was initiated in 2002. The TSCTP also involves smaller, regular training exercises conducted by US Army Special Forces personnel throughout the region. Although changing budgetary methodology makes it difficult to be certain, it appears that the TSCTP received some $31 million in FY 2006, nearly $82 million in FY 2007, and $10 million in FY 2008.

East Africa Counter-Terrorism Initiative (EACTI)

The East Africa Counter-Terrorism Initiative is a training program similar to the TSCTP. Established in 2003 as a multi-year program with $100 million in funding, the EACTI has provided training to Kenya, Uganda, Tanzania, Djibouti, Eritrea, and Ethiopia.

Africa Contingency Operations Training and Assistance (ACOTA) program

ACOTA, which began operating in 2002, replaces the African Crisis Response Initiative (ACRI) launched in 1997 by the Clinton administration. In 2004, it became part of the Global Peace Operations Initiative (GPOI). ACOTA is officially designed to provide training to African military forces to improve their ability to conduct peacekeeping operations, even if they take place in hostile environments. But since the training includes both defensive and offensive military operations, it also enhances the ability of participating forces to engage in police operations against unarmed civilians, counter-insurgency operations, and even conventional military operations against the military forces of other countries.

By FY 2007, 19 African countries were participating in the ACOTA program (Benin, Botswana, Burkina Faso, Ethiopia, Gabon, Ghana, Kenya, Malawi, Mali, Mozambique, Namibia, Niger, Nigeria, Rwanda, Senegal, South Africa, Tanzania, Uganda, and Zambia). In 2004, ACOTA became a part of the GPOI and the Bush administration's FY 2008 budget includes a request for a little more than $40 million for ACOTA activities. The GPOI itself, a multilateral, five-year program that aims to train 75,000 troops – mostly from African countries – by 2010, will receive more than $92 million under the president's FY 2008 budget, which also provides $5 million to reorganize the armed forces of the Democratic Republic of Congo (DRC), $16 million to reorganize the Liberian military, and $41 million to help integrate the Sudan People's Liberation Army into the national army as part of the peace process for Southern Sudan.

International Military Education and Training (IMET) program

The IMET program brings African military officers to military academies and other military educational institutions in the United States for professional training. Nearly all African countries participate in the program – including Libya, for the first time in FY 2008 – and in FY 2006 (the last year for which country figures are available – it trained 14,731 students from the Africa (excluding Egypt), at a cost of $14.7 million.

US private military contractors in Africa

In FY 2003, the State Department awarded five-year contracts worth $500,000 each to DynCorp and to Pacific Architects and Engineers to train and equip the new Liberian armed forces; to train and equip the Southern Sudanese military as part of the implementation of the peace agreement for Southern Sudan; and to train and equip African troops from all over the continent as part of the GPOI and ACOTA programs. In February 2008, the State Department announced that it would be awarding more than $1 billion worth of contracts in Africa for the next five-year period (2009–13) to as many as four private military contractors.[4]

Foreign Military Sales (FMS) program

The FMS sells US military equipment to African countries. Such sales are conducted by the Defense Security Cooperation Agency of the DoD. The US government provides loans to finance the purchase of virtually all of this equipment through the Foreign Military Financing (FMF) program, but repayment of these loans by African governments is almost always waived, meaning they amount to free grants. In FY 2006, sub-Saharan African countries received a total of nearly $14 million in FMFP funding, and the Maghrebi countries of Morocco and Tunisia received almost another $21 million; for FY 2007, the Bush administration requested nearly $15 million for sub-Saharan Africa and $21 million for Morocco and Tunisia; and for FY 2008, the administration requested nearly $8 million for sub-Saharan Africa and nearly $6 million for the Maghreb.

Direct Commercial Sales (DCS) program

Under the DCS program, the Office of Defense Trade Controls of the State Department licenses the sale of police equipment (including pistols, revolvers, shotguns, rifles, and crowd-control chemicals) by private US companies to foreign military forces, paramilitary units, police, and other government agencies. In FY 2008, American firms are expected to deliver more than $175 million worth of this kind of hardware to Algeria through the DCS program, along with $2 million worth for Botswana, $3 million worth for Kenya, $19 million worth for Morocco, $17 million worth for Nigeria, and $61 million worth for South Africa. Citing the commercial nature of these sales, the State Department refuses to release any further information on these transactions to the public on the grounds that it is "proprietary information," i.e. this information is the private property of the companies involved.

African Coastal and Border Security (ACBS) program

The ACBS program provides specialized equipment (such as patrol vessels and vehicles, communications equipment, night-vision devices, and electronic monitors and sensors) to African countries to improve their ability to patrol and defend their own coastal waters and borders from terrorist operations, smuggling, and other illicit activities. In some cases, airborne surveillance and intelligence training also may be provided. In FY 2006, the ACBS program received nearly $4 million in FMF funding, and the Bush administration requested $4 million in FMF funding for the program in FY 2007. No dedicated funding was requested for FY 2008, but the program may be revived in the future.

Excess Defense Articles (EDA) Program

This program is designed to conduct ad hoc transfers of surplus US military equipment to foreign governments. Transfers to African recipients have included the transfer of C-130 transport planes to South Africa and Botswana, trucks to Uganda, M-16 rifles to Senegal, and coastal patrol vessels to Nigeria.

Anti-Terrorism Assistance (ATA) program

The ATA program was created in 1983 – under the administration of the State Department Bureau of Diplomatic Security – to provide training, equipment, and technology to countries all around the world to support their participation in America's GWOT. In FY 2006, sub-Saharan Africa received $9.6 million in ATA funding; for FY 2007 the administration requested $11.8 million; and for FY 2008 the request was $11.5 million.

The largest ATA program in Africa is targeted at Kenya, where it helped create the Kenyan Anti-terrorism Police Unit (KAPU) in 2004, designed to conduct anti-terrorism operations, and the Joint Terrorism Task Force in 2004 to coordinate anti-terrorism activities (although the unit was disbanded by the Kenyan government in 2005 and is now training and equipping members of a multi-agency, coastguard-type unit to patrol Kenya's coastal waters). Between 2003 and 2005 (the most recent years for which this information is available), the ATA program provided training both in Kenya and in the United States to 454 Kenyan police, internal security, and military officers via courses on "Preventing, interdicting, and investigating acts of terrorism," "Crisis response," "Post-blast investigation," "Rural border operation," and "Terrorist crime scene investigation." The creation of the KAPU was financed with $10 million from the FY 2003 Peacekeeping Operations Appropriation for Kenya, along with $622,000 from the ATA program; the ATA program spent $21 million on training for Kenya in FY 2004, $3.5 million in FY 2005, and another $3.2 million in FY 2006. The administration requested $2.9 million for FY 2007 and an additional $5.5 million in FY 2008.

The second largest ATA program in Africa at present is one used to help fund the TSCTP. For FY 2007, the administration requested $7.2 million in ATA funding for the TSCTP. For FY 2008 it requested another $6 million in ATA funding for African regional activities, most of which may be used to fund the TSCTP.

ATA programs are also being used to train and equip police, internal security, and military forces in a number of other African countries, including Tanzania ($2.1 million in FY 2006), Mauritius ($903,000 in FY 2006), Niger ($905,000 in FY 2006), Chad ($625,000 in FY 2006), Senegal ($800,000 in FY 2006), Mali ($564,000 in FY 2006), Liberia ($220,000 in FY 2006), and Ethiopia ($170,000 in FY 2006). Training courses provided to these countries includes topics such as "Investigation of terrorist organizations," "Rural border operations," "Anti-terrorism instructor training," "Terrorist crime scene investigation," and "Explosive incident countermeasures." In Djibouti, this training helped to create the country's National Crisis Management Unit within the Ministry of the Interior, to respond to major national emergencies.

The ATA program utilizes training facilities at three International Law Enforcement Academy (ILEA) centers, one located in Botswana. In 2003, students from Botswana, Ethiopia, and Tanzania attended a course on "Terrorist investigations" at the Botswana ILEA center. In 2004, students from Djibouti, Malawi, Uganda, and Zambia took the same course there. In 2005, students from Botswana, Ethiopia, Kenya, and Tanzania attended a course on "Combating domestic and transnational terrorism" at the Botswana ILEA center. Students from Angola, Mozambique, Uganda, and Zambia took a course on the "Police executive role in combating terrorism."

Section 1206, 1207, and 902 programs

These programs are funded through the DoD budget and are named for provisions approved by Congress in the FY 2006 and FY 2007 National Defense Authorization Acts. The Section 1206 program – known as the Global Equip and Train program – was initiated in FY 2007 and permits the Pentagon – on its own initiative and with little congressional oversight – to provide training and equipment to foreign military, police, and other security forces to "combat terrorism and enhance stability." The program received $200 million in FY 2007 and has been authorized to spend $300 million in FY 2008 for programs in 14 countries, including Algeria, Chad, Morocco, Nigeria, Senegal, and São Tomé and Príncipe. In addition to paying for the cost of sending private military contractors to recipient countries to provide training, the fund is also being used to supply radar systems, surveillance equipment and sensors, GPS navigation devices, radios and other communications systems, computers, small boats, trucks, and trailers.

The Section 1207 program – known as the Security and Stabilization Assistance program – was also started in FY 2007. It allows the DoD to transfer equipment, training, and other assistance to the State Department to enhance its operations. The program received $100 million in FY 2007 and has been authorized to spend another $100 million in FY 2008. It has been used in Somalia and in trans-Saharan Africa. The Section 902 program – known as the Combatant Commanders' Initiative Fund – was created by Congress in FY 2008. It can be used by the commanders of AFRICOM and other combatant commands to fund their own relief and reconstruction projects, rather than relying on the State Department or USAID to undertake these efforts. The program received $25 million in FY 2008.

The Bush administration's FY 2009 budget request calls for total funding for these programs to be increased to $800 million: $500 million for the Equip and Train program, $200 million for the Security and Stabilization Assistance program, and $100 million for the Combatant Commanders' Initiative Fund. Of this, an estimated $300–400 million will go to provide training and equipment to military, paramilitary, and police forces in Africa.

Combined Joint Task Force – Horn of Africa

In October 2002 CENTCOM played the leading role in the creation of the CJTF-HOA, which was designed to conduct naval and aerial patrols in the Red Sea, the Gulf of Aden, and the eastern Indian Ocean as part of the effort to detect and counter the activities of terrorist groups in the region. Based at Camp Lemonier in Djibouti, long the site of a major French military base, the CJTF-HOA is made up of approximately 1,400 US military personnel – primarily sailors, Marines, and Special Forces troops – that work with a multi-national naval force composed of American naval vessels and ships from the navies of France, Italy, Germany, and other NATO allies.

The CJTF-HOA provided intelligence to Ethiopia in support of its invasion of Somalia in January 2007 and used military facilities in Djibouti, Ethiopia, and Kenya to launch air raids and missile strikes in January and June of 2007 and May of 2008 against alleged al-Qaeda members involved in the Council of Islamic Courts in Somalia. The command authority for CJTF-HOA, currently under CENTCOM, will be transferred to AFRICOM by 2008. Under the initial five-year agreement with Djibouti the CJTF-HOA base occupied less than 100 acres, but under a new five-year agreement signed in 2007, the base has expanded to some 500 acres.

In addition, the CJTF-HOA has established three permanent contingency operating locations that have been used to mount attacks on Somalia, one at the Kenyan naval base at Manda Bay and two others at Hurso and Bilate in Ethiopia.[5] A US Navy Special Warfare Task Unit is currently based at Manda Bay, where it is providing training in anti-terrorism operations and coastal patrol missions.[6]

Joint Task Force Aztec Silence (JTFAS)

In December 2003 EUCOM created the JTFAS under the command of the US Sixth Fleet (Europe) to carry out counter-terrorism operations in North and West Africa and to coordinate US operations with those of countries in those regions. Specifically, the JTFAS was charged with conducting surveillance operations using the assets of the US Sixth Fleet and to share information, along with intelligence collected by US intelligence agencies, with local military forces. The primary asset employed in this effort was a squadron of US Navy P-3 Orion based in Sigonella, Sicily. In March 2004 P-3 aircraft from this squadron, reportedly operating from the southern Algerian base at Tamanrasset, were deployed to monitor and gather intelligence on the movements of Algerian Salafist guerrillas operating in Chad and to provide this intelligence to Chadian forces engaged in combat against the guerrillas.[7]

In a particularly ominous incident in September 2007, an American C-130 Hercules cargo plane stationed in Bamako, Mali, as part of the Flintlock 2007 exercises, was deployed to re-supply Malian counter-insurgency units engaged in fighting with Tuareg forces and was hit by Tuareg groundfire. No US personnel were injured and the plane returned safely to the capital, but the incident constitutes a major extension of the US role in counter-insurgency warfare and highlights the dangers of America's deepening involvement in the internal conflicts that persist in so many African countries.[8]

Naval operations in the Gulf of Guinea

Although American naval forces operating in the oil-rich Gulf of Guinea and other areas along Africa's shores are formally under the command of the US Sixth Fleet, based in the Mediterranean, and other US Navy commands, AFRICOM will also help coordinate naval operations along the African coastline. As US Navy Admiral Henry G. Ulrich III, the commander of US Naval Forces (Europe) put it to reporters at Fort McNair in Washington in June 2007, "We hope, as they [AFRICOM] stand up, to fold into their intentions and their planning," and his command "will adjust, as necessary" as AFRICOM becomes operational.[9]

The US Navy has been steadily increasing the level and pace of its operations in African waters in recent years, including the deployment of two aircraft carrier battle groups off the coast of West Africa as part of the "Summer Pulse" exercise in June 2004, when identical battle groups were sent to every ocean around the globe to demonstrate that the United States was still capable of bringing its military power to bear simultaneously in every part of the world, despite its commitment to the wars in Iraq and Afghanistan.

More recently, American naval forces led an unprecedented voyage by a NATO fleet that circumnavigated the Africa from August to September 2007. Under the command of its flagship, the guided-missile cruiser USS *Normandy*, the ships of Standing NATO Maritime Group One – composed of warships from Denmark, Portugal, the Netherlands, Canada, Germany, and the United States – conducted what were described as "presence operations" in the Gulf of Guinea, then proceeded to South Africa, where they participated in the Amazolo exercises being held by the South African Navy. They then sailed to the waters off the coast of Somalia to conduct more "presence operations" in a region that has experienced an upsurge in piracy. Later that same month, the guided-missile destroyer USS *Forrest Sherman* arrived off South Africa to engage in a separate joint training exercise with the South African Navy frigate SAS *Amatola*.

In another significant expansion of US Navy operations in Africa, the USS *Fort McHenry* amphibious assault ship began a six-month deployment to the Gulf of Guinea in November 2007, the first phase of the Africa Partnership Station (APS) initiative. The USS *Fort McHenry* was accompanied by the high speed vessel HSV-2 "Swift" (the prototype for a new fast-assault ship capable of operating in shallow, coastal waters) and two maritime prepositioning ships. The were the USNS 2nd Lieutenant John P. Bobo and USNS Lance Corporal Roy M. Wheat, from Maritime Prepositioning Ship Squadron 1, one of three prepositioning squadrons used to stockpile equipment at strategic locations around the world. The ships made ports of call in Senegal, Liberia, Ghana, Cameroon, São Tomé and Príncipe, Gabon, and Angola, and trained more than 1,200 sailors and other military personnel from these countries.

During their deployment, the ships conducted three weeks of amphibious assault exercises off Monrovia, Liberia (known as Western Africa Training Cruise 2008) in March 2008 and conducted similar exercises off of Dakar, Senegal in April 2008, before returning to Norfolk, Virginia. Its mission was to serve as a "floating schoolhouse" to train local forces in port and oil-platform security, search-and-rescue missions, and medical and humanitarian assistance. According to Admiral Ulrich, the deployment matched up perfectly with the work of the new AFRICOM: "If you look at the direction that the Africa Command has been given and the purpose of standing up the AFRICOM, you'll see that the [Gulf of Guinea] mission is closely aligned," he told reporters in June 2007.[10]

In February 2008, the US Sixth Fleet conducted seven days of joint maritime exercises (known as Exercise Maritime Safari 2008) at Nigeria's Ikeja Air Force Base with the Nigerian Navy and Air Force as part of the APS initiative. The American forces involved included P-3 Orion aerial surveillance aircraft from the squadron based in Sigonella, and elements of the Sixth Fleet's Maritime Patrol Operations Command Center. The highlight was a search-and-rescue exercise off of Lagos.

The USS *Forrest Sherman* and the USS *Normandy*, as part of the Sixth Fleet's Southeast Africa Task Force, made the first tour by American warships of the waters off East Africa in 2007, with a visit to eight countries. The Southeast Africa Task Force made its second voyage in April 2008, when the dock landing ship USS *Ashland* visited Madagascar, Mauritius, and Reunion.

Base access agreements for cooperative security locations and forward operating sites

Over the past few years, the Bush administration has negotiated base access agreements with the governments of Botswana, Gabon, Ghana, Kenya, Mali, Morocco, Namibia, São Tomé and Príncipe, Senegal, Sierre Leone, Tunisia, Uganda, and Zambia. Under these agreements, the United States gains access to local military bases and other facilities so that they can be used by American forces as transit bases or as forward operating bases for combat, surveillance, and other military operations. They remain the property of the host African government and are not American bases in a legal sense, so the US government officials are telling the truth – at least technically – when they deny that the United States has bases in these countries.

In addition to these publicly acknowledged base access agreements, the Pentagon was granted permission to deploy P-3 Orion aerial surveillance aircraft at the airfield at Tamanrasset in southern Algeria under an agreement reportedly signed during Algerian President Aldelaziz Bouteflika's visit to Washington in July 2003.[11] Brown & Root-Condor, a joint venture between a subsidiary of the American company, Halliburton, and the Algerian state-owned oil company, Sonatrach, is currently under contract to enlarge the military air bases at Tamanrasset and at Bou Saada. In December 2006 Salafist forces used an improvised mine and small arms to attack a convoy of Brown & Root-Condor employees who were returning to their hotel in the Algerian town of Bouchaaoui, killing an Algerian driver and wounding nine workers, including four Britons and one American.[12]

Where will AFRICOM's headquarters be based?

Over the coming year, there is one major issue related to the new command that remains to be resolved: whether and where in Africa AFRICOM will establish a regional headquarters. A series of consultations with the governments of a number of African countries – including Morocco, Algeria, Libya, Egypt, Djibouti, Nigeria, and Kenya – following the announcement of AFRICOM found that none of them were willing to commit to hosting the new command. The public response throughout Africa was so unanimously hostile to the idea of a permanent and highly visible American military presence on the continent that no African government – except that of Liberia – was willing to take the political risk of agreeing to host the new command.

This constitutes a signal victory for civil society all across the continent and an important demonstration that the dynamics of global relations and political relations within states have changed radically since the end of the Cold War. Even in Africa – once treated as a convenient arena for manipulation and intervention by both superpowers – the United States can no longer rely on compliant regimes to do its bidding and faces growing opposition from popular political organizations and civic institutions (political parties; newspapers and other independent media; churches, mosques, and other religious institutions; trade unions; community associations; human rights organizations; environmental groups; and private business interests) that are gaining more and more power to challenge US policy. Privately, however, many African rulers have assured the United States that they are still eager to collaborate with the Pentagon in less visible ways, including participating in US security assistance programs and agreeing to allow US forces to use local military bases in times of crisis.

As a result, the Pentagon has been forced to reconsider its plans, and in June 2007 Ryan Henry, the Principal Deputy Under-Secretary of Defense for Policy, told reporters that the Bush administration now intended to establish what he called "a distributed command" that would be "networked" in several countries in different regions of the continent.[13] Under questioning before the Senate Africa Subcommittee on 1 August 2007, Deputy Assistant Secretary Whelan said that Liberia, Botswana, Senegal, and Djibouti were among the countries that had expressed support for AFRICOM – although only Liberia has publicly expressed a willingness to play host to AFRICOM personnel – which suggests that at least some of these countries may eventually agree to accommodate elements of AFRICOM's headquarters staff.[14]

For the time being, therefore, AFRICOM's headquarters will be set up in Stuttgart, Germany. In its FY 2009 budget request, the Bush administration is asking for $398 million to create and staff the new command. This will cover the cost of: creating an AFRICOM intelligence capacity, including a JIOC; launching a stand-alone TSOC for AFRICOM; deploying support aircraft to Africa; building a limited presence on the continent that is expected to include the establishment of two of the five regional offices projected by AFRICOM; and conducting training, exercises, and theater security cooperation activities over the coming year.

However, the Pentagon is already experiencing enormous difficulty assembling a staff for AFRICOM – which was originally expected to total some 1,300 personnel – because it has so few officers with the required training and expertise. Moreover, the Pentagon has had to cut back its ambitious plan to undertake more development and relief work in Africa because of growing resistance from the State Department and USAID, as well as increasing opposition from private US aid agencies. Even Defense Secretary Robert M. Gates recently conceded, "I think in some respects we probably didn't do as good a job as we should have when we rolled out AFRICOM." Gates noted that AFRICOM was created by his predecessor, Donald H. Rumsfeld, and argued that as the United States proceeded with the creation of AFRICOM, "I don't think we should push African governments to a place they don't really want to go in terms of relationships."[15]

What is to be done with AFRICOM?

AFRICOM became fully operational on 1 October 2008, just a month before the election of Senator Barack Obama, successor to President Bush. Thus, it will be up to president-elect Barack Obama to decide whether or not to follow the path marked out by the Bush administration – a strategy based on a determination to depend upon the use of military force in Africa and elsewhere to satisfy America's continuing addiction to oil. The alternative is to chart a new path based on an international and multilateral partnership with African nations and with other countries that have a stake in the continent (including China and India) to promote sustainable economic development, democracy, and human rights in Africa, and a new global energy order based on the use of clean, safe, and renewable resources.

The best indications that we have about what course the Obama administration will pursue on AFRICOM come from the answers that Senator Obama gave to the Leon H. Sullivan Foundation in response to their Presidential Town Hall Meeting Africa Questionnaire in October 2007, and in the remarks made by Whitney W. Schneidman (Deputy Assistant Secretary of State for African Affairs in the Clinton administration and adviser on Africa to the Obama campaign) to the Constituency for Africa's 2008 Ronald H. Brown African Affairs Series at the National Press Club on 24 September 2008.

In his response to the Sullivan Foundation questionnaire, Senator Obama maintained that AFRICOM "should serve to coordinate and synchronize our military activities with our other strategic objectives in Africa." But he contended "there will be situations that require the United States to work with its partners in Africa to fight terrorism with lethal force." And he went on to assert "having a unified command operating in Africa will facilitate this action."[16]

This statement, can be considered alongside Senator Obama's campaign statements on the need to intensify US military efforts in Afghanistan and on the right of the United States to make unilateral military strikes into Pakistan against alleged members of al-Qaeda, the Taliban, and other terrorist organizations in violation of that country's sovereignty. Such statements demonstrate that he is genuinely convinced of the necessity and legitimacy of the GWOT and, at least implicitly, of the necessity and legitimacy of recent US military attacks on Somalia. Since Vice Admiral Moeller cites the attacks on Somalia as a model for the type of activity that AFRICOM expects to conduct all across the continent,[17] this suggests that the Obama administration will continue to expand the entire spectrum of US military operations in Africa, including increasing US military involvement in the internal affairs of African countries (including both counter-terrorism and counter-insurgency operations) and the direct use of US combat troops to intervene in African conflicts.

Therefore, according to Whitney Schneidman, the Obama administration "will create a Shared Partnership Program to build the infrastructure to deliver effective counter-terrorism training, and to create a strong foundation for coordinated action against al-Qaeda and its affiliates in Africa and elsewhere." He explained that the proposed program "will provide assistance with information sharing, operations, border security, anti-corruption programs, technology, and the targeting of terrorist financing." In particular, Schneidman argued "in the Niger Delta, we should become more engaged not only in maritime security, but in working with the Nigerian government, the European Union, the African Union, and other stakeholders to stabilize the region."[18]

In addition, President Obama is certain to come under pressure from business interests and lobbyists (especially from the oil companies); certain think-tanks and NGOs; officials at the State Department, USAID, and the Pentagon; and from some African governments to pursue the plan for AFRICOM initiated by the Bush administration. It is likely, therefore, that the Obama administration will continue the militarization of US policy toward Africa unless it comes under pressure to change direction. However, members of the US Congress are now beginning to give AFRICOM the critical scrutiny it deserves and to express serious skepticism about its mission and operations. Moreover, a number of concerned organizations and individuals in the United States and in Africa – the Resist AFRICOM Campaign – came together in August 2006 to educate the American people about AFRICOM and to mobilize public and congressional opposition to the creation of the new command. The Resist AFRICOM Campaign will continue to press the Obama administration to abandon the Bush plan for AFRICOM and to pursue a policy toward Africa based on a genuine partnership with the people of Africa, multilateralism, democracy, human rights, and grass-roots development.[19]

Appendix: memo on Obama administration budget request for AFRICOM operations and request for security assistance programs in Africa in FY 2010

The budget request submitted to Congress by the Obama administration for FY 2010 proposes significant increases in US security assistance programs for African countries and the operations of AFRICOM. This suggests that, at least initially, the Obama administration is following the course laid down for AFRICOM by the Bush administration, rather than putting these programs on hold until it can conduct a serious review of US security policy towards Africa. For more information, see the State Department's *Summary and Highlights for International Affairs Function 150: Fiscal Year 2010 Budget Request* (www. state.gov/documents/organization/122513.pdf) and the DoD's *Fiscal Year 2010 Budget Request: Summary Justification* (www.defenselink.mil/comptroller/def-budget/fy2010/fy2010_SSJ.pdf).

Foreign military financing

The Obama administration proposes maintaining or significantly increasing funding for the FMF program to pay for the sale of weaponry and other military equipment to a number of African countries, raising the total funding for arms sales to Africa from $8.3 million in FY 2009 to $25.6 million in FY 2010.

The new funding includes funding for arms sales to Chad ($500,000), the DRC ($2.5 million), Djibouti ($2.5 million), Ethiopia ($3 million), Kenya ($1 million), Liberia ($9 million), Nigeria ($1.4 million), South Africa ($800,000), and African regional programs ($2.8 million).

International military education and training

The Obama administration proposes small increases in IMET programs for African countries, raising the total funding for this program from $13.8 million in FY 2009 to $16 million in FY 2010. Significant increases in funding are requested for Chad ($400,000), Djibouti ($350,000), Ethiopia ($775,000), Ghana ($850,000), Kenya ($1,050,000), Liberia ($525,000), Mali ($350,000), Niger ($250,000), Nigeria ($1,100,000), Rwanda ($500,000), Senegal ($1,100,000), South Africa ($900,000), and Uganda ($550,000).

Table 3.1 US foreign military financing

Country	FY 2009 estimate ($)	FY 2010 request ($)
Chad	0	500,000
DRC	600,000	2,450,000
Djibouti	2,000,000	2,500,000
Ethiopia	843,000	3,000,000
Kenya	250,000	1,000,000
Liberia	1,500,000	9,000,000
Nigeria	1,350,000	1,350,000
South Africa	0	800,000
Africa regional	1,412,000	2,800,000
Africa total	8,255,000	25,550,000

Table 3.2 US international military education and training

Country	FY 2009 estimate ($)	FY 2010 request ($)
Chad	275,000	400,000
Djibouti	300,000	350,000
Ethiopia	700,000	775,000
Ghana	600,000	850,000
Kenya	770,000	1,050,000
Liberia	400,000	525,000
Mali	280,000	350,000
Niger	100,000	250,000
Nigeria	850,000	1,100,000
Rwanda	420,000	500,000
Senegal	1,000,000	1,100,000
South Africa	845,000	900,000
Uganda	575,000	550,000
Africa total	13,795,000	16,020,000

Peacekeeping operations

The Obama administration proposes major new funding for security assistance provided through the Peacekeeping Operations program. The FY 2010 budget proposal includes increasing funding for the TSCTP – from $15 million in FY 2009 to $20 million in FY 2010 – and for the East Africa Regional Strategic Initiative – from $5 million in FY 2009 to $10 million in FY 2010. It also includes $42 million to continue operations in support of the CPA in Southern Sudan, $10 million to continue operations to create a professional 2,000-member armed force in Liberia, $21 million to continue operations in the DRC to reform the military (including the creation of a rapid-reaction force for the eastern Congo), and $3.6 million for the Africa Conflict Stabilization and Border Security Program, which will be used to support monitoring teams, advisory assistance, training, infrastructure enhancements, and equipment in the Great Lakes region, the Mano River region, the Horn of Africa, Chad, and the Central African Republic. The budget request also includes $67 million to support the African Union Mission in Somalia. It contains a request for $96.8 million for GPOI; this request includes funding for the ACOTA program, which provides training and equipment to African military forces to enhance their peacekeeping capabilities, although the specific amount requested for ACOTA is not provided in the budget summary.

International narcotics control and law enforcement

The budget request for International Narcotics Control and Law Enforcement (INCLE) programs contains $24 million to support implementation of the CPA and assist programs to stabilize Darfur by providing technical assistance and training for Southern Sudan's criminal justice sector and law enforcement institutions. It is also to contribute to UN civilian police and help form police units in Southern Sudan and Darfur. It also includes funds for police reforms in the DRC, for training, infrastructure, and equipment for police units in Liberia, to operate the American-run ILEA in Gaborone, Botswana, and to create a Regional Security Training Center for West, Central, and North Africa. The Obama

Table 3.3 Peacekeeping operations

Program	FY 2009 estimate ($)	FY 2010 request ($)
DRC	35,500	21,000
Liberia	49,650	10,000
Somalia	118,600	67,000
Sudan	38,000	42,000
East Africa Regional Strategic Initiative	5,000	10,000
Africa Conflict Stabilization and Border Control	2,500	3,600
TSCTP	15,000	20,000
GPOI	105,950	96,800

Table 3.4 International narcotics control and law enforcement

Country	FY 2009 estimate ($)	FY 2010 request ($)
Cape Verde	500,000	2,000,000
DRC	1,500,000	1,700,000
Guinea-Bissau	100,000	3,000,000
Liberia	4,130,000	8,000,000
Nigeria	720,000	2,000,000
Sudan	15,400,000	24,000,000
African regional	3,000,000	4,500,000

administration is also asking for funding to be provided through the INCLE programs for the first time to provide security assistance to countries participating in the TSCTP: Morocco, Algeria, Tunisia, Mauritania, Senegal, Mali, Niger, Chad, and Nigeria.

Nonproliferation, anti-terrorism, demining, and related programs

The Obama administration proposes to almost double funding for counterterrorism programs. These include the ATA program, which provides training to countries throughout the world; the Terrorist Interdiction Program/Personal Identification, Secure Comparison, and Evaluation System Program, which supports identification-and-watch listing systems to 18 countries (including Kenya); the Counterterrorism Financing Program, which helps partner countries throughout the world stop the flow of money to terrorists; and the Counterterrorism Engagement Program, which is intended to strengthen ties with key political leaders throughout the world and "build political will at senior levels in partner nations for shared counterterrorism challenges."

AFRICOM

The Obama administration's proposed FY 2010 budget for the DoD requests some $300 million in operation and maintenance funds to cover the cost of AFRICOM operations and Operation Enduring Freedom-TSCTP operations at the AFRICOM headquarters in Stuttgart, Germany. The administration is also requesting $263 million to provide additional manpower, airlift, and communi-

Table 3.5 Nonproliferation, anti-terrorism, demining, and related programs

Program	FY 2009 estimate ($)	FY 2010 request ($)
ATA program	161,300,000	228,385,000
Terrorist Interdiction Program	10,500,000	54,550,000
Counterterrorism Engagement Program	1,200,000	6,000,000
Counterterrorism Financing Program	8,500,000	21,865,000

cations support to AFRICOM. The budget also includes a request for a total of $451 million to replace or upgrade facilities at enduring CENTCOM and AFRICOM locations, but does not provide separate figure for AFRICOM. According to the budget, the administration intends to carry out significant investment at Camp Lemonier in FY 2010. In addition, the administration is requesting $30 million to pay the annual lease for the 500-acre base at Camp Lemonier in Djibouti and $170 million to cover the annual operational budget of the base.

The administration is requesting approximately $400 million for Global Train and Equip (Section 1206) programs, approximately $200 million for Security and Stabilization Assistance (Section 1207) programs, and approximately $1 million for the Combatant Commander's Initiative Fund. This money will be used primarily to pay for emergency training and equipment, the services of personnel from the State Department, and humanitarian assistance to the Iraqi and Afghani armed forces. It will also be available for the use of AFRICOM. The administration's budget request also contains $1.9 billion to buy three Littoral Combat Ships and another $373 million to buy two joint high speed vessels, ships that will play a crucial role in US Navy operations off the coast of Africa. It also includes $44 billion to fund US Navy operations throughout the world – of which a significant proportion will be needed to cover the costs of US Navy operations in African waters. However, but the budget does not provide enough information to estimate these costs.

Notes

1 Whelan 2007a.
2 Ward 2008a, pp. 6–9 *Congressional testimony*
3 Moeller 2008, pp. 3–4.
4 Office of Logistics Management 2008; see also, Walsh 2007.
5 Barnett 2007a, 2007b.
6 Cline 2008.
7 *Jane's Islamic Affairs Analyst* 2004; *Jane's Defence Weekly* 2004.
8 Diallo 2007; Cisse 2007.
9 Gilmore 2007.
10 Ibid.
11 *Jane's Islamic Affairs Analyst* 2004; *Jane's Defence Weekly* 2004; Smith 2004.
12 Smith 2006.
13 Tisdall 2007; Whitlock 2007.
14 Tate 2007.
15 De Young 2008, p. 18.
16 Senator Barack Obama, "Presidential Town Hall Meeting Africa Questionnaire," undated, but posted in October 2007, electronic version accessed at www.thesullivan-foundation.org/foundation on 9 July 2008.
17 Moeller 2008.
18 Schneidman 2008.
19 For more information about the Resist AFRICOM Campaign, go to the website at www.resistafricom.org.

4 AFRICOM

Terrorism and security challenges in Africa

J. Peter Pham

In ordering the stand-up of the US Africa Command (AFRICOM) as America's sixth geographic unified combatant command, President George W. Bush gave it a rather unusual mission for a military structure: "To enhance our efforts to bring peace and security to the people of Africa and promote our common goals of development, health, education, democracy, and economic growth in Africa" by strengthening bilateral and multilateral security cooperation with African states and creating new opportunities to bolster their capabilities.[1] Subsequently, especially as criticisms of the initiative mounted – some perhaps misinformed, but understandable given both historical sensibilities and mismanaged communications – some of AFRICOM's supporters have sought to further soft-pedal its creation as "primarily an internal bureaucratic shift, a more efficient and sensible way of organizing the US military's relations with Africa."[2] While it is true that AFRICOM is intended both as "a post-Cold War experiment that rethinks security in the early 21st century based on peace building lessons learned since the fall of the Berlin Wall,"[3] and as a much-needed updating of the structural framework that has long handicapped efforts by the US military to build bilateral and multilateral partnerships in Africa, it is also very unlikely that the initiative would have come about in the absence of a shift in the calculations of America's policymakers and analysts about Africa's strategic significance, especially with respect to terrorism and other security challenges.

Almost seven years to the day before he announced the creation of AFRICOM, Bush had actually responded negatively when PBS news anchor Jim Lehrer asked him whether Africa had a place in his understanding of the strategic interests of the United States: "At some point in time the President's got to clearly define what the national strategic interests are, and while Africa may be important, it doesn't fit into the national strategic interests, as far as I can see them."[4] As Princeton Lyman, a former Assistant Secretary of State who had also served as a US ambassador to South Africa and to Nigeria, has observed, as galling as Bush's comment was to Africanists, it nonetheless reflected "what had in fact been the approach of both Democratic and Republican administrations for decades."[5] With the exception of the preoccupation with countering Soviet attempts to secure a foothold on the continent during the Cold War, American interests in Africa have historically been framed almost exclusively in terms of preoccupation over the humanitarian consequences of poverty, war, and natural disaster, rather than strategic considerations. These moral impulses, however, rarely had the staying power to sustain long-term commitments.

Broadly conceived, there are three major areas in which Africa's significance for America – or at least the public recognition thereof – has been amplified in recent years. The first is Africa's role in the Global War on Terror (GWOT) and the potential of the poorly governed spaces of the continent to provide facilitating environments, recruits, and eventual targets for terrorists who threaten Western interests in general, and those of the United States in particular. The second important consideration is Africa's abundant natural resources, particularly those in its burgeoning energy sector. The third area of interest remains the humanitarian concern for the devastating toll which conflict, poverty, and disease – especially HIV/AIDS – continue to exact in Africa. This chapter will focus primarily on the first area, briefly touching upon the second insofar as the security challenges it poses relate to the challenge of terrorism, and leaving the third for the relevant chapter in this volume.

Terrorism's long shadow over Africa

There is no denying that US security policy for the foreseeable future, irrespective of the results of the 2008 elections, will remain largely determined by the strategic contours of the GWOT, the "Long War," or whatever the designation *du jour* for America's struggle against extremist violence happens to be.

According to the 2002 *National Security Strategy of the United States of America*, the 11 September 2001 attacks on the Unites States drove home to Americans the lesson that

> weak states ... can pose as great a danger to our national interests as strong states. Poverty does not make poor people into terrorists and murderers. Yet poverty, weak institutions, and corruption can make weak states vulnerable to terrorist networks and drug cartels within their borders.[6]

With the possible exception of the Greater Middle East, nowhere did this analysis appear truer than Africa, where – as the document went on to acknowledge – regional conflicts arising from a variety of causes, including poor governance, external aggression, competing claims, internal revolt, and ethnic and religious tensions all "lead to the same ends: failed states, humanitarian disasters, and ungoverned areas that can become safe havens for terrorists."[7] The spectacular attacks by al-Qaeda on African soil – including the 1998 bombings of the US embassies in Dar es Salaam, Tanzania, and Nairobi, Kenya, as well as the 2002 bombing of an Israeli-owned hotel in Mombasa, Kenya and the simultaneous attempt to down an Israeli commercial airliner in 2002 – only underscore the deadly reality of extremist threats in Africa, as has the recent "rebranding" of the Algerian Islamist terrorist group, the Salafist Group for Call and Combat (usually known by its French acronym GSPC), as a part of the al-Qaeda network.[8]

Extremism, however, requires opportunity if it is to translate radical intentionality into terrorist effect. Jakkie Cilliers, executive director of the Institute for Security Studies, succinctly summarized the situation in the following manner:

> The opportunity targets presented by peacekeepers, aid and humanitarian workers, donors and Western NGOs active in the continent are lucrative targets of subnational terrorism and international terrorism. Africa is also replete with potentially much higher value targets ranging from the massive oil investments (often by US companies) in the Gulf of Guinea to the burgeoning tourist industry in South Africa.[9]

Africa's burgeoning hydrocarbon sector and the growing American interest in it illustrates this point well.[10] West African hydrocarbons are particularly attractive to American companies for a variety of reasons, not least of which is the higher marginal profit rates to be made per unit, both because of ease of extraction and transport and because, in the case of oil, the quality of the crude is particularly adapted to US refineries.[11] The strategic value to the United States of access to this supply is magnified when one considers the objective, articulated in President Bush's 2006 State of the Union address, of "replac[ing] more than 75 percent of our oil imports from the Middle East by 2025" and "mak[ing] our dependence on Middle Eastern oil a thing of the past."[12] In fact, in 2007, according to data from the US Department of Energy's Energy Information Administration, African countries accounted for more of America's petroleum imports than the states of the Persian Gulf region: 969,722,000 barrels (19.8 percent) versus 791,928,000 barrels (16.1 percent).[13] Nonetheless, there is a very real risk to America's newfound source of oil, one that is increasing with time if one looks at its three constituent elements of threat, vulnerability, and cost.

"Threat" is the frequency or likelihood of adverse events. Sporadic attacks by a small group with local grievances, such as the Movement for the Emancipation of the Niger Delta (MEND), have nonetheless succeeded in cutting oil production by America's fifth-largest supplier, Nigeria, by an estimated 500,000 barrels per day, or approximately 25 percent, since the beginning of 2006.[14]

"Vulnerability" is the likelihood of success of a particular threat category against a particular target. With a few exceptions, like the Chad–Cameroon pipeline, which stands at more than 1,000 km in length, most hydrocarbon production in West Africa is littoral, either in delta regions like those found in Nigeria, or in offshore fields like those found in Equatorial Guinea. While this fact marginally lessens vulnerability to the type of hit-and-run attacks that have plagued Iraqi production since the US invasion, it also makes vigilance harder because it calls for the type of blue-water and naval capacities that African countries can only dream of acquiring. Even a regional powerhouse like Nigeria boasts more admirals and commodores than actual vessels in its fleet. So it is not surprising that, according to the International Maritime Bureau, two of the most dangerous bodies of water in the world in terms of attacks on commercial transport are the coasts of Somalia and Nigeria. If al-Qaeda could successfully attack an armed vessel of the US Navy, like it did the USS *Cole* in 2000, causing some $287 million in damage with just one explosive-laden speedboat, imagine how much easier it would be to assault an oil platform or tanker manned by non-military personnel.

"Cost" is the total cost of the impact of a particular threat experienced by a vulnerable target, including both the "hard costs" of actual damages and the "soft costs" to production, the markets, etc. Although the price of a barrel of crude oil has reduced recently, the global market is so tight that any shocks caused by cuts to production or supply would be devastating economically. Conversely, viewed from the perspective of the terrorists, the physical damage to the USS *Cole* alone was an extraordinary return on their investment, as would be the global economic fallout from any successful maritime attack on the oil supply. In fact, from the point of view of the economic warfare strategy laid out by bin Laden, an attack on commercial targets in the water makes much more sense than any land-based disruptions. David Goldwyn, who served as Assistant Secretary of Energy in the Clinton administration, for example, testified at one Senate hearing:

> While the region's geological prospects are good, the risk of an oil supply disruption from the region is rising from internal and external sources. We are in no position to endure a serious oil disruption from the Gulf of Guinea today. The global oil market is stretched to capacity.[15]

In short, the combination of these three factors – threat, vulnerability, and cost – raises the overall risk considerably. And this is just one sector.

One of the most eloquent reminders of the particular allure of the continent to terrorists came from an online magazine for actual and aspiring global *jihadis* and their supporters, *Sada al-Jihad* ("*Echo of Jihad*"), which took the place of *Sawt al-Jihad* ("*Voice of Jihad*") as the publication of al-Qaeda in Saudi Arabia after Saudi authorities shut down the presses of the latter. In its June 2006 issue, the publication featured an article by one Abu Azzam al-Ansari, entitled "Al-Qaeda is Moving to Africa,"[16] in which the author asserted:

> There is no doubt that al-Qaeda and the holy warriors appreciate the significance of the African regions for the military campaigns against the Crusaders. Many people sense that this continent has not yet found its proper and expected role and the next stages of the conflict will see Africa as the battlefield.

With a certain analytical rigor, Abu Azzam then proceeded to enumerate and evaluate what he perceived to be significant advantages to al-Qaeda of shifting terrorist operations to Africa, including: the fact that *jihadi* doctrines have already been spread within the Muslim communities of many African countries; the political and military weakness of African governments; the wide availability of weapons; the geographical position of Africa vis-à-vis international trade routes; the proximity to old conflicts against "Jews and Crusaders" in the Middle East, as well as new ones like Darfur, where the author almost gleefully welcomed the possibility of Western intervention; the poverty of Africa which "will enable the holy warriors to provide some finance and welfare, thus, posting there some of their influential operatives"; the technical and scientific skills that potential African recruits would bring to the *jihadi* cause; the presence of large Muslim communities, including ones already embroiled in conflicts with Christians or adherents of traditional African religions; the links to Europe through North Africa "which facilitates the move from there to carry out attacks"; and the fact that Africa has a wealth of natural resources, including hydrocarbons and other raw materials, which are "very useful for the holy warriors in the intermediate and long term." Abu Azzam concluded his assessment by sounding an ominous note:

> In general, this continent has an immense significance. Whoever looks at Africa can see that it does not enjoy the interest, efforts, and activity it deserves in the war against the Crusaders. This is a continent with many potential advantages and exploiting this potential will greatly advance the jihad. It will promote achieving the expected targets of Jihad. Africa is a fertile soil for the advance of jihad and the *jihadi* cause.

It would be a mistake to dismiss Abu Azzam's analysis as devoid of operational effect. Shortly before the publication of the article, the Islamic Courts Union, an Islamist movement whose leaders include a number of figures linked to al-Qaeda, seized control of the sometime Somali capital of Mogadishu and subsequently overran most of the country.[17] While intervention by neighboring Ethiopia in late December 2006 dislodged the Islamists, Somalia's internationally recognized but otherwise ineffective "transitional federal government" has yet to assert itself in the face of a burgeoning insurgency that has adopted the same nonconventional tactics that foreign *jihadis* and Sunni Arab insurgents have used to great effect in Iraq. Considerable evidence has emerged of links between the Somali Islamists and fugitive al-Qaeda leaders in Pakistan, not least of which was the subsequent capture and transfer to the US detention facility at Guantanamo Bay of Abdullahi Sudi Arale, who was apparently dispatched from Pakistan to Somalia in September 2006 and who, according to a Pentagon statement, "played a significant role in the reemergence" of the militants after their initial rout.[18]

Another al-Qaeda "franchise" has sought to reignite conflict in Algeria and spread it to the Sahel, the critical boundary region where sub-Saharan Africa meets North Africa and where vast empty spaces and highly permeable borders are readily exploitable by local and international militants alike, both as a base for recruitment and training and as a conduit for the movement of personnel and material. In 2006, after years of decline during which they had been squeezed by intense pressure from the outside, while beset by defections from within, members of the GSPC formally pledged allegiance to Osama bin Laden and al-Qaeda and began identifying themselves in communiqués as "Al-Qaeda Organization in the Islamic Maghreb" (AQIM). The link to al-Qaeda was confirmed by bin Laden's deputy, Ayman al-Zawahiri, who, in the "commemorative video" the terrorist group issued on the fifth anniversary of the 9/11 attacks, declared:

> Our *mujahid* Sheikh and the Lion of Islam, Osama bin Laden ... has instructed me to give the good news to Muslims in general and my *mujahidin* brothers everywhere that the Salafist Group for Preaching and Combat has joined al-Qaeda organization.[19]

The Egyptian terrorist hailed the "blessed union" between the GSPC and al-Qaeda, pledging that it would "be a source of chagrin, frustration and sadness for the apostates [of the regime in Algeria], the treacherous sons of [former colonial power] France," and urging the group to become "a bone in the throat of the American and French crusaders" in the region and beyond. Since its "rebranding" the group has been responsible for a number of spectacular attacks, including an assassination attempt against Algerian President Abdelaziz Bouteflika, as well as assaults on the Algiers offices of Prime Minister Abdelaziz Belkhadem and the United Nations. The US State Department's annual report on terrorism described the high-profile attacks as underlining "the substantial shifts in strategy made by [AQIM] towards mass-casualty attacks employing suicide tactics and targeting Western interests" and acknowledged that "we have witnessed a shift in Algeria to tactics that have been successfully employed by insurgents and terrorists in Iraq and Afghanistan."[20]

And while transnational terrorist challenges have been the preoccupation of America's policymakers, intelligence analysts, and military planners, most African governments are more concerned with the threat of "domestic terrorism," cases that rarely receive any press in the Western media. The problem actually begins with the definition of terrorism. Most African states are parties to the former Organization of African Unity's Convention on the Prevention and Combating of Terrorism, which defines "terrorism" as:

> Any act which is a violation of the criminal laws of a State Party and which may endanger the life, physical integrity or freedom of, or cause serious injury or death to, any person, any number of group of persons or causes or may cause damage to public or private property, natural resources, environmental or cultural heritage and is calculated to:
>
> i   intimidate, put in fear, force, coerce or induce any government, body, institution, the general public or any segment thereof, to do or to abstain from doing any act, or to adopt or abandon a particular standpoint, or to act according to certain principles; or
>
> ii disrupt any public service, the delivery of any essential service to the public or to create a public emergency; or
>
> iii create a general insurrection in a State.[21]

The emphasis is less on transnational phenomena and more on acts confined to national boundaries and involving neither targets nor agents abroad. As noted earlier, lack of both government capacity and social and economic opportunity, on top of political, ethnic, and religious tensions, makes many in Africa potentially candidates for radicalization.[22] An example of this is Nigeria, where the religious question that has had Africa's most populous country dancing very close to the precipice since 1999 when 12 predominantly Muslim northern states (out of a total of 36 states plus the federal capital territory of Abuja) began adopting separate legal codes based on Islamic *shari'a* law, over the objections of their own Christian and other religious minorities, as well as other states in the federation. The resulting communal riots have taken an estimated 10,000 lives and, unless the underlying social pathology is resolved, there is the risk of the country turning into *the* front line of a "clash of civilizations" between Islamist militancy and those who oppose it. While the underlying conflict in Nigeria – as elsewhere in sub-Saharan Africa – is largely a "mix of competition for scarce resources, legacies of corrupt government and collapsing state institutions, and political entrepreneurs who compete with one another to arm marginalized youth to press increasingly radicalized agendas,"[23] the sectarian terms in which it is cast risks embroiling Nigeria in a far wider conflict. (In fact, there are worrisome indicators that at least some parts of the country have already been drawn in[24] as well as the troubling news of late 2007 arrests by Nigeria's State Security Services of al-Qaeda-linked militants in three northern states.[25])

The U.S response

AFRICOM's overall objectives, focused on the nexus between security concerns, including terrorism prevention, as a prerequisite for development, and development as a bulwark against insecurity, including the "root causes" of extremist ideologies, dictate that AFRICOM will focus on working with African nations to build their regional security and crisis response capacity. Senior Pentagon officials have emphasized that "AFRICOM will promote greater security ties between the United States and Africa, providing new opportunities to enhance our bilateral military relationships, and strengthen the capacities of Africa's regional and sub-regional organizations."[26]

In fact, even before the announcement of AFRICOM, the United States was conducting a number of security cooperation efforts across Africa, responsibility for which will be assumed by the new command. In late 2002 the State Department launched the Pan-Sahel Initiative (PSI), a modest effort to provide border security and other counter-terrorism assistance to Chad, Mali, Mauritania, and Niger using personnel from US Army Special Forces attached to the Special Operations Command Europe (SOCEUR). Funding for PSI was modest, amounting to under $7 million in FY 2004, most of which was spent on training military units from the four partner countries. US Marines were also involved with certain aspects of the training and Air Force personnel provided support, including medical and dental care for members of local units, as well as neighboring residents. The program's modest funding was stretched to provide non-lethal equipment, including Toyota Land Cruisers, uniforms, and global positioning system (GPS) devices for participating military forces.[27]

The first test of the units that benefited from this training program, as well as of the counter-terrorism cooperation agreement Algeria, Chad, Niger, and Nigeria had signed with American encouragement in July 2003, came in early 2004 when a band of fighters from the GSPC were spotted moving in a convoy of Toyota SUVs and were waylaid by Algerian military forces in the deserts of northern Mali. While many of the fighters were slain, those who managed to escape were tracked by US personnel, who passed the information on to the parties to the counter-terrorism partnership. As a result, Chadian forces, backed by Nigerian units, engaged the fugitives in northern Chad and wiped the party out, killing nearly four dozen terrorists. Subsequent investigations revealed that the dead GSPC fighters included nationals from several Sahelian states, confirming the PSI's underlying presupposition that there was a radical movement which bridged the harsh Saharan divide.

As a follow-up to the PSI success, as well as to overcome what Deputy Assistant Secretary of Defense for African Affairs Theresa Whelan called its "band-aid approach,"[28] the State Department-funded Trans-Sahara Counterterrorism Initiative (TSCTI) was launched in 2005 with support from the Department of Defense's (DoD) Operation Enduring Freedom-TransSahara (OEF-TS). The TSCTI added Algeria, Nigeria, Morocco, Senegal, and Tunisia to the original four PSI countries. The new initiative was inaugurated in June 2005 with an exercise dubbed "Flintlock 05," whose goal was to help "participating nations to plan and execute command, control and communications systems in support of future combined humanitarian, peacekeeping and disaster relief operations."[29] The training was "to ensure all nations continue developing their partnerships" while further enhancing their capabilities to "halt the flow of illicit weapons, goods and human trafficking in the region; and prevent terrorists from establishing sanctuary in remote areas."[30] Funding for the TSCTI has increased steadily from $16 million in 2005 to $30 million in 2006, with incremental increases up to $100 million per year through 2011.

In addition to the Pentagon-led efforts, as part of the TSCTI (which was renamed the Trans-Sahara Counter-terrorism Program (TSCTP) in late 2007), the Sahel countries have also received support from State Department programs – especially the Anti-Terrorism Assistance (ATA) program and the Terrorist Interdiction Program (TIP) – and other US government agencies, including the US Agency for International Development (USAID) and the Department of the Treasury.

While the United States has historically deployed naval forces to Africa only to rescue stranded expatriates – Commodore Matthew Calbraith Perry's Cape Verde-based transatlantic slave trade-interdicting Africa Squadron in the 1840s being a notable exception[31] – the US Sixth Fleet, the naval component of the European Command (EUCOM) which, until the creation of AFRICOM, had responsibility for most of Africa, has taken the lead in maritime engagement in the Gulf of Guinea. In May 2003, Marine General James Jones, then NATO Supreme Commander and Commander of EUCOM, speculated that US carrier battle groups in his command would be shortening their Mediterranean deployments to "spend half the time going down the west coast of Africa."[32] While the general's promise has not quite been fulfilled, there have been a series of both impressive and substantive demonstrations of American naval commitment off the African littoral.

As part of "Summer Pulse '04," the unprecedented deployment of seven US aircraft carrier strike groups to five different theaters in a demonstration of the Navy's ability to carry out combat operations with partners around the globe in response to simultaneous crisis contingencies, the aircraft carrier USS *Enterprise* led a battle group of some 30 vessels from nine countries, including Morocco, in exercises in the Atlantic Ocean off the western coast of Africa in July 2004. Three months later, EUCOM hosted the first-ever "Gulf of Guinea Maritime Security Conference" in Naples, Italy, headquarters of the US Sixth Fleet. The three-day meeting brought together African diplomatic and naval officials from Angola, Benin, Cameroon, Equatorial Guinea, Gabon, Ghana, Nigeria, the Republic of Congo (Brazzaville), São Tomé and Príncipe, and Togo, as well as representatives from the United States, France, Italy, the Netherlands, Portugal, Spain, and the United Kingdom. The conference participants pledged to continue dialogue and cooperation to combat common threats like piracy, smuggling, and drug trafficking, as well as terrorism.

As an immediate result of the Naples conference, at the beginning of 2005 the submarine tender USS *Emory S. Land* deployed to the Gulf of Guinea with some 1,400 sailors and Marines for a two-month training operation involving officers and sailors from Benin, Cameroon, Gabon, Ghana, and São Tomé and Príncipe.[33] Between May and July of that year, the US Coast Guard cutter, *Bear*, deployed to the same waters on a similar training mission.[34]

Subsequently, in late 2005, the dock landing ship USS *Gunston Hall* and the catamaran HSV-2 *Swift* conducted five weeks of joint drills with forces from several West African nations, including Ghana, Guinea, and Senegal. The drills included live-fire exercises, small-boat maneuvers, and amphibious landings – the very type of activity naval forces would be called upon to undertake against pirates, smugglers, and terrorists in those waters. In early 2006, the *Emory S. Land* returned to the region, again with some 1,400 sailors and Marines, to boost maritime security and strengthen partnerships, calling on ports from Senegal to Angola. Last November, the Department of State and the DoD co-sponsored a ministerial-level conference in Cotonou, Benin on "Maritime Safety and Security in the Gulf of Guinea," which included representatives from 11 Gulf of Guinea countries, as well as delegates from the United States, Europe, Senegal, South Africa, the African Union (AU), and regional and international organizations.

In late 2007, the dock landing ship USS *Fort McHenry* was stationed in the Gulf of Guinea on an extended seven-month deployment through the spring of 2008 as part of a multinational maritime security and safety initiative that partners with West African countries to train teams from 11 African countries along the gulf, helping them to build their security capabilities, especially in maritime domain awareness. The Sixth Fleet's commander at the time, Admiral Henry G. "Harry" Ulrich III, described the *Fort McHenry*'s mission, which he characterized as within "the spirit of AFRICOM and the initial operating capacity of AFRICOM," as "the tipping point for us [which will] move this whole initiative of maritime safety and security ahead."[35] The *Fort McHenry*'s West Africa deployment, where it was joined by the *Swift*, is a new international inter-agency effort known as the African Partnership Station (APS) in which European and African sailors join their American counterparts, as well as civilian personnel, onboard. It is aimed at enhancing regional and maritime safety and security in West and Central Africa through assistance in developing maritime domain awareness, maritime professionals and infrastructure, maritime enforcement capabilities, legal and regulatory regimes, sub-regional cooperation, and public awareness of maritime security issues.

Targeted grants from the State Department's International Military Education and Training (IMET) program have also been effective in building the capacities of America's African partners. During FY 2007 alone, some 1,400 African military officers and personnel received professional development at US military schools, as well as other training assistance. On a significantly broader scale, the Global Peace Operations Initiative (GPOI), which in 2004 subsumed the Clinton administration's African Crisis Response Initiative (ACRI) and the Bush administration's earlier Africa Contingency Operations Training and Assistance (ACOTA) program, aims at training and equipping 75,000 military troops, a majority of them African, for peacekeeping operations on the continent by 2010.[36] The five-year, $660 million GPOI is especially important, not only because of the generally reluctant attitude of the American public toward deployment of troops to conflict situations in an Africa lacking explicit threats to US interests, but also because it responds to Africans' aspirations to build capacity in their own emergent continental and regional peace and security institutions.

The shape of things to come

In testimony before the US Congress in early 2008, AFRICOM commander General William E. "Kip" Ward outlined his vision for the command:

> AFRICOM is pioneering a new way for a Unified Command to fulfill its role in supporting the security interests of our nation. From inception, AFRICOM was intended to be a different kind of command, designed to address the changing security challenges confronting the U.S. in the 21st Century. We are integrating interagency personnel into our structure to improve both the planning and execution of our duties. By incorporating interagency representatives into our structure, we will provide better informed and more effective support to initiatives led by civilian Departments and Agencies, such as the Department of State and the U.S. Agency

for International Development. Through persistent engagement with our African partners and integration of this kind of [U.S. Government]-wide expertise into our structure, AFRICOM will improve support to US policy objectives in Africa.[37]

According to the commander, "AFRICOM's number one theater-wide goal is to promote security and stability" within its area of responsibility (AOR) in order to "deny terrorists freedom of action and access to resources, while diminishing the conditions that foster violent extremism."[38] In practice, what would such a theater strategy look like? The largest pre-existing commitment the new command will assume perhaps gives some indication of the counter-terrorism approach that AFRICOM as a whole might possibly take.

The Combined Joint Task Force – Horn of Africa (CJTF-HOA), established in 2002 under the aegis of Central Command (CENTCOM), is presently the largest American military operation in Africa and is perhaps an exemplar of what one might come to expect of AFRICOM's efforts to counter terrorism and build capacity. Headquartered at Camp Lemonier, a one-time French Foreign Legion post in Djibouti which, in May 2003, became the only US base on the continent, the approximately 2,000 sailors, soldiers, airmen, and Marines, as well as civilian government employees and contractors of the CJTF-HOA, have seen their mission evolve considerably since its initial inception as a kinetic anti-terrorism operation. As it is currently articulated, the CJTF-HOA's mission is to conduct "unified action in the Horn of Africa combined joint operation area of the Horn of Africa to *prevent* conflict, *promote* regional stability, and *protect* US and Coalition interests, in order to *prevail* against extremism."[39]

Thus while US Special Operations forces and other combat-oriented elements are present and actively engaged in fighting terrorism in the Horn of Africa – witness the strike in May 2008 which killed Adan Hashi 'Ayro, the al-Qaeda-trained leader of the armed wing of the Somali Islamists – the CJTF-HOA has a separate mandate focused on a long-term approach aimed at denying extremist ideologies, as well as individuals and groups, the ability to exploit the vulnerabilities of the nations and societies in the sub-region. To this end, the CJTF-HOA's commanders have stressed the importance of inter-agency collaboration in its "area of interest" as the key to success in achieving US strategic objectives, as well as those of other members of the Coalition and other partners.[40] Within this framework, the CJTF-HOA's function is to be the defense element of the "3Ds" approach to US foreign policy (defense, diplomacy, and development), using civil–military operations, civil affairs, and military-to-military training to strengthen security and stability across its AOR.[41] Hence its operational concept includes a number of measures to foster inter-agency integration, including: close coordination with US diplomatic missions throughout the sub-region by posting of liaison teams at each of the embassies, as well as a senior military advisor to the US Mission to the African Union in Addis Ababa, Ethiopia; and the presence in the CJTF-HOA's command element of a senior State Department officer as the commander's foreign policy advisor and a veteran USAID officer as senior development advisor.

In addition to US personnel, the CJTF-HOA embeds military personnel from a number of Coalition partner countries, including, as of the beginning of 2008, Djibouti, Egypt, Ethiopia, France, Kenya, Pakistan, Romania, Seychelles, Mauritius, South Korea, Uganda, Yemen, and the United Kingdom in its staff, involving them in all operational phases, including strategic and operational planning and execution. During his tour as commander of the CJTF-HOA, which concluded in February 2008, Rear Admiral James Hart hosted conferences with his counterparts from some of America's long-time allies, including France and Great Britain. The CJTF-HOA has carried out an extensive series of regional senior-level engagements on both a bilateral footing at the Minister-of-Defense and Chief-of-Defense levels, and on multilateral bases as when, in September 2007, it organized the East Africa and Southwest Indian Ocean (EASWIO) Maritime Security Conference and Port Security Seminar in Mombasa, Kenya.

The CJTF-HOA has worked closely with African sub-regional institutions and, in fact, the recent inclusion of Rwanda in its activities is a purposeful attempt to align its AOR with the frontiers of African sub-regional self-created organizations, in this case the East African Community (EAC),[42] with which the CJTF-HOA collaborates in the biennial "Natural Fires" joint exercise. The CJTF-HOA has moved beyond traditional bilateral security cooperation to work closely with the Eastern Brigade (EASBRIG) of the African Standby Force (ASF), especially its coordinating element, strategic planning cell, and training organizations. The CJTF-HOA has also cooperated with the Intergovernmental Authority on Development (IGAD) initiative to establish a Conflict Early Warning and Response Mechanism (CEWARN) for the IGAD countries.[43] According to Lange Schermerhorn, who served as US ambassador to Djibouti and later as political advisor to the CJTF-HOA, the establishment and ongoing mission of the task force

> acknowledged the potential for terrorism both within and infiltrating into the area, demonstrated a commitment to deal with it aggressively, and provided a focus around which the efforts of nations in the region could coalesce on a regional and cooperative basis, rather than on a bilateral basis.[44]

In addition to training with partner militaries in the region, CJTF-HOA personnel have been involved in the building or rehabilitation of schools, clinics, and hospitals; conducted medical civic action programs (MEDCAPs), dental civic action programs (DENCAPs), and veterinary civic action programs (VET-CAPs); drilled and refurbished wells for communities; and assisted in nearly a dozen major humanitarian assistance missions. Funding for humanitarian assistance programs comes under the aegis of Overseas Humanitarian Disaster and Civic Aid (OHDACA), generally local contracts, and Humanitarian Civic Assistance (HCA), carried out by US and Coalition personnel, with the balance favoring the former. As of early 2008, some 50 humanitarian projects were being implemented by the CJTF-HOA.

Conclusion

The creation of AFRICOM at this time is due to a confluence of factors, among which concerns about terrorism and security challenges on the continent are significant. AFRICOM's architects envision it representing not only a new institutional framework for US engagement with Africa, but also a significant shift in America's strategic paradigm from military reaction to threats to a preventative approach that fosters human security by privileging conflict prevention and, where necessary, post-conflict stabilization operations. Whether or not the nascent structure and its new paradigm will prove sustainable ultimately remains to be seen. If AFRICOM does succeed, however, it will be because it embraced a strategic vision whereby the internal and regional security priorities in Africa are addressed in concert with America's partners on the ground, both at the state level and below.

The reality is that as globalization continues apace, its currents will inevitably lap onto the shores of Africa, bearing not only commerce and innovation, but also extremist ideologies and violence. Against the latter, the United States, motivated by a newfound appreciation of Africa's strategic significance, has begun laying the foundations for partnerships with Africans, which presents both sides with a historic opportunity to engage each other well beyond the current War on Terror.

Notes

1   White House 2007.
2   Mills *et al.* 2007, 1.
3   McFate 2008: 10.
4   George W. Bush, interview by Jim Lehrer, *NewsHour*, PBS, 14 February 2000, www.pbs.org/newshour/bb/election/jan-june00/bush_2–16.html.
5   Lyman 2006, 49.
6   White House 2002.
7   Ibid.
8   Pham 2007a, 39–54.
9   Cilliers 2003a: 100.
10 See Morris 2006, 225–38.
11 See Cedoz *et al.* 2005).
12 State of the Union Address by the President (31 January 2006), www.whitehouse.gov/stateoftheunion/2006.
13 US Department of Energy, Energy Information Administration 2008.
14 See Pham 2007b, 97–100.
15 Goldwyn 2004.
16 Azzam al-Ansari 2006, 27–30. For a full translation of the article along with analysis, see Paz and Terdman 2006, 1–6.
17 See Shay 2008.
18 US DoD 2007.
19 The video was posted to the www.alhesbah.org website on 11 September 2006. A partial translation of the transcript prepared by the Middle East Media Research Institute is available at http://memritv.org/Transcript.asp?P1=1269.
20 US Department of State 2008.

21 Organization of African Unity Convention on the Prevention and Combating of Terrorism (adopted 14 July 1999), art. 1 §3 (a), www.africa-union.org/Official_documents/Treaties_%20Conventions_%20Protocols/Algiers_convention%20on%20Terrorism.pdf#search=%22african%20unity%20convention%20terrorism%22.
22 See Davis 2007, 1–14.
23 Reno 2004, 236.
24 Terdman 2007, 29.
25 Last 2007.
26 Whelan 2007b.
27 Ellis 2004, 459–64.
28 Quoted in Miles 2005).
29 EUCOM 2005).
30 Ibid.
31 Canney 2006.
32 Quoted in Klare and Volman 2006, 619.
33 See Burnley 2005.
34 See *Navy Newsstand* 2005.
35 Gilmore 2007.
36 See Franke 2007, 1–13.
37 Ward 2008a.
38 Ibid.
39 CENTCOM 2007.
40 See CJTF-HOA 2007.
41 As a subordinate command of CENTCOM, the CJTF-HOA's operational area is circumscribed by the former's AOR; however, its wider "area of interest" aligns with the AU's regional organization to include the Comoros, Djibouti, Ethiopia, Eritrea, Kenya, Mauritius, Madagascar, Rwanda, Seychelles, Somalia, Sudan, Tanzania, and Uganda, as well as Yemen for geographical and strategic reasons.
42 The EAC's members are Burundi, Kenya, Rwanda, Tanzania, and Uganda.
43 IGAD's current effective members are Djibouti, Ethiopia, Kenya, Somalia, Sudan, and Uganda, Eritrea having announced in April 2007 that it was suspending its participation in the sub-regional organization.
44 Schermerhorn 2005, 57.

5 An African perspective on security

M.A. Mohamed Salih

Introduction

African regional and sub-regional organizations were originally formed to foster economic and social development and political and cultural integration. However, in recent years, their objectives and programmes have become increasingly dominated by peace and security issues as major defining elements of their objectives. Africa's regional and sub-regional organizations' shift towards establishing military commands and standby forces has occurred at a time when the social conditions of a large proportion of Africa's population have deteriorated. Unwittingly, a skewed logic privileging militarized security has become the dominant form of security, with the negative peace as the preferred course of action, knowing that African fundamental social problems, including conflict, are not caused by the lack of militarized notions of security, but by abject poverty and destitution.

In this chapter I argue that an African perspective that can be defended and justified should not and could not be nurtured by the same logic of military security arrangements that have, through decades of conflict, obliterated African people's well-being and subjected a large number of them to intolerable levels of violence and poverty. I argue the case for an African perspective on security premised on the virtues of human security as an alternative to the current dominant militarized peace and security arrangements. The chapter commences with defining human security and then proceeds to delineate the compelling case for a human security perspective by interrogating the human conditions in Africa. Then, the chapter explains the current retreat of African regional and sub-regional organizations from development to a militarized security. The chapter closes with an exploration of the linkages with the AFRICOM debate from this perspective.

A debate has often ensued as to whether an African perspective on security espouses one of the two dominant conventional perspectives on hard and soft security. I commence by contrasting the basic elements of hard and soft security. Hard security implies: (1) the presence, at any given time, of formidable military forces and other capabilities to respond to external and inter-state security threats; and (2) a build-up of forces, including alliances to secure the force needed to ensure strategic advantage, whereby an arms race becomes unavoidable.[1]

On the other hand, soft security implies: (1) an inward-looking security concerned with internal security issues emanating from intra-state conflicts, organized crime, human trafficking, weapons or drugs and money laundering etc.; and (2) outcomes that are often less destructive, less discernible and, to an even lesser degree, determinable in terms of success or failure. This is in sharp contrast to the usage of hard security, where the result in terms of victory or defeat is conspicuous and unavoidable.[2]

Neither a hard nor soft security perspective is appropriate for defining an African perspective on security. These perspectives are blurred, irrelevant and to a large extent reminiscent of the Cold War. They are blurred because many African states have resorted to hard security in order to resolve soft security threats, such as ethnic, religious and nationalist conflicts and concerns. The distinction between an outward function for the use of the military and inward functions for the use of the police for solving soft security problems is really irrelevant in countries where such a distinction does not exist. In many African and other developing countries, the state operators assign to the military many police functions, such as road blocks and curbing violent riots and demonstrations. The notion that the outcome of soft security policies and interventions is less destructive is also grossly erroneous.

While it is possible for Africans to be amenable to living under conditions where soft security prevails, history has shown that some African states have systematically and sometimes deliberately compromised the soft security of their citizens; they have compounded soft security provision, with the state itself becoming a source of fear. Soft security alone cannot respond to people's security needs, which are, to a large measure, human security needs. It privileges the punitive role of the internal security organs and their ability to punish the symptoms while leaving the underlying social and material root causes intact. This is exactly what the African state has been capable of doing, i.e. responding to intractable social problems, legitimate resentment and grievances with force, using policy and armies' monopoly over the use of power and coercion.

Instead of using cliché definitions originating in competing perspectives within conventional security definitions, an African perspective of security ought to be human and people-centred. This chapter offers a human security perspective as an alternative to both soft and hard security. Therefore, I commence with explaining human security and its enduring relevance and implications for Africa.

In 1994, the United Nations Development Programme (UNDP) *Human Development Report* contrasted the dominant conventional notions of security with human security in this way:

> For too long, the concept of security has been shaped by the potential for conflict between states. For too long, security has been equated with threats to a country's borders. For too long, nations have sought arms to protect

their security. For most people today, a feeling of insecurity arises more from worries about daily life than from the dread of a cataclysmic world event. Job security, income security, health security, environmental security, security from crime, these are the emerging concerns of human security all over the world.[3]

The UNDP also defined chronic threats such as hunger, disease and repression and 'sudden and hurtful disruptions'. In a more expansive treatment of the relevance of human security to the African experience, Caroline Thomas has alerted us to the significance of human security as a fundamental departure from an orthodox international relations security analysis. In international relations the dominant notion of security has the state as the exclusive primary referent object, whereas in human security, human beings and their complex social and economic relations are given primacy with or over states.[4] This notion of human security also implies that human security is about citizenship, where citizens enjoy fundamental rights (human, civil, political and economic) with practicable provisions to redress violations of these rights. These rights can be guaranteed only by states that recognize the sanctity of citizen rights and where state security is subservient to that of the citizens from whom it draws its legitimacy.

In Africa, the relevance of human security from a citizenship perspective dates back to the colonial period where the struggle for independence meant the struggle for citizenship rights. In the following section, I explore the continued relevance of this notion to the African perspective on security.

The antecedence of an African perspective on security

In my earlier writings, I argued that an African perspective on security is different from the dominant Western-inspired perspectives in that most Africans are yet to satisfy their basic human needs, are poor and are incapable of harnessing their human and natural resources for the betterment of their standards of living.[5] Above all, Africa is technologically under-developed and, for the most part, militarily dependent on external powers with higher conventional security capabilities. This is, in itself, sufficient reason why an African perspective on security should be human. Hansen has succinctly argued for the African perspective on security as follows:

> For us [Africans] the perspective on the peace problematic which we can defend and justify is that which makes it possible for the majority of the people in this planet to enjoy physical security, a modicum of material prosperity, the satisfaction of the basic needs of human existence, emotional wellbeing, political efficacy and psychic harmony.[6]

Clearly this perspective underscores the interconnection of African security with broader human security arrangements based on development and regional security, understood in terms of the elimination of the sources of direct and structural violence. Furthermore, the industrially and militarily advanced countries' concept of security is militarily inclined, while the African perspective is based on managing mere survival on a continent with very little, if any, bargaining power other than its commodities, minerals, oil and other natural riches.

This perspective is not new. It dates back to the colonial experience, where the colonial might left them with few options other than rejecting a notion of security that had never taken their desire to live in dignity on their continent into account. The prevalent security arrangement during the colonial legacy was that of the empires and their citizens, not that of the colonies. I illustrate this point in the following synoptic depiction of the persistence of an African perspective on security from colonialism through independence until today.

Africa has been the victim of colonization by societies that mustered formidable command of military technology, with Africans disadvantaged and therefore having to assign security a different meaning from that of the colonialists. For the colonialists, security meant advancing their own well-being and improving their capabilities to deter rebellion and subdue the unruly in societies alienated from their resources and even the possibility of enjoying the fruits of their own land and labour.

Supported by slavery as a supplier of plantation workers and forced labour, colonization undermined one of the most cherished aspects of human security, 'the achievement of human dignity, which incorporates personal autonomy, control over one's life, and unhindered participation in the life of the community'.[7] It is natural that the decolonization struggle was meant to restore Africans' human dignity, which was infringed upon for more than four centuries of conquest. The struggle was most profound, unrelenting and absorbing against a security arrangement that denied them freedom and left them meagre, if any, social amenities, technological development or independent trade outlets.

After the attainment of independence and self-rule, the most pressing issue for African countries has been, and still is, development, initially defined as basic human needs (food, health, water and shelter). Basic human needs are basic human security needs as recently defined by the UNDP: 'Safety from chronic threats such as hunger, disease, and repression and protection from sudden disruption in the pattern of daily life.'[8]

Ake laments that, despite the difficulties that confronted the independent African states, the elite could not abandon development 'because it was the ideology by which the political elite hoped to survive and to reproduce its domination'.[9] A false dawn has masked reality and turned citizens' aspirations away while the elite competed for office, self-enrichment and power, using the state and its resources to ensure their political and even physical survival. I add to Ake's contention that, as the development crisis intensified, the elite and state have lost people's allegiance and a second liberation for the restoration of dignity and human security ensued. The state institutions (law and order, the administrative structures and institutions, the meagre development that was achieved since independence) suffered the wrath of angry and disappointed counter currents. From Somalia to Sudan, from Sierra Leone to Liberia and from the Democratic

Republic of Congo (DRC) to Chad and Rwanda and others, civil wars and conflicts, and the destruction of the basis of human security were unrelenting. With war and civil strife, the gap in perception of security between the African elite, both civilian and military, that controlled the state and the African people has increased, nurturing at least two contradictory security objectives:

1   The elite and operators of the state perceived state security to be paramount, often misconstrued to mean their own security. In many cases, the attainment of state security meant silencing political opponents, suppressing genuine grievances by opposing political parties, ethnic or religious groups. For the majority of the African people, state or national security has not been translated into physical security or respect for social, economic and political rights. The deployment of state security organs (policy and the army) in pursuance of citizens perceived as enemies of the state has resulted in gross human rights abuses, thus undermining state legitimacy and, in some cases, justified taking up arms against an oppressive authoritarian state; and

2   While basic human needs have persisted as the major security concern for the majority of the African people, skewed national security priorities have also persistently diverted substantial human, financial and other resources to military security. The war of vision between the African people and their political elite and leadership has played a significant role in the quest to order the state priorities and its intrusive manner in regulating its citizens' affairs.

Therefore, it is plausible to argue that under divergent state and society interests, the African people's struggle for democracy cannot be separated from their struggle to humanize the state by making it more responsive to a security perspective premised on improving human security provisioning. Elsewhere I argue that, had the African people not resisted state oppression, no external force, no matter how powerful or endowed with infinite resources, would have ever been able to rescue such a socially, religiously, culturally and ethnically complex continent as Africa.[10] The relevance of the struggle for democracy for African people's security resonates with the contention that, as part of human development, democracy makes them more secure in freedom and in dignity, with equality and protection of human rights.[11]

It is from this perspective I argue that Africa needs security arrangements different from those which dominated the continent from the colonial to the post-colonial rule. These new security arrangements are informed by and responsive to the fundamental social problems confronting the African people. This I will attempt to explain with reference to prevailing social conditions in Africa.

Why Africa needs a different perspective on security?

Africa suffers an apparent human security deficit in terms of satisfaction of basic human needs. Out of the 50 least developed countries (LDCs) in the world, 34

(68 per cent) are African.[12] Income poverty has fallen in all regions of the world since 1990, except in sub-Saharan Africa, which is the only region that has witnessed an increase both in the incidence of poverty and in the absolute number of the poor. Some 300 million people – almost half of Africa's total population – live on less than US$1 per day.[13] Sadly, in 25 of Africa's LDCs the gross domestic income (GDI) per capita is less than US$500. In countries such as Burundi (US$90), Liberia (US$110), the DRC (US$120), Eritrea (US$180) and Chad (US$260), the GDI per capita is too low to maintain a life.[14]

Behind these statistics there is real human misery, revealed by two recent reports on the human conditions in Africa: the *Human Development Report*[15] and *The Millennium Development Goals* Report.[16] These reports make grim reading and, due to their importance for making the case for human security in Africa, I synthesize their major findings in detail in order to be able to make the case for an African perspective on security.

The *Human Development Report* developed an elaborate Human Development Index (HDI) which consists of a composite index that measures a country's average achievements in three basic dimensions of human development: a long and healthy life; access to knowledge; and a decent standard of living. These basic dimensions are measured by life expectancy at birth, adult literacy and combined gross enrolment in primary-, secondary- and tertiary-level education, and gross domestic product (GDP) per capita in purchasing power parity US dollars (PPP US$), respectively.[17]

Table 5.1 shows some alarming trends in terms of Africa's total African population, which has more than doubled from 341.1 million in 1975 to 722.7 million in 2005. An annual population growth rate of 2.8 per cent and 2.3 per cent during 1975–2005 and 2005–15, respectively, is almost five times higher that the average GDP growth during the same period, noting that the GDP growth rate was negative during 1975–2005. Illiteracy remains high and the number of people with access to sources of clean drinking water is low, with 32 per cent of the population malnourished. As if this level of misery is not enough, it was reported in 2008 that, in 2005 slightly more than one-third of the urban population in developing regions lived in slum conditions; in sub-Saharan Africa, the proportion was over 60 per cent. In sub-Saharan Africa, half of the slum households suffered from two or more shelter deprivations, lacking a combination of access to improved water, improved sanitation, durable housing or sufficient living area.[18]

The *Millennium Development Goals Report* prognosis of the levels of poverty and Africa's progress in the field of poverty reduction are shocking. According to the report, the proportion of people in sub-Saharan Africa living on less than $1 per day is unlikely to be reduced by the target of one-half in 2015. The goal of cutting in half the proportion of people in the developing world living on less than $1 per day by 2015 remains within reach. In contrast, previous estimates suggest that little progress was made in reducing extreme poverty in sub-Saharan Africa. Overall, higher food prices are expected to push many more people into absolute poverty, with estimates suggesting that the increase will be as many as

Table 5.1 Population, GDP and HDI trends in Africa

Population/GDP and HDI	Year and values
Population (millions)	1975 (314.1) 2005 (722.7)
Annual population growth rate (%)	1975–2005 (2.8) 2005–15 (2.3)
GDP per capita (PPP US$)	2005 (1,998)
GDP per capita, annual growth rate (%)	1975–2005 (−0.5) 1990–2005 (0.5)
Life expectancy at birth (years)	2005 (49.6)
Adult literacy rate (% aged 15 and above)	1995–2005 (60.3)
Combined gross enrolment ratio for primary, secondary and tertiary education (%)	2005 (50.6)
MDG population using improved sanitation (%)	1990 (32.0) 2004 (37.0)
MDG population using improved water source (%)	1990 (48.0) 2004 (55.0)
MDG population under-nourished (%)	1990–2 (36.0) 2002–4 (32.0)

Source: UNDP Human Development Report 2007/2008, compiled from table 1, p. 232; table 5, p. 246; table 7, p. 254; and table 14, p. 280.

100 million. Most of the increase will occur in sub-Saharan Africa and Southern Asia, already the regions with the largest numbers of people living in extreme poverty.[19]

Maternal mortality remains unacceptably high across much of the developing world. In 2005, more than 500,000 women died during pregnancy, childbirth or the six weeks after delivery. Of these deaths, 99 per cent occurred in the developing regions, with sub-Saharan Africa and South Asia accounting for 86 per cent of them. In sub-Saharan Africa, a woman's risk of dying from treatable or preventable complications in pregnancy and childbirth over the course of her lifetime is 1 in 22, compared to 1 in 7,300 in the developed regions of the world. Sub-Saharan Africa accounts for approximately half the deaths of children under five in the developing world. Between 1990 and 2006, about 27 countries – the significant majority in sub-Saharan Africa – made no progress in reducing childhood deaths.[20]

Employed persons living in a household where each member earns less than $1 per day are considered to be the 'working poor'. In sub-Saharan Africa, over half the workers fall into this category.[21] The generally low and volatile changes in productivity in sub-Saharan Africa have limited the decline in working poverty in Africa. The majority of countries making the least progress in reducing child malnutrition are in sub-Saharan Africa. In sub-Saharan Africa, however, the net enrolment ratio has only recently reached 71 per cent, even after a significant jump in enrolment that began in 2000. Around 38 million children of primary-school age in this region are still out of school. In sub-Saharan Africa, only one-quarter of children of secondary-school age are in secondary school.[22]

The presentation of these serious human security problems confronting Africa should not give the impression that Africans have not been struggling to redress these problems. Elsewhere I have drawn attention the poverty–human security nexus in Africa, comparing and contrasting New Partnership in African Development (NEPAD), Africa's home-grown initiative and the MDGs. By-and-large, NEPAD objectives coincide with those of the MDGs (eradicate extreme poverty and hunger; achieve universal primary education; promote gender equality and empower women; improve maternal health; combat HIV/AIDS, malaria and other diseases; and develop a global partnership for development). The common thread of strategic thinking cutting across both NEPAD and the MDGs is that peace and security are also part of a new development conception concerned with human development-cum-human security issues. In other words, the negative consequences of violent conflict on human security and its potential for exacerbating poverty are too well demonstrated to be left unattended.[23] I deal with these in the following section on the human security elements of African security architecture.

Obviously, the dire social conditions in Africa require a security approach devoid of the conventional security arrangements, which are by-and-large premised on military security as a means to ensure national security. In the introduction to this chapter I have attempted to elucidate the fact that conventional security arrangements have not benefited the African people, and have largely been used by the state to oppress its opponents under the pretext of national security. Despite several calls for disarmament and reduction in military expenditure, the business-as-usual approach to security still prevails in many African countries. Unfortunately, recent statistics do not show that a shift from military to human security has been contemplated in many African countries. For example, in 2005, countries such as Eritrea spent over 24.1 per cent of their GDP on military expenditure, with Ethiopia following at 8.5 per cent, Angola at 5.7 per cent and Burundi at 6.2 per cent. Africa's better-performing economies (Ghana, Uganda, Tanzania, Nigeria and Mauritius) spent 0.7–1 per cent of their GDPs on military expenditure.[24] Apart from Nigeria, which is confronted with the Niger Delta rebellion, the rest of the low military expenditure countries are relatively more peaceful than those with higher military expenditures.

In short, due to these social conditions in Africa, the case for human security rather than clichés of hard or soft security is compelling and self-evident. It is more so because very few African countries have been engaged in inter-state wars. The majority of African post-independence wars were intra-state, which makes the case for a military-based national security rather obsolete while the majority of the African people live under conditions of absolute poverty. As Stephan Kingebiel has purported, security is bound to remain – and rightly so – one of the major issues in Africa, partly as a reflection of post-Cold War conditions.[25] But a policy that concentrates solely on military security would be too limited and myopic. There is a need to enlarge the options for short-term responses and peace missions. Seen in these terms, there is still a great deal of work to do. But long-term efforts must be assigned high priority. To be sure, an African perspective on security ought to be human, a negation of the very security structures that breed conflict rather than people, destruction rather than development, and exclusion and abuse of human rights rather than inclusion and social justice.

From regional development organizations to military commands and standby forces

This section of the chapter is not intended to provide a detailed history of the development of African regional and sub-regional organizations as there are several publications on this subject.[26] I rather aim at establishing the fact that, from an African perspective, these regional organizations were originally established to foster development and political integration rather than develop into military establishments with formal command structures and brigades. Therefore, I argue that it is only later during their development that African regional and sub-regional areas begin to acquire more prominent security characteristics.

To be sure, African regional organizations from the Organization of African Unity (OAU) and its successors the African Union (AU) to the Economic Community of West African States (ECOWAS), the Southern African Development Community (SADC), the East African Community (EAC) and the Intergovernmental Authority on Development (IGAD) were never originally established as peace and security organizations with the tacit intent to establish regional military commands and structures. For example, the OAU was originally established to enhance the decolonization process and protect the African independent states from external intervention. The 1972 proposal to establish a pan-African defence force to act as a peacekeeping force based on the UN model, capable of intervening in African inter-state conflicts with an African high command to defend African states against outside powers and South African aggression, was rejected due to ideological differences, amongst other things, among the African states. In 1981 the idea of a defence pact was discussed to support the frontline states against South Africa's racist regime. Divisions among African leaders were between those who argued for the sanctity of sovereignty and non-interference in the internal affairs of other states and those who argued for a continental military command to deter external attacks, to intervene in domestic disorders, to prevent or suppress military coups, and to counter the forces of racist South Africa.

This, however, does not mean that the OAU was aloof or not engaged in peace negotiations, or supportive of the organization of military forces and peacekeeping operations, notably taking part in a peacekeeping operation in Chad during the Chad–Libya war. More significant is the OAU's support for the Group of Frontline States (GFLS) against the South African white supremacist regime's destabilization policies and its surrogate pro-Portugal counter-revolutionary fronts in Mozambique and Angola.[27] In fact, the establishment of the Southern African Development Coordination Conference (SADCC) in 1980 was, to a large extent, inspired by the support GFLS had gained from the OAU at the continent level and internationally. Moreover, the OAU's 1980 Lagos Plan of Action encouraged sub-regional economic cooperation as building blocks for a continental economic union. The SADCC adopted a project-based approach, with each member taking responsibility for a particular sector (e.g. Angola for energy, Mozambique for transport, Swaziland for human resources development), focusing attention on the coordination of members' development initiatives, rather than on formulating a regional economic development strategy. The aim was to boost the activities of the individual states in the areas of infrastructure and productive sectors. Cooperation in the field of transport infrastructure was, however, the prime concern of the organization, given the region's landlocked countries' dependence on South Africa for the transport of goods. Developments in this sector became one of the main targets of South Africa's destabilization policy of the 1980s.[28]

In January 2004, African ministers of defence and security, meeting at the AU headquarters in Addis Ababa, Ethiopia, adopted the Draft Framework for a Common African Defence and Security Policy. The ministers reviewed progress made in developing an African standby peacekeeping force and an early-warning system to detect and prevent potential conflicts and to ensure rapid humanitarian relief during disasters. In July 2004, the AU Assembly (heads of state or government), meeting in Addis Ababa, formally adopted the defence and security policy as Africa's 'blueprint' in the search for peace, security and stability on the continent.[29] Today, the AU has established a Peace and Security Council (PSC) as an implementation mechanism within a wide-ranging Common Africa Defence and Security Policy (CADSP); an end to the pan-African non-intervention pact which was the hallmark of the OAU, the predecessor of the AU; and entered into regional security arrangements, such as the involvement of the AU/UN forces in Sudan/Darfur and Somalia.[30]

However, the SADCC remained an informal institution, without treaty or constitution, and operated on an ad hoc basis. The transformation of the SADCC from 'conference' to 'community' (the creation of the SADC via the Windhoek Treaty 1992) signalled a major shift in its objectives, structure and mode of operation. Key among the many objectives of the SADC is the desire of its members to achieve development and economic growth; alleviate poverty; enhance the standard and quality of life of the people of southern Africa; support the socially disadvantaged through regional integration; evolve common political values, systems and institutions; promote and defend peace and security; promote self-sustaining development on the basis of collective self-reliance and the interdependence of member states; and develop policies aimed at the progressive elimination of obstacles to the free movement of capital and labour, goods and services, and of the people of the region generally, among member states.[31]

The Intergovernmental Authority on Drought and Development (IGADD) was founded in 1986 as a sub-regional response to the recurring and severe droughts and other natural disasters which precipitated hunger and famine amongst a large proportion of the population.[32] It was succeeded in 1996 by the IGAD, with expanded areas of regional cooperation and a new organizational structure. In its new revitalized form and structure, the IGAD set itself a vision for becoming 'the premier regional organization for achieving peace, prosperity and regional integration in the IGAD region'. This vision is supported by a three-pronged mission to assist and complement the efforts of the member states to achieve, through increased cooperation: (1) food security and environmental protection; (2) promotion and maintenance of peace and security and humanitarian affairs; and (3) economic cooperation and integration.

The IGAD's main objective is to promote joint development strategies and gradually harmonize macro-economic policies and programmes in the social, technological and scientific fields; harmonize policies with regard to trade, customs, transport, communications, agriculture, and natural resources, and promote free movement of goods, services, and people within the region; create an enabling environment for foreign, cross-border and domestic trade and investment; and achieve regional food security and encourage and assist efforts of member states to collectively combat drought and other natural and man-made disasters and their natural consequences.

Also, like other regional and sub-regional organizations and with the collapse of one of its member states (Somalia) and wars in Sudan, northern Uganda, and even an inter-state war involving Eritrea and Ethiopia, the IGAD has shifted its emphasis from development to peace negotiations and peacekeeping operations, under the auspices of the AU. In April 2005, IGAD member states, in addition to the Comoros, Madagascar, Rwanda and the Seychelles, signed the Memorandum of Understanding on the Establishment of the Eastern African Standby Brigade (EASBRIG). Article 3 stipulates that EASBRIG's objective is 'to carry out in a timely manner the functions of maintenance of peace and security as mandated by the Peace and Security Council of the African Union (AU) in accordance with the Consultative Act of the African Union'.[33] By now the full integration of the IGAD in an enlarged East African regional military structure is complete, and its involvement in the conflicts in Sudan and Somalia are testimony to this major shift of emphasis from development to an organization dominated by the military security agenda.

Likewise, ECOWAS was established in May 1975[34] with the main objective of promoting cooperation and integration in economic, social and cultural activity, ultimately leading to the establishment of an economic and monetary union through the total integration of the national economies of member states. It also aims to raise the living standards of its people, maintain and enhance economic stability, foster relations among member states and contribute to the progress and development of the continent. However, in 1980 and owing to the emergent conflicts in the West African sub-continent, 13 of its members signed a mutual defence pact providing for collective military response to attack from non-ECOWAS countries, mediation and peacekeeping missions in the event of armed conflict between member states, and defence against external states that initiate or support insurgencies within member states. It also provided for a Defence Council, a Defence Commission, and joint exercises, but no standing regional force or command structure. Gradually ECOWAS evolved into a regional organization with a Defence and Security Commission, a West African standby force of 6,500 soldiers that could deploy rapidly in response to crisis or threats to peace and security in the West African sub-region. By 2004 it had replaced the ECOWAS Cease-Fire Monitoring Group (ECOMOG) as a new military structure capable of launching peacekeeping or even intervention missions at short notice.

In short, during the last decade, there have been at least four developments in African regional security arrangements. A major emphasis on African regional and sub-regional organizations establishes joint military commands and standby forces. This is evidenced by an increase in African regional security organizations' engagement in peace negotiations, intervention and peacekeeping. The emphasis on security also signals a shift of internal and external development resources from societal to security issues. For instance, peacekeeping operations and humanitarian emergency take priority over development, and even development itself has, in some instances, been militarized. The fear here is that, in the process of responding to real or imagined security threats, the securitization of Africa's regional and sub-regional organizations has made human security issues subservient to military security.

The AFRICOM connection

Other contributors to this volume have already introduced AFRICOM, its strategic objectives and possibility of reshaping Africa's future role in the emergent global security architecture. In this brief section, I will introduce a few intersections and correlates in respect of the AFRICOM debate from a human security perspective, reflecting on the added value of Africa's emergent regional and sub-regional military command and standby forces. I will ask the same question in respect of AFRICOM and its potential role for enhancing regional and sub-regional military command and standby forces, and whether it is desirable at all to militarize human security.

The starting point of my contention is that I cast doubt on whether the proliferation of African regional and sub-regional military commands and standby forces will have a positive effect on the maintenance of peace and security in Africa. This is so mainly because the root causes of African conflicts cannot be explained in terms of a lack of military security to respond to external military threats. If military security refers to the ability to quell rebellion or defeat liberation movements on the battlefield, then it is not really the security priority of the African people. The security priority, as I argued earlier, is human development (food security, health, education, clean drinking water, shelter, etc.). Poverty, exclusion and destitution are major factors explaining the prevalence of conflict. Furthermore, the African states have abused their monopoly over the use of force and coercion to protect corrupt and oppressive state apparatus rather than protecting citizens' rights.

If the role of African regional and sub-regional military commands and standby forces is intervention in conflicts in other African states, so far their experiences with these ventures leave much to be desired. Evidently, African regional and sub-regional organizations are lacking in the military capabilities to mount such interventions on their own, are largely dependent on foreign financial and technical resources, and have so far contributed a dismal proportion of the peacekeeping in operations in which they have participated.[35]

Some of the security threats the African regional and sub-regional military commands and standby forces are supposed to fight or respond to are global in nature (terrorism, international crime networks, maritime piracy, humanitarian intervention, peacekeeping, etc.) and require globally shared responsibility. Africans often ask the question of whether they should use their own meagre economic resources for combating global security issues given the rampant human security deficit. It is here where the connection between African regional and sub-regional military commands and standby forces and AFRICOM becomes apparent.

The African military and their political masters expect AFRICOM to provide technical and financial resources to the regional and sub-regional military commands and standby forces, thus freeing up their own resources for other purposes, including improving the dire social conditions of the military forces. In some countries, low-paid military forces have mutinied, participated in looting and erected roadblocks for extortion and collecting illicit payments to boost their incomes.

Some African civilians, military, security experts and researchers have come to realize the utility of AFRICOM's technical and military capabilities in confronting global security threats that no single country or even region can fight alone. The African militaries are under-resourced and therefore more vulnerable than most to threats posed by terrorists, internal criminal networks, human and drug trafficking and money laundering. From this perspective, it is very difficult, if not impossible, for poor countries, the majority of whose population live in absolute poverty, to match the military capabilities and resources of AFRICOM. The possibility of collapsed or failed states (Liberia, Sierra Leone and the DRC) defending themselves against internal adversaries, let alone external threats of a global nature, is inconceivable.

That AFRICOM could be effective in supporting the capacity of countries emerging from conflict – with active civil militia, warlords and light and small weapons beyond state control – to maintain peace and security on their own is impossible. In these circumstances, Africans may contemplate the idea that their regional and sub-regional military commands and standby forces would ensure a sense of ownership with a measure of autonomy in regional security policy and decision making structures. Unfortunately, they do not command the resources to do so on their own. Several fault-lines have emerged in almost all peacekeeping operations undertaken by Africa's emergent regional security structures. Few countries are ready to commit troops or use their meagre human and financial resources for peacekeeping operations, let alone intervention – with the exception of Ethiopia's intervention in Somalia.

If the African states have failed in delivering human security to their people, the question many Africans will ask is whether AFRICOM will fare better than their own military and become an engine for peace and human security. Two factors hamper this type of thinking: (1) The African countries pose no military threat to each other, let alone the United States, but this does not mean that the United States has no legitimate interests in Africa; and (2) African conflicts and security problems are a result of internal and external factors which could be resolved by non-military means.

The best scenario in this case is that AFRICOM and the African regional and sub-regional commands and standby forces develop joint military programmes and leave the human security issues to international development agencies. AFRICOM and African regional and sub-regional military commands and standby forces can mount joint operations in support of the delivery of humanitarian emergency programmes and fight global security threats, which the African states are incapable of confronting alone.

Conclusion

In short, an African perspective on security is a human security-based negation of conventional security perspectives, which in the African context have historically privileged the security of the state over its citizens, and military security over human security. From this perspective, the more human security is securitized and militarized, the more it is taken away from people and put in the hands of the military, security personnel and state operators who have no contact with the lives of ordinary African people.

To be sure, human rather than military security is what would deliver peace and security to Africa. Militarizing human security through an alliance between AFRICOM and African regional and sub-regional commands and standby forces would enable AFRICOM to buy only short-term loyalty, with unpredictable long-term achievements. Worst of all, in the long-term, a militarized human security would make AFRICOM partly responsible for any future development.

Notes

1 Wallace 1999: 219.
2 Herd 2006.
3 UNDP 1994: 3; also see: Suhrke 1999; Liotta 2002; Commission on Human Security 2003; Glasius 2009.
4 Thomas 2001: 161. For a more recent application of human security to NEPAD and the MDGs, see Mohamed Salih 2008a.
5 Mohamed Salih 1989, 1990.
6 Hansen 1987: 1–2.
7 Thomas 1999: 3; Shakleina 2007: 1.
8 UNDP 1994: 23.
9 Ake 2006: 7.
10 Mohamed Salih 2001.
11 Ramcharan 2002: 9.

12 UNCTAD 2005: 6.
13 Ibid.
14 UNCTAD 2005: 6, 7, 20, 21, 23, 26, 27, 28, 30, 35, 37.
15 UNDP 2007/8.
16 UN 2008.
17 UNDP 2008: 225.
18 UN 2008: 43.
19 MDG 2008: 6.
20 Ibid.: 20–4.
21 Ibid.: 9.
22 Ibid.: 13–14.
23 For more on the poverty–conflict nexus, refer to Humphreys and Varshney 2004; Miguel *et al.* 2004; Collier and Hoeffler 2004; Collier *et al.* 2003; Sachs and Warner 2001.
24 UNDP 2008: 296–7.
25 Kingebiel 2005.
26 See Francis 2006 for more comprehensive coverage of the development of African regional peace and security systems.
27 Evans 1984; Neethling 2005a.
28 Evans 1984.
29 Neethling 2005a: 65.
30 Mohamed Salih 2008b; Mlambo 2006; Kaldor 2007; Mwangiru 2004.
31 SADC-PF 1995, 2005.
32 Governments of Djibouti, Ethiopia, Kenya, Somalia, Sudan and Uganda met in Djibouti in January 1986 to sign the agreement, which officially launched the IGADD with headquarters in Djibouti. The State of Eritrea became the seventh member after attaining independence in 1993.
33 The main organs of EASBRIG are the Assembly of East African Heads of States and Governments, the Assembly of East African Council of Ministers of Defence and Security, and the East African Committee of Chiefs of Defence Staff.
34 ECOWAS member states are: Benin, Burkina Faso, Cape Verde, Cote D'Ivoire, Gambia, Ghana, Guinea, Guinea Bissau, Mali, Niger, Nigeria, Sierra Leone, Togo.
35 Dorn 1998; Jackson 2000; Ghebremeskel 2002.

6 Solutions not yet sought

A human security paradigm for twenty-first-century Africa

Shannon Beebe

A few years ago, while working as the senior Africa analyst on the US Army general staff, I was tasked by the Chief of Staff to conduct an open-ended research project exploring how Africans view security and whether our current strategic security paradigm adequately addresses the concerns of Africa. A fair question, since Africa is often considered a country rather than a continent in Western security circle parlance. Indeed, there is a reason Africa is shaped like a question mark when it comes to our understanding of what drives security in Africa. In short, although the US strategic security narrative is necessary for traditional types of threat – the primary role of the military will always be to defend and protect against all enemies, foreign and domestic – it is insufficient for addressing the security concerns of Africans, thus marginalizing the influence of the United States. Why is this? While US security is driven through a lens of kinetic-based threat, African security – or insecurity – is best seen as conditions-based, falling along the strategic seams of Western security institutions. These conditions in and of themselves aren't threats, but are best seen as creeping vulnerabilities. However, left unchecked, these vulnerabilities become increasingly interdependent, combining over time into intractable, hydra-type threats defying traditional monolithic security responses, thus creating a vortex of violence incapable of being halted without great expenditure of resources.

This chapter seeks to challenge traditional thinking about what security means for Africa and explore solutions not yet sought in the form of a twenty-first-century human security paradigm. This will be accomplished through looking at how the United States – and by extension most of the West – has viewed security. We then transition to what Africans have said are their primary security concerns. With the imbalance between how the West has viewed security and the views on the continent, I then discuss how it might be we can bridge this gap for a more substantial partnership arriving at sustainable security arrangements: a human security paradigm. In the final section, I discuss the "what might be" should a shift towards a human security paradigm occur.

Traditional Western views of security

To begin this discussion, it is important to think about how the West has traditionally viewed security in modern times. Modern Western security has been driven through understanding threat from a state-centric, realist paradigm. In the twentieth century, threats were normative, conventional, and militarily quantifiable. From a Western perspective, security has been very much about defense and protection against these "kinetic" threats. Which is to say, we have developed a security system to protect against similar (symmetric) types of threat architecture. Central points to this paradigm, briefly outlined, were: an international system based on state sovereignty; protection of territorial borders; protection of economic viability through defense of technology and infrastructure; large standing, professional militaries oriented toward engagement with other like-type military forces; and alliances based on similar views of economic principles. This was the "system" we (the developed world) bought in to – both East and West – and the developing world had to suffer.

In this system, the state reigned supreme and was the focal object of international discourse and military protection/defense. Conventional militaries were responsible for creating security on one side to protect the state, thus creating the tangible threats to other states of an opposing bent. In the twentieth century, the state maintained relative hegemony over what has been called "elements of national power": diplomatic tools, control of information and its dissemination, military power projection, economic viability. State sovereignty was paramount, with additional legal frameworks being constructed to adjudicate international infractions of this rule set. The United States led the development of most of these international agencies, organizations, and bodies after the end of World War II. A rule set based on a grouping of states was important to this structure. Leaders of these states were recognized to be the sovereign decision makers for those states. Although often times many of these leaders were known to be ruthless, oppressive, and dictatorial, because the world was divided into two poles, intervention in these countries was only carried out when it was in the self-interest of one – or both – of those poles. Seldom were actions carried out based on the needs of people within various countries. Rather, intervention was an exercise of realist state interest. Populations had little voice in their own affairs in these oppressive states and information as such was difficult to project in or extract out.

A corollary to this was the protection of the state's territorial borders and those of its allies. NATO was formed along these lines, with Article 5 explicitly stating that an attack on one ally would be constituted as an attack on all. Territorial integrity has traditionally been viewed seriously within the United States. If one doesn't think territorial sovereignty is important to the United States, all one has to do is look at the US flag: 13 stripes for the 13 original colonies, 50 stars for 50 states. Most important to understand here, is that military and security systems were oriented to look for conventional threats that might have power projection capabilities to infringe on sovereign territory and were designed to attack other militaries in order to capture or destroy territory and industrial capacity.

During the twentieth century, a discussion of security would have been incomplete without a brief mention of protecting the economic viability of the state. In the past, elements of economic power were assured through military protections of the state. During the era of multinational corporation (MNC) growth, these lines soon became blurred but still important. Economic ties were formed with allies and like-systems, with an understanding that each state had a vested interest in protecting those economic lines. This was normally insured through militaries such as the United States or funding for military actions in support of protecting the economic system.

As mentioned throughout this section, a multi-trillion dollar military-industrial complex was developed to support and defend this system. It worked well as the world was bipolar and the other guys were doing the same thing. In short, we all played with the same rule book, bending and breaking the rules where we could, and it was only a sin if you got caught. This was the enemy and threats we were prepared to face. Yet, what happened to the United States – and the world – on 11 September 2001, was an attack not launched from inside the system, not instigated by a state following the rules of sovereign interaction, and certainly not symmetric. It was the manifestation of long-standing collective vulnerabilities which had come together as a hydra-type threat operating along the periphery of our strategic focus. There will be volumes written on ascertaining the "failures of intelligence" to identify such a threat. Yet in final analysis, this threat began not as a system – nor is it a system to this day as many within the traditional defense community would lead us to believe – but as conditions of insecurity leveraging twenty-first-century technologies to create international networks.

Why the conventional paradigm of security is no longer relevant

So what has changed so dramatically, allowing an attack such as 9/11 to happen relatively undetected prior to the attack? If one were to look at international relations and interactions as a three-dimensional plane, with the X, Y, and Z axes represented as Political, Economic, and Information (closely mirroring the D-I-M-E elements of national power), what we discover is that the world has systemically changed along all three axes. Normally, a system is capable of adjusting to shock along one or two axes, but when there is shock along all three cardinal axes, the system becomes inherently unstable. Instability is an exponential factor for insecurity. This is what has happened to the structure of the twentieth-century system. Politically the world transitioned after the Cold War from a bipolar to a briefly unipolar then multipolar world. A multipolar world creates instability of its own. Economically, the world continues down the road of uneven globalization. The effects of this new economic system are still undetermined. What can be said is this: globalization has impacted not only upon economic systems, but also the cultural and societal structures within states. The final axis is Information. Traditionally, the state had control over most information dissemination or, at a minimum, information was passed at a much slower rate and through fewer sources than today. With the information revolution, the state has lost a great deal of control over information flow and thus a reduction of one element of national power. The twenty-first century might very well become the age of the individual and those groups that are most capable of manipulating information technology. This fact is well documented with the success of al-Qaeda in the run-up to 9/11. Virtual, international societies can be established with little more than a cell phone these days.

In short, what this means to the twentieth-century security system is that the "threat" has shifted from the state to just about anything, anywhere. This has untethered the conventional, international security landscape. It is now impossible to plan for every possible contingency with twentieth-century doctrine, defense structures and thinking. This fact has untethered the international security architecture. Although we still try to conduct a Global War on Terror (GWOT) using most of the same rules of engagement as we used during the Cold War, international security has inherently shifted from system-based drivers to conditions-based drivers. If we fail to adapt ourselves to this new system, we run the risk of, at best, becoming less relevant in world affairs and, at worst, adding to world instability through misperceived and misguided actions.

Security of systems versus security survival

To best illustrate the difference between the way the West views security and the way Africans view security, I am reminded of something one African ambassador told me. I was at a conference on terrorism and weapons of mass destruction (WMD) in Africa. The conference was in Washington, DC and attended by most of the African diplomatic and military attaché community. Numerous high-level officials from the US government were present, admonishing the African diplomatic community to help the United States identify terrorists in Africa and locate potential elements of WMD. I noticed one of the ambassadors whom I had known for several years shaking his head in disbelief. During a break, I approached him and asked his views of the conference thus far. His response to me was telling and has stuck with me as a poignant example of our differing views of security. He said:

> You Americans are always looking for terrorists and weapons of mass destruction. Yes, we have those things in Africa. We have terrorism. It is poverty, HIV/AIDS and malaria. We have weapons of mass destruction as well. It is an AK-47 usually carried by a child. All of this is played out every day in an environment we don't even control.

This would not be the last time during this research that I would hear much the same sentiments. Most Africans would talk to me about security in terms of security sector reform (SSR), health, poverty, and environmental shock caused by climate change as being their top security concerns.

I've thought a great deal about that statement and wondered, if we were to look at security through this lens rather than our state-centric threat lens, how would our world change? A simplified way of doing this is to look at a standard political relief map representing the way the United States has traditionally viewed security and compare that with cartograms representing the way Africans view their security. On a simple political relief map, we can see the traditional twentieth-century view of security – territorial borders, neatly displayed showing the world with the state as the referent object of that element, giving and taking security. Yet, were we to look at a cartogram of the world, how would it change? Cartograms are simply graphical representations of data injected within the state borders to show the impact of factoring in that specific set of variables relative to other states. These cartograms come from a group called *Worldmapper.org*. I have used their work over the past few years to show what the world through African eyes might look like. Figures 6.1–6.5 are examples of the ambassador's statement to me, graphically represented. Should we shift our view of terrorism and WMD to HIV/AIDS, malaria, poverty, child labor, deforestation, and the like, how significant to security issues do they now become?

These challenges for a developed country are stressors on the legitimacy of the government, but when dealing with these same challenges in the context of an African state, it is important to understand that at best, the state has minimal capacity to handle such challenges and, at worst, no political will. This is for multiple reasons, which fall outside the scope of this chapter; volumes have been written on the evils of colonialization. Suffice to say, the geo-political borders of

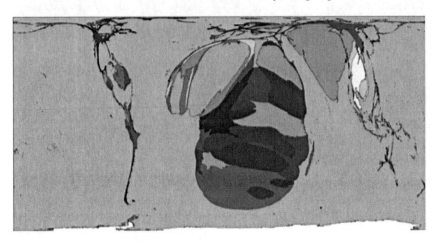

Figure 6.1 HIV/AIDS deaths (source: *Worldmapper.org*). Copyright 2006 SASI Group (University of Sheffield) and Mark Newman (University of Michigan).

Note
Territories are sized in proportion to the absolute number of people who died from HIV/AIDS in one year.

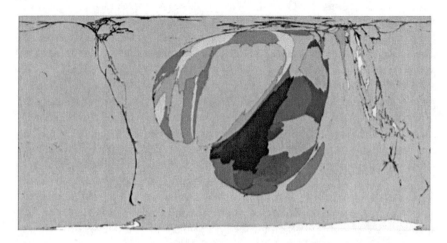

Figure 6.2 Malaria deaths (source: *Worldmapper.org*). Copyright 2006 SASI Group (University of Sheffield) and Mark Newman (University of Michigan).

Note
Territories are sized in proportion to the absolute number of people who died from malaria in one year.

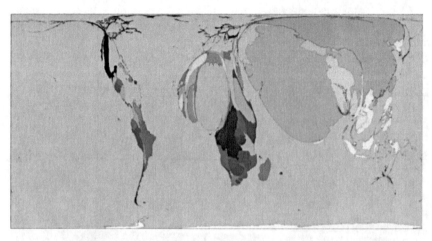

Figure 6.3 Populations living on US$1 per day (source: *Worldmapper.org*). Copyright 2006 SASI Group (University of Sheffield) and Mark Newman (University of Michigan).

Note
Territory size shows the proportion of all people living on less than or equal to US$ 1 in purchasing power parity per day.

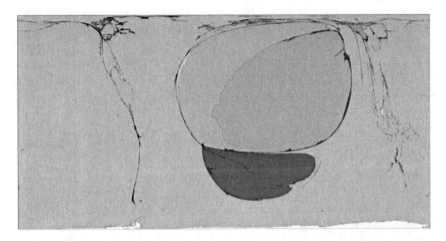

Figure 6.4 Populations killed by drought (source: *Worldmapper.org*). Copyright 2006 SASI Group (University of Sheffield) and Mark Newman (University of Michigan).

Note
Territory size shows the proportion of all people who have died in disasters due to drought, who died there. A disaster is an event which overwhelms local resources.

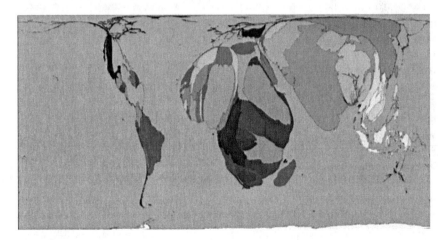

Figure 6.5 Child labor (source: *Worldmapper.org*). Copyright 2006 SASI Group (University of Sheffield) and Mark Newman (University of Michigan).

Note
Territory size shows the proportion of worldwide child work force (aged 10–14) that live there.

most African states were not a result of input from Africans, but rather the carving up of the continent at the Berlin Conference in the late 1800s. What this means is that although these borders make sense from a Western perspective, they have little relevance to cultures divided between two countries with an artificial line, little impact on herdsmen traveling with their herds in search of fertile grazing lands and water, little real significance for indigenous populations whose societal habits cross multiple borders as part of their everyday lives. What this means is that the governments in power are not necessarily representative of the entirety of the state, rather groups and sub-groups within the state. This can most readily be seen in today's context with the ongoing strife between the government of Sudan, government of Southern Sudan, and Darfur. This is a microcosm of challenges to security in Africa. First, the state of Sudan was created by the British with little thought that Darfur culturally had never belonged to the rest of Sudan. Second, the cultural divide between Arab north and Nubian south. Third, the division between pastoralists and herdsmen, with the impacts of global warming forcing the herdsmen further south in search of water for their herds. Finally, the lack of government capacity for power projection and the apparent unwillingness to provide personal security for its citizens. This all adds up to a very different type of security architecture that defies Western explanation.

Should we begin to see the world through this lens rather than our traditional state-centric lens, what becomes readily apparent is that security is something more than protection against kinetic-based threats. The question then becomes "what security and whose definition?" Should the West continue to demand adherence to a traditional view of security, we risk becoming marginalized in the eyes of those who most need a sustainable definition for security. Much like going to the doctor with a sore throat, only to have the doctor set one on the examination table, break one's leg, then proclaim the problem really isn't a sore throat but a broken leg: how often would one return for this treatment? This is an, admittedly far-fetched, anecdote that describes how many times the West has denied Africans the opportunity to define security for themselves because it fell outside the West's definition of what security should be. To maintain relevance in the eyes of Africans, the West will have to shift from imposing what it sees as the *right* definition for security on to Africa, to what Africans see as a *relevant* definition for their own security.

Toward a relevant security architecture for Africa: a human security paradigm

So, if a traditional Western security model is insufficient for explaining security from an African context, how best to do this? Again, I go back to the quote from the African ambassador and what so many Africans have discussed with me as their top security concerns in the forms of security sector reform, health, poverty, climate change, and lack of infrastructure. The security challenges of Africa can't be measured through quantifiable, kinetic metrics. The most relevant security narrative for Africa is found in a discussion of *human security*. What is human security? In 1994, the United Nations Development Program (UNDP) introduced the concept in their annual *Human Development Report*. Although the concept has been around for a number of years, this was the first attempt to codify and operationalize variables of this concept. What the report stated was:

> The concept of security has far too long been interpreted too narrowly: as a security of territory from external aggression, or as protection of national interests in foreign policy or as global security from the threat of nuclear holocaust. It has been related to nation-states more than people ... forgotten were the legitimate concerns of ordinary people who sought security in their daily lives. For many of them, security symbolized protection from the threat of diseases, hunger, unemployment, crime [or terrorism], social conflict, political repression and environmental hazards. With the dark shadows of the cold war receding, one can see that many conflicts are within the nations rather than between the nations.
>
> (UNDP 1994)

The report received little attention in Western security circles as we were still basking in "winning" the Cold War. Francis Fukuyama had proclaimed the end of history with the triumph of capitalism. Just a few years earlier, President George Bush had proclaimed this new era of democracy and freedom to be one of a "thousand points of light" to the West Point graduating class of 1991. As the West maintained its focus on state-based threats, this was all correct. The threat from states had dramatically decreased, with just a few "rogue" states remaining. Yet, the world was becoming inherently less stable.

What the *Human Development Report* of 1994 attempted to do was shift the security focus from the state as the referent object to focus more on populations and the insecurities which they would face. It was also prescient in identifying that the conflicts of the twenty-first century would have little to do with state rivalries, but rather with instabilities within the state which could be projected internationally through networks of despair. It went on to discuss the seven critical components of human security:

1 economic security – the threat from poverty;
2 food security – the threat emanating from hunger, famine, and global warming;
3 health security – the threat from pandemic disease and injury;
4 environmental security – the threat emanating from natural and manmade environmental shock, environmental degradation, and natural resource depletion;
5 personal security – threats emanating from acts of violence such as rape;
6 cultural security – threats targeted at specific groups impacting cultural integrity;
7 political – the threat of political oppression and lack of political freedoms.

The report went on to state: "The battle of peace has to be fought on two fronts. The first is the security front where victory spells freedom from *fear*. The second is the economic and social front where victory means freedom from *want*." This was translated into the concepts of freedom from want and freedom from fear.

This was, of course, a paradigm shift on a number of fronts. First, the report suggested that the referent object for security be shifted away from the nation-state as a focus and hegemon of power projection as it would become less and less relevant in the twenty-first century, moving to more closely concentrate on collective humanity grouped along lines of the above seven components. The second shift was from the way security had been measured and shared in the past. Human security is best exercised as a proactive, inclusive approach rather than a "siloed" approach with little inter-agency coordination or consideration for other organizations which might play larger roles, provided with accurate information. The need for this type of approach is simply because the seven components of human security are interrelated and no single organization/agency has sole purview or comparative advantage in all areas. This requires more of a joined-up approach.

This idea permeates into the way intelligence operations have been structured and oriented. Traditionally, intelligence collection was done through clandestine methods focused on state strengths and weaknesses, compartmentalized and shared sparingly. With human security, this idea is turned on its head and intelligence/information, call it what you will, should be openly shared and activities should be transparent to the greatest extent possible to all parties involved.

This leads to another important point, which was probably the most resounding point of the report. What the report identified for the first time was that an inextricable link between defense and development would be required for meaningful international security for the twenty-first century. In short, meaningful security for the twenty-first century would no longer be the sole purview of a department or ministry of defense from a Western capital. Rather, it would be an effort amongst a collection of non-traditional security actors attempting to find proactive ways of creating a security architecture developed on working *toward* an end-state rather than attempting to *avoid* the inevitable instability or, worse yet, picking up the pieces after the fact.

Douche.

The house of cards and Faberge rice bowls

As mentioned earlier, human security recognizes the interdependence of each component. This is important to understand for several reasons. First, this interaction between the various components is not readily measured and may fester for years before becoming a true security concern. This is a primary difference between human security and traditional security paradigms. Traditional state-based security could be measured by counting planes, tanks, and battleships; human security is about conditions. As mentioned at the beginning of this chapter, human security shifts from focusing on quantifiable metrics such as standing armies amassing along the borders, and tries to identify those conditions creating vulnerabilities that fall along the strategic seams of our understanding/With the unknown interaction amongst the variables, what might have been seen as security algebra has moved to security calculus.

To appreciate this, think of a house of cards or a spider's web. If you pull on one strand of the web, it changes the complexity and composition of the web entirely. Or, pull one card out of a house of cards and what happens? What is uncertain is which way the house will fall, how quickly it will fall, or if it will fall entirely, but what is guaranteed is that the house will no longer be left standing and will break down to a lesser common denominator. This is true also in looking at security in Africa. What is unknown is which component left unchecked will be the proverbial straw to break the camel's back. What was the final straw to begin the spiraling vortex of violence in Darfur? What spurred the latest round of violence in Eastern Congo? What next in Somalia? Although important discussions, one and all, this line of debate misses the first order point of the dynamic relation amongst each variable. Looking back at the analogy of the house of cards, it makes little sense working to strengthen any one card without strengthening the whole.

Herein lies the strength of human security, and at the same time its greatest potential shortcoming. In looking at how bureaucracies function, one thing is clear: there are plenty of Faberge rice bowls that no one wants to have broken or stolen. One short example: while working on the research project for the Army Chief of Staff, we convened a small working group of around 20 various US agencies working in Africa. One area that Africans had expressed to us as a security concern was SSR (being defined as military, police, judicial reform, rule of law, and established and enforceable penal system). The military is restricted by US Title X from engaging in police training. So, if the United States wanted to truly get at the whole of SSR, it was important to know who else was or might be willing to train police in Africa. We asked this question of the agencies present. The usual suspects – FBI, Homeland Defense, and the Department of Justice – all said they had training programs ongoing. What was informative was that there were five other organizations there that also said they were training police. Upon further questioning, we discovered these organizations had trained the same police in the same country less than six months apart without the others knowing about it. In the course of our research, this surfaced again and again. Why? Mostly because there was little traditional need to coordinate or talk across agency boundaries for various operations. I began calling this the "Who's on First" syndrome, named after the classic Abbott and Costello routine. Not only will there need to be coordination across various intergovernmental agencies, international organizations, and host nation agencies, there will also need to be a reaching out to non-traditional security partners in the non-governmental community of interest. Each agency and organization must come to a realization that twenty-first-century security requires working together rather than working individually or against each other.

Since the first days of the newest US unified command, US Africa Command (AFRICOM), being billed as a new way of doing business in the security arena, there has been an inherent tension amongst the Department of Defense (DoD) and elements of the development and NGO communities. Charges leveled against the command before the guidon was ever planted were that this command would be a military invasion of humanitarian space and this would be a progressive militarization of foreign policy. Before the command even had a designated commander, AFRICOM was doing more explaining about what it wouldn't be rather than what it would be. There was a certain call-to-arms to protect the parochial rice bowls and turfs that had been carved out over the years, and real concern that somehow this new command would break all the good work and programs that had been created throughout the years on the African continent. Regretfully, this argument carried far more weight than it ever should have, simply because the first order question of "what defines security on the African continent?" was overshadowed by arguments over base location on the continent, the "hidden agenda" for AFRICOM's stand up, and other lesser political dramas. Had a lens of human security been put on the task at hand, the discussion most certainly would have shifted from fears of the 800 lb DoD gorilla steamrolling across years of hard work by other organizations to more of an open discussion of how the interrelated components of human security require an open, transparent dialogue and some heavy intellectual lifting to lay out a framework of how each community of interest could best leverage their comparative advantage to create a sustainable security framework. What is meant by sustainable security?

I've often been asked to speak at various conferences and symposia discussing sustainable development in Africa. I tend to be the skunk at the party, however. I contend there can be no such thing as sustainable *development* until there is a sustainable *security*. Sustainable development is a strategic goal and one that I most certainly agree with. However, populations aren't concerned about next year's growing season, opening a bank account, saving for their children's education and the like when they are faced with imminent mortal danger. There is a reason you cannot yell "fire!" in a crowded theater. It is much the same for the daily lives of Africans who fear death from violence, disease, and pestilence. Their focus is on tactical, daily survival at the cost of strategic sustainable development. What must be understood is that populations with little hope of a tomorrow, living in fear, are very willing to mortgage their tomorrows for today's survival. Until these populations perceptually believe they are safe, have relative stability, and live in freedom of fear, there will be little concern for anything other than immediate steps to assure survival.

Yet, sustainable security and sustainable development are not independent of one another. As the *Human Development Report* of 1994 indicated, development and defense in the twenty-first century will be inextricably linked. So, instead of battening down the hatches and defending twentieth-century bureaucracies, what we should be looking for are ways of working together proactively to prevent conditions from becoming vulnerabilities; vulnerabilities from becoming crises; and crises from becoming open hostilities. The greatest strength of human security is the spirit of cooperation and openness to address problems in a transparent manner, leveraging the comparative advantages of various communities. Human security allows for looking at security and development challenges on their own merits, and not simply applying a cookie-cutter approach to our foreign policy and security actions. In the long run, this will also mean more efficiency in the use of resources. Again, going back to most of the events I attend on Africa, I often hear the lamentation of the West not doing *enough* in Africa. I often wonder if that is the real issue, or rather should we be asking if we are doing enough *together* in Africa.

Toward a more sustainable global security

If we are to have a meaningful, long-term, positive impact on African security, we must first shift from a Western view of what is *right* for Africa to what Africans are saying is *relevant* for their security. In my many discussions with African leadership and the average citizen on the street, Africans most often define their security in terms of SSR, health, poverty, and environmental shocks spurred by climate change on the continent. After the summer of 2008, food security would most certainly have moved up the list. With the exception of SSR, the other top concerns have not been viewed by traditional security architectures as "threats" or security concerns. Understanding through a human security lens that these elements make for the conditions of insecurity, then, begs the question of how best to approach a more sustainable global security. The answers aren't as complicated as one might think and are certainly achievable.

The second component to address is what many Western policymakers view as roadblocks to African development and security: lack of political will and corruption. There are numerous examples pointing to the intentionally weak political institutions designed to serve the "big man" rather than the people. Reinforcing this is the traditionally weak civil society that provides the checks and balances seen in most developed nations. This is partly due to the perceptions of the average African, still viewing themselves as servants to the state rather than citizens of the state. Corruption, by and large, can be viewed as endemic uncertainty on the part of the leaders in power that they will stay in power and a winner-takes-all attitude. This goes from the highest levels of government down to the local customs official, police officer, and even a teacher requiring bribes from their students. Is this because they are bad people or simply have a low-level perception of personal security and fear for the survival of themselves and their families from one day to the next?

Solutions not yet sought?

To get to new synergistic answers, the first myth we have to overcome is that Africa has to somehow pass through the twentieth century to make it into the twenty-first. While visiting with Mohammed Yunus, the Nobel Peace Prize recipient for his work on microfinance in Bangladesh, he said the key to success in working in the developing world is to "Let go of the present and don't fear the impossible." In short, when arguments are made that Africa has little infrastructure and this is holding back their development, it might be true, but the answer all too often is that we attempt to give Africans our twentieth-century solutions – or rather our definition of "right."

So, if we are to believe Africans know what is relevant for their security and the top four security concerns are SSR, poverty, health, and environmental shock, what would a human security architecture possibly be to address these issues? First, we would look at the root causes or drivers of the security challenge. With SSR, for example, there are numerous challenges, and one might even argue the term "reform" to be inaccurate, since in many instances there are no institutions in place to "reform" in the first place. But, looking at some of the top challenges of SSR, most Western eyes come away with the need for professionalization of the military, training in peacekeeping operations, police training, training the judiciary in rule of law, training in anti-corruption, and border security. Yet from a human security perspective, it makes little sense to have both a military force and a police force competing for scarce resources. What is needed is a civil protection corps made up of engagement brigades serving the most pressing needs of the people. This force would resemble the Gendarmerie of France or Caribinerri of Italy in most respects. When speaking with African military leaders, most suggest the training most needed by security forces is in infrastructure development and medical training. Why? This adds to the development of the country and helps with internal perceptions that these military forces are actually a value added to the country and not a drain on resources. Often times overlooked is how very few times in modern history one African country has actually invaded or started a war with another. So, instead of preparing to defend the country against an enemy that will never materialize, these military forces could be blended into a security force that addresses the security concerns of the people. This civil protection corps would have a standard policing mission and emergency response for environmental disasters such as floods. A new idea would be to create other engagement brigades which focused on agricultural development. Yes, security forces focused on ensuring food security.

The West could mirror these engagement brigades for training such a force composing of military civil engineering teams, medical/dental training teams, and military police, while other agencies such as USAID, DFID, and agricultural agencies could provide experts in agricultural development. The United States Coast Guard could provide training in coastal patrolling to countries along the coast suffering from the decimation of the territorial waters by fishing fleets and pirates. Much as the United States does with its foreign military sales contracts, deals could be struck with host nations to provide trucks, tractors, and farming implements to these countries with maintenance contracts. This would help Western companies such as John Deere, Caterpillar, and others. The program would be designed to train the civil protection corps on the use and maintenance of this equipment, then leave it with the host nation.

Another idea along these lines is to have civil protection corps equipment sets prepositioned in case of a humanitarian disaster. Much like the US military has prepositioned war stocks to quickly respond to crises of a military nature, a civil protection corps equipment set would be designed to meet the needs of populations in crisis. Equipment could include bulldozers, tractors, well-digging equipment, bridging equipment, tentage, water purifying equipment, and so on.

Countries would no longer simply train on peacekeeping missions with a traditional military set, but on full-spectrum sustainable security missions based on a civil protection corps.

Important to mention at this juncture is one of the greatest concerns of training military and police in Africa today. So often I've heard that the police and military add to the instability and insecurity of a country rather than reinforce security, even after training by Western countries, the UN or other international organizations, because they are predatory. This is in part due to lack of pay or that the pay system is so corrupted that monies never hit the pockets of the soldiers and policemen for which they're intended. Again, why not look at twenty-first-century solutions to such problems? Instead of having monies funneled from one ministry to the next, have direct pay systems implemented through the concept of mobile banking. This is to say, money is directly transferred through mobile banking technologies to the civil protection corps members. This alleviates the ability for the system to be corrupt.

Mobile banking and mobile government should be encouraged not only for the civil protection corps, but implemented across the whole of Africa. Almost everyone in Africa has or will have access to a cell phone over the next ten years. Indeed, it is easier for me to get a call in the Virginia National Park than in some parts of Virginia. The technology is there. It must simply be leveraged at the "whole scale" level. The power of mobile banking and mobile government is that it takes away the incentive for corruption. How? No longer does a citizen needing a document stamped or other action which can be done electronically have to pay a bribe. This can be done without the need for human interface, alleviating the chance for corruption. No longer do police and military members have to prey on populations due to their pay going into the pockets of ministers. This isn't pie in the sky. It's been implemented successfully in many provinces in India. Another promise of mobile banking is through microfinance operations. A nationally instituted mobile banking system opens the doors for greater microfinance investment in that country. As has been proven time and again, microfinance is a powerful tool of economic stimulus but also, more importantly, sustainable security. People empowered with the dignity of work and providing for their families will tend toward peaceful existence far more often than taking up hostilities. This allows non-traditional security partnerships with organizations such as Kiva.org – one of the finest microfinance organizations – to exist and flourish in the darkest and most challenging of circumstances.

Mobile technologies also would aid in providing greater health for Africans. Villages and towns could designate certain individuals to get training in community health practices sponsored by well-established organizations such as Project Hope, and then be networked into hospitals, doctors and universities. When issues arose in towns, these community practitioners could contact these resources. Also beneficial would be early notice of severe outbreaks of Ebola, avian bird flu, or other pandemics. This could be networked into the work of international health agencies and non-governmental organizations (NGOs) for better situational awareness, allowing for greater response times.

The challenge of environmental shock brought on by climate change is a real and imminent vulnerability that will quickly turn into a threat in Africa. However, this vulnerability can also be turned into an opportunity for engagement with Africa. Through the use of the civil protection corps, nations can be taught greater responsibility for protection and sustainable use of natural resources. Military forces in countries such as Kenya, Botswana, and Gabon have already received training as park rangers in protecting their natural resources and have turned this into eco-tourism opportunities. This civil protection corps would also be trained on natural disaster response, preventing containable events from spiraling out of control and destabilizing a country. Additionally, resources could be provided to these countries for monitoring weather trends, allowing for more accurate prediction and early warning of floods and droughts. Promising in this area is the development by Lockheed Martin of the High Altitude Airship. This unmanned "super blimp" is designed to go up to 60,000 feet in the air and be able to remain in place for up to three months, powered by solar energy, taking reading on weather trends. It can also be fitted with transponders which could increase cell phone coverage and wireless communications, complementing such areas as education, health, and others.

So how would a long-term human security program look? If we took Angola for instance, this provides for a strong case of security and development based along human security lines. Angola, a country of some 16 million people, emerged from one of the longest and bloodiest civil wars in Cold War history in 2002. The country is still recovering from the aftershock, but blessed with numerous natural resources such as oil, uranium, and diamonds, it has the fiscal resources to begin the journey to becoming one of Africa's regional powers. Yet, it is also plagued with a number of problems ranging from allegations of endemic corruption, lack of an educated work force, over-inflated bureaucracies, and populations of four million in the capital city built for 500,000 inhabitants due to lack of jobs and basic services in the provinces. Large, unemployed populations in capital cities are tinder boxes of discontent and tend to create a level of instability. So, how best to assure the continued upward progress of Angola, increase stability, and re-integrate and return populations to their traditional homes? Through a human security perspective, we would first understand the reasons populations don't want to return home: no economic future, no education, danger of disease, and landmines. None of these issues fall within the sole purview of one organization, yet expertise in these fields is resident to a number of them. What we understand is this: continued delay in engaging in these areas creates more instability with the seeds of conflict already planted.

An opportunity to engage this from a human security perspective would suggest negotiations with the government to create a number of free trade zones in several provinces. A free trade zone would allow for import and export of goods duty free, alleviating much of the endemic corruption afflicting the country. With a great deal of human capital available, it would then benefit large multinational corporations to put operations within these free trade zones, as has been demonstrated in the country of Jordan. In particular, corporations could look at developing their supply chains through a sustainable business model. In other words, look at creating departments within the corporation to provide microloans to small business entrepreneurs in these areas, as well as larger-scale production. Work would be done to create the mobile banking and mobile governance structures, allowing for quick processing of transactions and alleviating potential corruption.

These free trade zone areas could be paired with a number of NGOs and international organizations working in the health and human services field. Again, reflecting on the house of cards, the whole of security and development must be considered if we are to reach a sustainable security model which could then set conditions for sustainable development. Concentrating efforts in one area, working within each community of interest's comparative advantage allows for a very powerful synergy to develop. This is done with a spirit of openness, transparency, and cooperation. Known as a "swarming" technique, this is much how a colony of bees works to get things done – highly concentrated efforts with each working within their area of expertise. With organizations concentrating efforts inside the areas of free trade zones, health services, water, sanitation, and education then work in harmony to create the basic tapestry of viable livelihoods. This, in turn, creates the opening for civil society and development of societies along democratic principles. No longer do people have to mortgage their futures for today's survival. The more developed these free trade zones become, the greater the need for human resources, thus returning people from impoverished living in the capital to provincial areas now strengthened and developing. The infrastructures that would be constructed would be zero-carbon emitting, renewable energy sources with particular attention paid to effective and non-threatening modes of transportation.

As many other African nations on the way up have desired, so too the Angolans are looking to transform their security architecture into something cutting edge for the twenty-first century. The Angolan military and police forces could be transformed not individually, but as one into a civil protection corps. This would help with the destruction of land mines, infrastructure development, health and human services, cargo transport, agricultural development, and patrolling along its coasts. Although Angola doesn't suffer from threat of invasion from neighboring countries, it has suffered from international fishing fleets robbing national waters of fish resources and endangering the ecosystem there. Conservation groups such as the World Wildlife Fund could partner with the Angolan navy to stop these illegal fishing operations. The Angolan civil protection corps could develop a twenty-first-century *naval-based* air force with seaplane capability to spot the illegal fishing activities, then pass this information to fast boats, which could apprehend these criminals. This could be used as a model for other parts of Africa, such as Mozambique, Nigeria, South Africa, Kenya, and Somalia.

Conclusion

Security of the twenty-first century will be less about kinetic threats and more about the conditions creating human insecurities and draining populations of hope. One thing is sure: people who have nothing to live for are willing to die for almost anything if they feel it might better protect their families and way of life. Individuals who commit criminal terrorist acts aren't born; they are created through years of deprivation, disenfranchisement, and desperation. Security of the twenty-first century will be less and less about sovereign state interactions and more about proactively identifying causes of instability and working with properly targeted groups to turn these vulnerabilities into opportunities. The lack of infrastructure and development on the African continent should not be seen as a liability, but an opportunity to leverage cutting-edge technologies to leapfrog Africa onto the forward edge of the twenty-first century. Human security shifts away from the zero sum gain of the Cold War and provides for two options: positive sum gain or all lose.

Part II

African responses

Threats and opportunities

7 AFRICOM

Its reality, rhetoric and future

Jeremy Keenan

Much of what has been written over the last 2–3 years about AFRICOM, the new United States Africa Command, is little more than rhetoric associated with the Pentagon's fairly sophisticated attempt to shift AFRICOM from the Global War on Terror (GWOT) discourse into the new security–development discourse and, while so doing, re-rewrite, or at least blur, the history of its development.

President Bush's authorisation of AFRICOM in December 2006 and its subsequent establishment as a new, independent, fully autonomous command on 1 October 2008, was much more than a post-Cold War rationalisation of America's global military command structure.[1] AFRICOM reflects the recognition of Africa's new strategic importance to the United States. This shift in US interest towards Africa did not come about overnight, but was, as AFRICOM's website states, 'the culmination of a ten-year thought process within the Department of Defense'.[2]

That 'thought process' began in 1997. Since then, Africa's strategic importance to the United States has undergone several reappraisals as a result of the United States' increased awareness of its own energy crisis, the post-9/11 GWOT and China's growing economic investment in Africa. The year 1997 was, in fact, a landmark year in contemporary US history for two related reasons: it saw the founding of the neoconservatives' ('neocons') 'Project for the New American Century' (PNAC 1997), and US dependency on foreign oil reached the psychologically critical 50 per cent. The threat posed to national security by the latter development was not lost on the neocons. They made it an election issue in 2000, with George W. Bush pledging to make energy security a top priority. One of his first executive decisions was to establish a National Energy Policy Development (NEPD) group under the Chairmanship of his Vice President, Dick Cheney. The 'Cheney Report' was published in May 2001 (National Energy Policy Group 2001). Its findings were stark: between 1991 and 2000, Americans had used 17 per cent more energy than in the previous decade, while domestic energy production had risen by only 2.3 per cent. It projected that, by 2020, US energy consumption would increase by about 32 per cent, with the oil share remaining at around 40 per cent, more than one-quarter of the world's total consumption.

The Cheney Report singled out sub-Saharan Africa as the key source of future US oil supplies. It forecast that by 2015, 25 per cent of US imported oil would come from the Gulf of Guinea. Some forecasts now put this figure at 35 per cent. In 2002 sub-Saharan Africa was already supplying 14 per cent of US oil imports; by 2006, the US imported 22 per cent of its oil from Africa; by 2007 the country was importing more crude oil from Africa than from the Persian Gulf (US Dept of Energy 2007). The Cheney Report highlighted the strategic importance of Africa, prompting Bush to define African oil as a 'strategic national interest' and thus a resource that the United States might choose military force to control (Volman 2003).

Taking the GWOT into Africa

To secure consistent access to and control over African oil, the Bush administration decided to create a US military structure for Africa. Instead of acknowledging that US military intervention in Africa was about resource control, the Bush administration opted to use the GWOT as the justification for its militarisation of the continent. However, launching the GWOT into Africa was tricky, as most of the continent, especially sub-Saharan Africa, had hitherto not suffered the atrocities of terrorism. The main terrorism incidents in Africa had been concentrated in Somalia, East Africa and the Maghreb.[3]

For the last ten years (1999–2009), I have undertaken continuous, detailed anthropological research on the developments within the Sahara–Sahel regions of southern Algeria, southern Libya, northern Mali, northern Niger, Mauritania and Chad, especially in regard to the development of the GWOT and the actions of the US military in this part of Africa. This research has formed the basis of my two books on the GWOT in Africa, *The Dark Sahara* (Keenan 2009) and *The Dying Sahara* (Keenan 2010). The two books together provide the field-based evidence which enabled me to understand how the US administration and its key ally, Algeria, overcame the problem posed by the lack of terrorism in Africa by fabricating it. In the first volume, *The Dark Sahara*, I document the circumstances and evidence of how Algeria's secret intelligence service, the Département du Renseignement et de la Sécurité (DRS), operating in alliance with US military intelligence services, orchestrated the abduction by Islamic extremists of 32 European tourists in the Algerian Sahara in February–March 2003. This research also reveals how the leader of this group of Islamic extremists, Amari Saifi (generally known as 'El Para'),[4] could only have been a DRS agent. Mine was not the only research to reach this conclusion. Two years before the publication of *The Dark Sahara*, Salima Mellah and François Gèze, Director of *Editions Le Découverte* and *Algeria Watch*, Algeria's respected human rights organisation, wrote:

> We have undertaken an in depth enquiry into the affair of the European hostages in the Sahara. A close study of the facts shows that there is no other explanation for this operation than the directing of the hostage-taking by the DRS, the Algerian army's secret service.
>
> (Gèze and Mellah 2007)

Through this and a number of related fabricated incidents in the northern Sahel regions of Southern Algeria, Mali, Niger and Chad during the course of 2003–4,[5] the Bush administration was able to justify the launch of a Sahara–Sahel front, or what became known as a 'second front' of the GWOT in Africa.

The idea of creating false-flag incidents to justify military intervention is not new in US history. In 1962, for example, the US Joint Chiefs of Staff drew up and approved plans, codenamed Operation Northwoods, that called for CIA and other operatives to commit acts of terrorism on innocent civilians in US cities and elsewhere, thus giving the appearance of a Communist Cuban terror campaign in Miami, other Florida cities and even Washington, which would create public support for a war against Fidel Castro's Cuba.[6] The plan, signed by all members of the Joint Chiefs of Staff, under the Chairmanship of General Lyman Lemnitzer, was presented to President Kennedy's Defense Secretary, Robert McNamara, on 13 March 1962. The plan was ultimately rejected by President Kennedy.

Forty years later, a not dissimilar plan was presented to the US Defense Secretary, Donald Rumsfeld, by his Defense Science Board (DSB) (2002). Excerpts of the DSB's 'Summer Study on Special Operations and Joint Forces in Support of Countering Terrorism' were revealed on 12 August 2002, with Pamela Hess (2002), William Arkin (2002) and David Isenberg (2002) publishing further details and analysis of the plan for UPI, the *Los Angeles Times* and *Asia Times*, respectively, on 26 September, 27 October and 5 November. The DSB recommended the creation of a 'Proactive, Preemptive Operations Group (P2OG)', a covert organisation that would carry out secret missions to 'stimulate reactions' among terrorist groups by provoking them to undertake violent acts that would expose them to 'counterattack' by US forces, along with other operations which, through the US military penetration of terrorist groups and the recruitment of local peoples, would dupe them into conducting 'combat operations, or even terrorist activities' (Floyd 2002; Ahmed 2009)

The budget of the P2OG programme was large. Hess (2002) reported that the entire DSB recommendation would require $7 billion in new spending, with the P2OG running at a minimum of $100 million per year. Isenberg (2002) reckoned the total envisaged cost as $3.3 billion annually. The P2OG programme raises huge questions about all terrorist actions since 2002, such as the Madrid and London bombings in March 2004 and July 2005, respectively, as well as the GWOT's Sahara–Sahel front. For example, in May 2008, George Bush was reported to have signed a secret finding authorising and requesting some $400 million of funding for terrorist groups across much of the Middle East–Afghanistan region in a covert offensive directed ultimately against the Iranian regime. An initial outlay of $300 million was approved by Congress with bipartisan support (Cockburn 2008; Ahmed 2009).

In his investigation of such operations, Nafeez Ahmed (2009) says that the US investigative journalist Seymour Hersh (2005) was told by a Pentagon advisor that the Algerian [El Para] operation was a pilot for the new Pentagon covert P2OG programme. While Ahmed and Hersh corroborate my field research findings (Keenan 2009, 2010), the timing of the developments between Washington and the Algerian Sahara are even more acute than the various dates mentioned above would suggest. The P2OG programme was 'leaked' on 16 August 2002, while the El Para operation began in February–March 2003. In fact, the P2OG 'leak' came two weeks after Marion E. (Spike) Bowman (2002), Deputy General Counsel for the FBI, presented crucial evidence to the Senate Select Committee on Intelligence in regard to proposed amendments concerning the Foreign Intelligence Surveillance Act, and two, not six, months before the first fabrication of terrorism in the Sahara. Until Bowman's evidence, the American intelligence community was anxious about working too closely with their Algerian counterparts for fear that they would pass sensitive information to Palestinian organisations. However, Bowman's statement, in which he presented the background and present nature of what the FBI called the 'International Jihad Movement', dispelled many of the anxieties about collaborating with the Algerians by showing how close Algeria was to the United States in its fight against al-Qaeda and terrorism.

The first attempt to fabricate terrorism in the Sahara–Sahel region was on 18 October 2002, when alleged Islamists, operating under the protection of the DRS, hijacked and abducted four Swiss tourists near Arak (Southern Algeria). The operation, however, was botched.[7] It is inconceivable, in the light of the very close 'post-Bowman' relationship between US and Algerian intelligence services, that the United States could have been unaware of the Arak operation. Why else were two officials from the State Department's Counterterrorism Office, AF DAS Robert Perry and S/CT Deputy Coordinator Stephanie Kinney, briefing the governments of Mali, Niger, Chad and Mauritania on the Bush administration's planned counter-terrorism Pan-Sahel Initiative (PSI), at the same time as the botched Arak operation?[8] Indeed, even though the PSI forces were not officially brought into the region until January 2004, US Special Forces, believed to be attached to the P2OG, were operating covertly in the region as early as November 2002. The State Department explained the PSI as:

> a program designed to protect borders, track movement of people, combat terrorism, and enhance regional cooperation and stability. It is a State-led effort to assist Mali, Niger, Chad, and Mauritania in detecting and responding to suspicious movement of people and goods across and within their borders through training, equipment and cooperation. Its goals support two U.S. national security interests in Africa: waging the war on terrorism and enhancing regional peace and security.

Prior to El Para's abduction of the 32 tourists in February–March 2003, four months after the Arak attempt, there had been no terrorism – by the conventional meaning of the term[9] – anywhere in this part of the Sahara–Sahel region of Africa. And yet, even before the hostages had been released, the Bush administration, following on from Perry and Kinney's briefing of the Sahel states, had designated the Sahara as a new front in the GWOT.[10] Bush described El Para as

'Bin Laden's man in the Sahel', while EUCOM's deputy commander, General Wald, described the Sahara as a 'Swamp of Terror', a 'terrorist infestation', which 'we need to drain' (Powell 2004).

The White House, the US Office of Counterterrorism and the Pentagon moved quickly. On 10 January 2004, President Bush's PSI rolled into action with the disembarkation in Nouakchott, capital of Mauritania, of a US 'anti-terror team' of 500 US troops. US Deputy Undersecretary of State Pamela Bridgewater, in Nouakchott to oversee what locals called the 'American invasion', confirmed that these troops would work in Mauritania and Mali, while 400 US Rangers would be deployed into the Chad–Niger border regions the following week, along with Los Angeles-based defence contractors Pacific Architects and Engineers.

Africa's new terrorist threat was portrayed as having spread across the wastelands of the Sahel, from Mauritania in the west, through the little known desert lands of Mali, Niger and Southern Algeria, to the Tibesti Mountains of Chad, with beyond them the Sudan, Somalia and, across the waters, the 'talibanised' lands of Afghanistan. Shortly after El Para's alleged escapades across the Sahel (Keenan 2009), western intelligence and diplomatic sources were claiming to be finding the fingerprints of this newly fabricated terrorist threat everywhere. It took only a few days after the Madrid train bombings (11 March 2004) for that atrocity to be linked to al-Qaeda groups lurking deep in the Sahara, with western intelligence and security services soon warning that al-Qaeda bases hidden deep in the world's largest desert could launch terrorist attacks on Europe.[11]

This new, fabricated front in the GWOT helped create the ideological conditions for Washington's militarisation of Africa. A key figure in this strategy was General James (Jim) Jones, recently appointed as President Obama's National Security Advisor. At that time, however, General Jones was Supreme Allied Commander, Europe (SACEUR) and Commander of EUCOM, which was responsible for most of Africa prior to the establishment of AFRICOM. General Jones envisaged a new concept of US military basing in Africa. With Cold War-style bases containing large numbers of US forces neither militarily appropriate nor politically feasible, General Jones was planning a far more flexible facilitative arrangement which would enable the US military to deploy quickly, as and when required, through what he called a 'family of bases'. These would include 'forward-operating bases', or what he called 'lilypads',[12] perhaps with an airfield nearby. These bases would house up to 3,000–5,000 troops. There would also be 'forward-operating locations', which would be lightly equipped bases where Special Forces, Marines or possibly an infantry rifle platoon or company could land and build up as the mission required.[13]

In 2002, at the same time as Bush was preparing his PSI, Central Command (CENTCOM) moved many of its facilities from Saudi Arabia to the old French colonial base of Camp Lemonier in Djibouti, making it the base for the Combined Joint Task Force in the Horn of Africa (CJTF-HOA) and the East African Counter-terrorism Initiative (EACTI). With the Horn and East Africa covered by CENTCOM, General Jones focused his attention on the Sahara and Sahel.

In May 2003, with the 32 European hostages making news headlines, he spoke of 'large ungoverned areas across Africa that are clearly the new routes of narco trafficking, terrorist training and hotbeds of instability'. Two months later, he was more specific:

> As we pursue the global war on terrorism, we're going to have to go where the terrorists are. And we're seeing some evidence, at least preliminary, that more and more of these large uncontrolled, ungoverned areas (vast swaths of the Sahara, from Mauritania ... to Sudan) are going to be potential havens for that kind of activity.[14]

In 2005 the United States expanded the PSI into the Trans-Saharan Counter-Terrorism Initiative (TSCTI), increasing the countries involved from four (Mauritania, Mali, Niger and Chad) to nine with the inclusion of Senegal, Nigeria, Morocco, Algeria and Tunisia. This new initiative created an overarching US military architecture to oversee the security of Africa's two largest oil- and gas-producing states.[15]

Rhetorical shift from terrorism to security and development

Around the turn of 2005–6, and with the idea of a dedicated US Africa Command beginning to take concrete shape, the Bush administration's justification for its militarisation of the continent began to reflect an apparent transformation in US military thinking, as its rhetoric shifted from the GWOT and counter-terrorism to a more humanitarian security–development discourse. This has enabled the US military to substitute the overly aggressive and militaristic image that EUCOM commanders had been displaying towards Africa for one that enabled President Bush to announce AFRICOM as a new command that 'will enhance our efforts to help bring peace and security to the people of Africa and promote our common goals of development, health, education, democracy, and economic growth in Africa'.[16]

Such seductive language, emphasising AFRICOM's development–humanitarian aims and stressing its goals of strengthening civilian agencies and civilian capacities, now characterises all US government references to, and descriptions of, AFRICOM. AFRICOM's own website, for example, states that:

> U.S. Africa Command will better enable the Department of Defense and other elements of the U.S. government to work in concert and with partners to achieve a more stable environment in which political and economic growth can take place.... Unlike traditional Unified Commands, Africa Command will focus on war prevention rather than war-fighting. Africa Command intends to work with African nations and African organizations to build regional security and crisis-response capacity in support of U.S. government efforts in Africa.

(www.africom.com)

This shift is seen in the content of the EUCOM and AFRICOM websites and associated publications before and after 2006. Whereas most of their news stories prior to 2005–6 reflected the US military's concerns with the GWOT, counter-terrorism and the associated training of African militaries, AFRICOM's news stories cover military involvement in medical training, provision of safe water, care of livestock, civilian capacity building, etc.

This apparent transformation in military thinking raises three immediate questions. First, what are its intellectual and political origins? Second, is it genuine or merely a new angle in the Bush administration's 'information' or 'propaganda' war? Third, what are its implications for the people of Africa?

New Labour's 'development–security' discourse

The Pentagon can claim little intellectual originality for its security–development discourse, which was shipped more or less wholesale across the Atlantic from Downing Street to Washington following the publication in March 2005 of Prime Minister Tony Blair's *Commission for Africa*.[17]

An analysis of New Labour's policies towards Africa (Abrahamsen 2005) revealed how Blair's securitisation of Africa enabled Britain's (and Europe's) dealings and interactions with the continent to shift from the category of 'development/humanitarianism' to one of 'risk/fear/security' in such a way that Africa became increasingly mentioned in the context of the 'war on terrorism' and the dangers it posed to Britain and the international community.

The UK's securitisation[18] of Africa began with Tony Blair's call to heal 'the scar on the conscience of the world' that is Africa.[19] A key element in New Labour's analysis of Africa was the interpretation of poverty and under-development as dangerous (ibid.). By emphasising the threat posed by the marginalised and excluded, Africa's 'dangerous classes', and the role of aid and 'development' in containing this threat, the British government succeeded in merging the development and security agendas so that the two have become almost indistinguishable. By means of such pronouncements, Africa and under-development has subtly shifted 'away from the categories of "development/humanitarianism" and along a continuum of "risk/threat"' (ibid.).

The securitisation of Africa has been further prioritised by drawing attention to the association between under-development and conflict and the various discourses on 'failed states', which, in no time at all, were linked directly to the 9/11 attacks. It took only a few steps – from 'poverty' and 'under-development' to 'conflict', 'fear', 'failed states' and the black holes of the 'ungoverned areas' – to recast Africa as the 'Heart of Darkness' and to transpose the GWOT into its vast ungoverned spaces: the DRC, Sudan, Somalia and EUCOM's infamous 'Swamp of Terror' – the Sahara.

The Pentagon and AFRICOM have readily adopted and developed New Labour's 'development and security' discourse, enabling them to argue that security and development are inextricably linked and mutually reinforcing. 'To deny the sanctuary in which armed groups incubate and thereby stave off internal conflict, governments must address the root causes of public grievances. These grievances are development based; therefore, the security solution must be development based' (McFate 2008a).[20]

The fundamental question regarding AFRICOM is whether the stories and news items on its websites, its mission statements and its professed concern for humanitarian development really do reflect a paradigmatic shift in US military thinking, of whether they are nothing more than a new twist in Washington's 'information war'.

The 'information war'

Before answering that question, let me make a brief digression to clarify what is meant by Washington's 'information war', as it is not something which either AFRICOM or the Pentagon, are keen to discuss.

Soon after the 9/11 attacks, the White House began running an information war through a host of shadowy disinformation or counter-propaganda units and organisations, such as the International Information Centre, the Pentagon's lavishly endowed 1,200-strong Psychological Operations group and the White House's Counter Terrorism Information Strategy Policy Coordinating Committee (Gerth 2005). These covert operations, little known to most Americans until 2005, have involved contentious means to 'keep doing every single thing that needs to be done', to quote the former US Defense Secretary, Donald Rumsfeld (Gerth 2005). One such operation involved giving contracts worth millions of dollars to private contractors, such as the Lincoln Group and the Rendon Group, to plant, fabricate or buy news stories favourable to US interests on an immense scale. In 2005 the Lincoln Group, to give just one example, admitted to having planted more than 1,000 articles in the Iraqi and Arab press.

Proof of this came out in June 2008 when the US Senate Select Committee on Intelligence published the final volume of its report into the use, abuse and faulty assessments of intelligence leading to the invasion of Iraq. It confirmed, in the words of its Chairman, Senator John D. Rockefeller IV, that: 'In making the case for war, the administration repeatedly presented intelligence as fact when it was unsubstantiated, contradicted or even nonexistent.'[21]

In North Africa, the US has been able to rely heavily on its main ally in the GWOT, Algeria, to promote disinformation. Nevertheless, the US Department of Defense (DoD), first through EUCOM and now through AFRICOM, has maintained a similar strategy in Africa as in the Iraq theatre, by sponsoring its own website, namely Magharebia.com. *Magharebia* looks like a regular online news service with numerous links to internationally known and respected news services. It is, however, a creation of the Pentagon. Founded in 2004, it is believed to be one of two such websites financed by, supervised by and accountable to EUCOM, before being transferred to AFRICOM. The other is *Today* (SETimes.com), founded in 1999, which covers southeast Europe. In June 2007, EUCOM was reported to be paying $4.7 million annually to General Dynamics Info Technologies to manage the *Magharebia* and *Today* websites (Al-khiyal

2007). *Magharebia* has played a significant role in propagating false information in relation to the fabrication of terrorism by the Algerian and US military intelligence services in the Sahara–Sahel. Altogether, since 2002 the number of 'false' media stories and reports on the Sahara–Sahel front, including their reiteration through wire and online agencies, runs into the thousands and is rising.

AFRICOM in action

AFRICOM is enmeshed in Washington's 'information war'. The question of whether it really does reflect a paradigmatic shift in US military thinking, or whether it is nothing more than a new twist in Washington's 'information war' can therefore only be asked and understood within that context. This requires cutting through the layers of contorted disinformation that inveigle both it and the GWOT, a task which is especially difficult in Africa as the GWOT used to justify the establishment of AFRICOM, especially its Sahara–Sahel front, is, as explained in the first half of this chapter, based substantially on the fabricated terrorism of the El Para operation (Keenan 2009). The answer can therefore only be found 'on the ground', by looking at what the US military is actually doing in Africa, as distinct from what it says it is doing. Outlined in the next few paragraphs are some of the engagements that have not been covered on AFRICOM's website.

On 7 January 2007, less than three weeks after AFRICOM's authorisation, US forces killed an unknown number, reportedly hundreds, of Somali fighters and innocent civilians trapped in the 'killing zone' between US-backed Ethiopian forces to the north and west, and US-backed Kenyan forces to the south and the sea. The operation, which was meant to have been secret, was widely publicised, reminding the world that the US presence sought to resolve conflicts in Africa by brute military intervention. The situation in Somalia has not only become a nightmare of American making, but has generated a major terrorism security threat, especially to those countries, such as the UK, which contain large immigrant Somali communities.

The gunship that carried out the 7 January 2007 bombardment is believed to have been launched from a secret airstrip in eastern Ethiopia. However, the US special operators sent into southern-most Somalia after the aerial attack to search out survivors among the supposed foreign fighters and al-Qaeda operatives were dispatched from America's new military base at Manda Bay in northeast Kenya, just south of the Somali border. Manda Bay was a strategically important base for AFRICOM operations in both the Horn and East Africa. However, its continued operation was heavily dependent on the pro-American Kenyan President, Mwai Kibaki, retaining office in the December 2007 presidential elections. His challenger, Raili Odinga, was not known to be so supportive of US counter-terrorism operations in the country. Odinga was widely expected to win the election, and both pre-election polls and exit poll evidence suggested that he should have won. However, in spite of international observers and a high US presence, the elections were believed by most Kenyans to have been rigged. The result was an explosion of violence that left more than 1,000 Kenyans dead. Now, in the wake of 'administration change' in the US, the evidence of US involvement in Kenya's vote-rigging is coming to light (McIntyre and Gettleman 2009).

The US military has been more successful in keeping its interventions in the Sahara–Sahel secret. On 23 May 2006 a group of Tuareg staged a rebellion in the Kidal region of northern Mali. In spite of extensive media coverage, two aspects of the rebellion have remained secret, namely that the Algerian DRS orchestrated it, and that it was supported by US Special Forces (Keenan 2010). On 15–16 February, some 100–200 Special Forces, accompanied by their dogs, flew from Stuttgart to Tamanrasset,[22] where they were garrisoned temporarily before crossing overland into Mali shortly before the rebellion. Why the US soldiers brought their dogs and what they were doing in Mali is not clear. Although denied by the State Department and Pentagon, the operation is confirmed by field research (ibid.), the flight details and subsequent 'verification' from a US State Department official.[23]

In February 2008, 21 months after US Special Forces had assisted Algeria in destabilising northern Mali, US Special Forces accompanied Malian soldiers in ransacking the desert border town of Tin Zaouatene (ibid.). Four days later, AFRICOM commander General Ward and Theresa Whelan, Deputy Assistant Secretary of Defense for African Affairs, attending an AFRICOM promotion in London,[24] denied the presence of US forces in northern Mali. The following week, General Ward was in Bamako to reassure the Malian government that the US was committed to helping Mali maintain the security of its northern regions.

The US military's presence and actions in the Sahara–Sahel have encouraged the regional governments of the PSI and TSCTI countries to provoke potentially 'rebellious' elements of local/indigenous populations, notably the Tuareg, to take up arms. Indeed, Washington's ability to justify its counter-terrorism operations and AFRICOM's presence in these countries has been predicated increasingly on the false premise that the government-provoked Tuareg rebellions that have engulfed much of the western Sahel (Niger–Mali–Mauritania–Southern Algeria) since early 2007 are linked to al-Qaeda. I will say more about this development later. For the moment, I should merely stress that this duplicitous strategy has little to do with security and development. On the contrary, the US post-2003 presence in the PSI–TSCTI region has been directly responsible for increasing political unrest, rebellion, war crimes against civilian populations and severe economic deprivation.[25]

As for the United States' contribution to the training of PSI countries' troops in counter-terrorism, etc., Niger's US-trained army now stands accused of genocide,[26] or what the local Tuareg term 'ethnocide'. In August 2007 a report commissioned by the United Nations High Commission for Refugees (UNHCR) (Keenan 2007) warned that Niger's President, Mamadou Tandja, was likely to unleash the Forces Armées Nigériennes (FAN) on the civilian population. By December, two international human rights organisations, the UK-based Amnesty International (2007) and the US-based Human Rights Watch (2007), had denounced Niger's armed forces for committing war crimes, including summary executions of the civilian population. By 2008 Niger's forces had taken to bombing civilian nomadic camps with grenades dropped from light aircraft, a common practice in Darfur.

AFRICOM's last military operation under the Bush administration was in December 2008 when AFRICOM, which had been training Ugandan troops in counter-terrorism for some years, advised, provisioned and part-financed a force of 6,000 Ugandan and Congolese troops to eliminate Joseph Kony and his estimated 700-strong Lord's Resistance Army (LRA).

About five years ago the Ugandan army drove the LRA into Southern Sudan. Over the previous 15 years the LRA had killed tens of thousands of people in northern Uganda. Kony subsequently set up camp in the DRC's remote Garamba National Park, abutting the Sudan border. Attempts to coax Kony into signing a peace treaty were unsuccessful, the stumbling block being his refusal to sign until his indictment by the International Criminal Court (ICC) on charges of crimes against humanity was dropped. Recently, elders of the Acholi tribe, from which Kony had originated and from which he had recruited his army of children, felt that they were making progress in overcoming the LRA problem by using traditional means to help rehabilitate many members of his 'army' and perhaps even Kony himself. They simply asked for more time. AFRICOM, however, had neither the patience for the 'tribal option', nor the time: it was champing for the opportunity to demonstrate its military effectiveness and to 'destroy' the LRA. Kony's refusal to sign a peace treaty in November gave AFRICOM the opportunity to use its long-sought military option (McCrae, 2008).

The operation was an unmitigated disaster. After US satellites and Ugandan field intelligence had located Kony's camp, the plan was for Ugandan helicopters to bomb the camp and for 6,000 Ugandan and Congolese ground troops to cut off LRA fighters. On 13 December, the day before the assault, US military advisors held a final coordination meeting close to the Congolese border. Unanticipated fog delayed the operation. By the time the helicopters bombed his camp, Kony had got wind of the attack and fled. For their part, the 6,000 ground troops failed to cut off the LRA's escape routes and to protect the nearby towns and villages from the slaughter the fleeing LRA inflicted upon them. An estimated 2,000 innocent Congolese civilians were slaughtered and hundreds more children abducted to become the latest LRA conscripts. The exercise was a grotesque demonstration of inept military planning and appalling execution.

In short, in those areas where AFRICOM has intervened militarily, either directly or though proxies, as in Somalia, Northern Kenya (where refugees fleeing the Somalia violence are now a major humanitarian concern), the DRC and the western Sahel (Niger and Mali), the outcomes have been disastrous for the civilian populations, and without any semblance of military 'victories' to be shown for them.

Implications of the development–security discourse for the people of Africa

Does AFRICOM have any prospect of bringing peace, security and development to Africa? While AFRICOM's commanders have been preaching 'security and development', their operations on the ground, as seen in these examples, have demonstrated the Bush administration's primary reliance on the use of military force to pursue its strategic interests. So far, AFRICOM's operations have merely created insecurity and undermined democratic expressions of civil society. If this 'reality' does not change under the Obama administration, it will have at least four serious consequences for the people of Africa.

First, and as Abrahamsen (2005) also emphasises, the link between under-development and terrorism has served to generate a negative image of fear around the continent, and has created suspicion and hostility towards its people, with a consequent deterioration in race relations, stricter Europe-wide immigration controls and asylum laws[27] and the erosion of civil liberties in the face of perceived terrorist threats. Through this discourse, 'under-development, chaos and state failure become the expression of "otherness", rather than an outcome and reflection of certain deficiencies and shortcoming in contemporary international relations between north and south' (ibid.). Above all, this new discourse explicitly links Africa's poor – her 'dangerous classes' – the marginalised and excluded to international 'security problems' and 'terrorism'. Second, it will militarise US relations with Africa and also militarise numerous African countries which, in turn, will be more likely to use force in obtaining their own objectives. Third, the presence of US bases and domestic governments' encouragement to use force in preference to more democratic means will create more militants and hence unrest and insecurity, as we are now seeing in most countries across the Sahelian zone. Fourth, the US administration's primary reliance on its military has effectively usurped the role of the State Department and specialised agencies such as USAID, whose skills and experience are better suited to achieving the 'peace', 'security' and 'development' that AFRICOM claims to espouse.

Indeed, when we examine AFRICOM's interventions, we can see that they are serving largely to protect unpopular, repressive regimes supportive of US interests. In the case of North Africa and the Sahel regions, the US military intervention of the last 6–7 years has served to reinforce the authoritarian and repressive means of states in the region, not only through the provision of more high-technology surveillance, weapons and security systems, but also by emboldening the state security services in their abuse of power. One prominent local citizen in southern Algeria expressed the views of many when he said: 'Now that they [the Algerian authorities] have the Americans behind them, they have become even bigger bullies' (Keenan 2010). The US intervention is thus prolonging and perhaps even entrenching fundamentally undemocratic regimes, while weakening or delaying the development of autonomous and more democratic civil societies.

In the same vein, the ruling regimes being supported by the United States in this way are in turn using the pretext of the GWOT to repress legitimate opposition by linking it with 'terrorism'. The ruling regimes of the North Africa–Sahara–Sahel region, as well as those in many other African countries, have provoked elements of civil society, usually minority groups of one sort or another, into civil unrest or taking up arms. Examples are the Kidal rebellion and the ransacking of Tin Zaouatene mentioned above, the Tamanrasset riots of July 2005 and the Aïr (Niger) uprising of winter 2004–5 (ibid.). The GWOT has provided these regimes with 'terrorism rents' in the form of military, financial and other largesse that stems ultimately from Washington.[28] More significantly, these local–regional outbreaks of civil unrest and rebellion ('incursions') by minority-cum-opposition groups, have served to legitimise the US military presence in Africa. However, the resulting instability is doing immense damage to local economies. In the Sahara–Sahel region, for example, as with parts of East Africa, it has destroyed the tourism industry on which many local people depend for their livelihood.

The tragedy of the Bush administration's Saharan–Sahel front, is that it has become a self-fulfilling prophecy. The same is now true of Somalia, parts of East Africa and perhaps also the northeast of the DRC. Six years of fabricated terrorism and provoked unrest have transformed large, hitherto relatively tranquil tracts of Africa into zones of more-or-less permanent instability, rebellion, war and 'terror'. Far from bringing 'peace and security' to Africa, the US military presence, first through EUCOM and now through AFRICOM, has been directly instrumental in creating conflict and insecurity. The way in which the United States and its military have intervened in Somalia (through Ethiopian proxy), Kenya, the DRC, Niger and Mali are not good advertisements for the US military and the role of AFRICOM in the future of Africa's development.

AFRICOM's future

AFRICOM is faced by three major problems. The first is that nobody really wants it. No African country, with the possible exception of Liberia, has been prepared to house AFRICOM's headquarters, which for the foreseeable future will remain in Stuttgart. While America has tended to put this down to the security difficulties that AFRICOM's presence would inflict on the host country, the truth is that America is seen by African countries as an imperialist power whose rhetoric about 'development and security' lacks credibility. There is widespread belief across the continent that AFRICOM is intended merely to protect US oil interests and 're-assert American power and hegemony globally'. (Malan 2008a)

The second problem is that AFRICOM does not have the means to accomplish its huge mandate. This has been confirmed by several authoritative sources. Sean McFate, a pre-eminent advisor on US military affairs in Africa, has confirmed that no dedicated or new military units will be created for AFRICOM. Nor will AFRICOM be able to 'borrow' troops because of the huge demand for troops in Iraq and Afghanistan (McFate 2008b). Mark Malan, a former military officer now working for Washington-based *Refugees International*, gave testimony to the US House of Representatives Subcommittee on National Security and Foreign Affairs that AFRICOM lacks 'the appropriate policy framework, the depth and balance of professional expertise, or the requisite funding mechanisms to deliver on active security'(Malan 2008b). Indeed, there is much opposition to AFRICOM from within Washington's own corridors of political power. The House of Representatives' Appropriations Committee, for instance, believes that 'traditional U.S. military operations are not an appropriate response to most or many of the challenges facing Africa' (McFate 2008a) and accordingly wants to cut AFRICOM's requested budget. For FY 2009, Congress allocated only $266 million of the $390 million requested by AFRICOM.[29] However, it should be noted that Obama has increased the AFRICOM budget significantly for FY 2010 (Volman 2009

How then will AFRICOM accomplish its mission? The answer, according to McFate, is what EUCOM and AFRICOM have been doing in Africa since at least early 2004, by outsourcing it to PMCs, whose propensity towards corruption (as seen in Iraq) and disregard of human rights are part of the package. That, as McFate knows from his own personal involvement with PMCs,[30] is exactly what PMCs have been waiting for: 'This [PMC] multi-billion dollar industry is looking for the next US-sponsored conflict market once the Iraq and Afghanistan "bubble bursts", and they see that market as Africa, a continent of crisis' (McFate 2008b).

If McFate is correct, and all the signs suggest that he is, we are thus facing the likely privatisation of AFRICOM's mission. While that is in keeping with the US administration's commitment to neoliberalism, it opens Africa up to the potentially horrific prospect of these mercenary forces, and not only American ones, turning Africa into their own 'plunder economy' where their self-interests will be served and their fortunes made through the promotion and maintenance of conflict. Will it come to that? The crisis currently working its way through western capitalism's financial system may mean that future US budgets may not stretch to the luxury of PMCs in Africa. That may, in a sense, let Africa off the imperial hook. But there is also the prospect that US budget constraints will encourage US PMCs to look towards Africa's 'plunder economy' to make themselves more financially 'self-reliant'. And that also means even more unaccountability.

The third problem, or perhaps question, for AFRICOM is whether the new Obama administration will countenance a continuation of the policies and practices outlined in this chapter. It is, of course, too early to say. However, with Africa still low on the new administration's radar, all the signs are that we should not expect any major changes in America's militaristic approach to Africa in the immediate future. In addition to McFate's warnings about privatisation,[31] there are signs that AFRICOM may be seeking to work more closely with, and to provide a more supportive military arm to European, notably French and British, interests in Africa. For example, AFRICOM's intelligence section is now reportedly relocated at RAF Molesworth, UK, the Joint Intelligence Centre (JAC) which serves as the focal point of military intelligence for the US

EUCOM. While this is not overly significant, as most of EUCOM's intelligence on Africa was undertaken through Molesworth, it comes at a time when US and British intelligence services are clearly working more closely together on African issues. For example, British counter-terrorism advisors are now,[32] for the first time in the very heart of AFRICOM's Trans-Saharan Counter-Terrorism Programme (TSCTP), while France and its parastatal corporations, notably Total, Areva, Lafarge, France Telecom and Vinci, are aggressively establishing and expanding their presence in West and Central Africa on the back, so it would seem, of the reactions to US militarisation, most notably in Niger, Mauritania and the DRC.

However, behind the signs of a more collaborative engagement between US, British and French interests in Africa, there are disquieting questions. Why, for example, has AFRICOM been training local troops in amphibious landings on the Cameroon coast? Is it a precursor to an invasion of the Niger delta? And what is going on within the TSCTP? The recent spate of kidnappings in the Algeria–Niger–Mali sector of the Sahara–Sahel region looks remarkably like a re-run of the 2003 hostage-takings, even down to the involvement of the same DRS-associated personnel.[33] The US military and intelligence services have many questions to answer about what they have done in Africa. With the Obama administration seemingly reluctant to dig over the past, there is a growing anxiety in Africa that the US Congress will fail to probe as deeply in Africa as it did in Iraq.

Notes

1   The Second World War and the subsequent Cold War led the United States to divide the world into five military commands covering North America; South America; the Pacific and Far East; the Middle East, Gulf and Central Asia; and Europe, including most of the former USSR. Prior to the creation of AFRICOM, Africa fell under the responsibility of three separate commands: EUCOM, CENTCOM and PACOM. EUCOM held responsibility for most of the continent; CENTCOM oversaw Egypt, Sudan, the Horn of Africa and Kenya, while PACOM administered Madagascar and other islands in the Indian Ocean. This 'poor relation' status reflected the United States' comparative lack of interest in Africa, especially in the immediate post-Cold War period. Africa was considered and treated as little more than an adjunct to US–European relations.

2   www.africom.mil/AboutAFRICOM.asp.

3   In 1993 18 US soldiers were killed in Mogadishu in an incident which some 'terrorism analysts' now attribute to 'Islamic terrorists'. In 1998 some 200 people were killed when US embassies were bombed in Nairobi and Dar es Salaam. In 2002 a hotel was bombed in Mombassa, allegedly by al-Qaeda 'terrorists', and two surface-to-air missiles were fired at an Israel-bound airliner. Northern Algeria has been subjected to both Islamist and state terrorism since the early 1990s. There have been incidents in Morocco (bombings in Casablanca on 16 May 2003) and Tunisia (el-Ghriba synagogue, April 2002).

4   El Para has at least 12 other aliases (Keenan 2009: 94).

5   Also documented in Keenan (2009), esp. chaps. 4 & 5.

6   U.S. Joint Chiefs of Staff, 'Justification for US Military Intervention in Cuba (Top Secret)', *US Department of Defense*, 13 March 1962. The Northwoods document was

published online in a more complete form by the National Security Archive on 30 April 2001: 'Pentagon Proposed Pretexts for Cuba Invasion in 1962' *National Security Archive*, 30 April 2001.

7 The tourists managed to escape and report their experience to the gendarmes at Arak, who immediately went after the kidnappers and tracked them down to the well at Tin Gherour. On radioing the DRS headquarters in Tamanrasset and reporting their success, the gendarmes were immediately ordered to release the 'terrorists'. I was at Tamanrasset, Arak and Tin Gherour during this period and was able to interview many of the parties concerned. See Keenan (2009: 172–4) for details of the incident.

8 Details of AF DAS Robert Perry and S/CT Deputy Coordinator Stephanie Kinney's mission were confirmed publicly by the Office of Counterterrorism, U.S. Department of State, Washington, DC on 7 November 2002.

9 By 'conventional', I mean that terrorism is the threatened or employed use of violence against civilian targets for political objectives.

10 In his State of the Union address of 29 January 2002, President Bush spoke of the expansion of the war on terror to new fronts. Since then, the term 'front', and especially the term 'second front', has become almost synonymous with the attempt to globalise the GWOT. Afghanistan is usually understood to be the first front. The term 'second front' has been applied at one time or another to most parts of the world, including Southeast Asia, Iraq, Latin America in the context of the election of left-wing presidents in Brazil and Ecuador, Colombia in terms of the FARC campaign and, after 2003, the Sahara. In the later case the 'first' front is sometime understood to be the Horn of Africa and East Africa. See, for example, Pyne (2002) and Clays (2003).

11 See, for example, Colonel Victor Nelson, responsible for overseeing the PSI, quoted by Jim Fisher-Thompson (2004) and General Charles Wald, quoted by Donna Miles (2004).

12 Although denied by both the United States and Algeria, it is clear that one such proposed 'lilypad' was the base being built by the Halliburton subsidiary, Brown & Root Condor (BRC), at Tamanrasset in southern Algeria, later abandoned after the company got involved in a corruption scandal in 2006 (Keenan 2006, 2010).

13 Eric Schmitt, quoting General Jones, in *New York Times*, 4 July 2003.

14 *World Tribune*, 6 May 2003; *New York Times*, 4 July 2003. EUCOM's second-in-command, air-force General Charles Wald described these groups as 'similar to al-Qaeda, but not as sophisticated or with the same reach, but the same objectives. They're bad people, and we need to keep an eye on that' (ibid.).

15 Burkina Faso was added in 2009. AFRICOM has also discretely changed the TSCTI to the TSCTP, by changing the word 'Initiative' to 'Partnership'. To add to the confusion of names, AFRICOM now has its OEF-TS Operation Enduring Freedom Trans Sahara which, according to AFRICOM, provides military support to the TSCTP. At this point, however, AFRICOM has seemingly managed to confuse itself with its many partnerships. On one page of its website it claims that OEF-TS comprises the ten TSCTP countries (www.africom.mil/oef-ts.asp) (last accessed 21 November 2009) while on another page (www.africom.mil/tsctp.asp) (last accessed 21 November 2009) the OEF-TS also includes Libya! This apparent confusion is possibly the result of mission creep.

16 The White House Office of the Press Secretary, 'President Bush Creates a Department of Defense Unified Combatant Command for Africa.' 6 February 2007.

17 www.commissionforafrica.org/english/report/introduction.html#report.

18 For the definition of securitisation, see Abrahamsen (2005) and Buzan *et al.* (1997)

19 Tony Blair, 'Speech to the Labour Party Conference', 2 October 2001. Reprinted in the *Guardian*, London, 3 October 2001. Quoted by Abrahamsen (2005).

20 Sean McFate is an Assistant Professor at the National Defense University, Washing-

ton, DC. He has served as a US army officer, Program Manager at DynCorp International (a PMC) and advisor to both the US State Department and Department of Defense. He is married to Montgomery McFate, generally regarded as the founder of the US military's Human Terrain System.

21 US Senate Select Committee on Intelligence, 'Report on Whether Public Statements regarding Iraq by U.S. Government Officials were Substantiated by Intelligence Information' (http://intelligence.senate.gov/080605/phase2a.pdf) and 'Report on Intelligence Activities Relating to Iraq Conducted by the Policy Counterterrorism Evaluation Group and the Office of Special Plans Within the Office of the Under Secretary of Defense for Policy' (http://intelligence.senate.gov/080605/phase2b.pdf), Washington, DC 5 June 2008. See also: Press Release of Intelligence Committee, 'Senate Intelligence Committee Unveils Final Phase II Reports on Prewar Iraq Intelligence', 5 June 2008 (http://intelligence.senate.gov/press/record.cfm?id=298775).

22 Details of the manifests of the three flights were given to me by Tamanrasset airport security. One flight carried listening and communications equipment; the other the dogs and their handlers. The exact number of Special Forces (100 or 200) was not clearly translated in the manifest.

23 In August 2006 I attended an ambassadorial briefing at the US State Department in Washington. In my address, I warned of the illegality of the role of the US Special Forces and their dogs in promoting the 23 May rebellion. Two years later, at a similar briefing at the US State Department, one of the State Department officials who had attended my 2006 address confirmed finding proof of the 2006 incursion of US Special Forces into Mali. Although the official had not been able to find records of the US troop movements, the veterinary records of the dogs were accessible and confirmed their passage from Stuttgart to Tamanrasset and into Mali.

24 18 February 2008, at the Royal United Services Institute.

25 Details of these operations are chronicled in Keenan (2010).

26 The UN was formally notified by the Tuareg representative on 29 March 2008.

27 On 18 June 2008, the European Parliament voted 369–197 (106 abstentions) in favour of the draconian, so-called 'Return Directive'. The measure allows undocumented migrants to be held in detention centres for up to 18 months and banned from the territory of the EU for five years.

28 The TSCTI budget, for example, was $100 million per year over five years.

29 Summary: 2009 Defence Appropriations, Washington, DC: House of Representatives. Committee on Appropriations, 22 September 2008.

30 McFate was Program Manager for DynCorp International.

31 The Pentagon has already outsourced the hiring of social scientists to its much-criticised Human Terrain Teams to British Aerospace Systems.

32 UK FCO counter-terrorism advisors visited Timbuktu in April 2009 following the kidnapping of a British citizen, Edwin Dyer, in January, allegedly by al-Qaeda in the Islamic Maghreb. Scotland Yard has also set up an office for Northwest Africa. Information provided by personal communication from FCO (Keenan, 2010).

33 Full details of these latest kidnappings and associated actions are given in *Sahara Focus* (2009: 4) and Keenan (2010).

8　The African Union and AFRICOM

Thomas Kwasi Tieku

Introduction

The establishment of the US Africa Command (AFRICOM) in October 2007 has created a cottage industry in policy discourse, campaigns of non-governmental organizations (NGO) and media discussions. Supporters of AFRICOM claim it will help African states prevent, manage and resolve intractable military conflicts in Africa, reduce endemic poverty and position Africa on the path of economic development. But those who loathe AFRICOM see it as a clear manifestation of the militarization of US foreign policy towards Africa. AFRICOM, in the view of the naysayers, is an instrument designed to help US policymakers exploit Africa's resources and impose American policies on Africans. The partisan nature of the discussions has obscured one of the most important questions – perhaps *the* most important question – in African security today: What relationships exist between AFRICOM and African Union (AU) security institutions? This question requires serious attention from those interested in both Africa and US security issues. Shedding light on it will help us to understand the challenges posed by, as well as the opportunities embedded in, the simultaneous operation of the two security institutions in Africa. This in turn will, first, enhance the ability of policymakers to serve the common interests of Americans and Africans and, second, put academics in a better position to develop a nuanced theoretical understanding of emerging security structures in Africa.

This chapter seeks to close the cavernous gap in the discussions on AFRICOM by examining the relationship between AFRICOM and AU security institutions. The analysis is carried out through the conceptual lenses of hard, soft and smart activities. Hard activities are coercive and aggressive military and economic instruments that undergird AFRICOM and AU security architectures. Soft activities are the cultural values and ideological tools that guide the work of AFRICOM and AU security institutions. Smart activities combine elements of hard power (Knorr 1973; Campbell and O'Hanlon 2006) and soft power (Nye 2004) in ways that are mutually reinforcing.

This chapter argues that while AFRICOM and AU security institutions appear to conflict in some hard activities, they have cordial relationships in the area of soft activities. Their relationship in the area of smart activities is virtually non-existent. They need to develop a solid partnership in the area of smart activities, in part because doing so has the best potential to be enduring, and in part because it will create room for AFRICOM to win the hearts and minds of stakeholders in Africa, particularly those in the security arena. The broad implication of the argument is that US policymakers have neglected to develop the areas of AFRI-COM that have the greatest chance of enhancing the AU security regime and winning the support of its key member states.

The chapter is organized into five main sections. The first gives an outline of the AU and shows its position within broader African politics. The second section teases out AU security architecture, paying particular attention to the normative, ideational and institutional structures of the nascent pan-African security regimes. The next section summarizes the major views on AFRICOM and pan-African security regimes. The penultimate part conceptualizes the relationship between AFRICOM and AU security institutions through the lenses of hard, soft and smart activities, examines each in turn and outlines the hurdles US policymakers need to overcome to secure the support and collaboration of the AU. The last section brings the entire argument together, and reflects on its implications.

Background to the AU security architecture

The new AU security architecture was established as part of the transformation of the Organization of African Unity (OAU) into the AU. Understanding the place of the AU security regime and its relationships with AFRICOM requires considerable insight into the formation of the AU. African leaders established the AU on 26 May 2001 in order to reflect a shift in the focus of the pan-African project.[1] Pan-Africanism as practised within the institutional framework of the OAU focused primarily on legitimizing and institutionalizing statehood in Africa. The institutionalization of the state across the African continent meant that Pan-Africanism needed a new focus and meaning; African leaders established the AU to give it just that. The new Pan-Africanism ideals seek to deploy indigenous African solutions to challenges facing ordinary Africans (Mandela 1994; Salim 1990).

One of the things that the new Pan-Africanism prioritized is conflict resolution (Salim 1995). As a result, Article 4(h) of the Constitutive Act of the AU gives the continental organization the right to intervene in member states in order to 'prevent war crimes, genocide and crimes against humanity.'[2] The specification of *war* crimes, genocide and crimes against humanity as grounds for intervention has provided a clearer set of criteria for intervening in a state to protect ordinary people in Africa from abusive governments (Malan 2002; Cilliers and Sturman 2002; Kioko 2003). These intervention thresholds go beyond the provision made for intervention in the internal affairs of a country in the UN Charter and other major international organizations (Weiss 2004; Schoeman 2003).

AU security institutions

Article 4(h) opened up the space for the creation of a 15-member Peace and Security Council (PSC) as a standing organ of the AU during the first session of the Assembly meeting in Maputo in July 2003.[3] The PSC absorbed the work and structures of the OAU's Mechanism for Conflict Prevention, Management and Resolution, and moved a step further by providing a collective security and early-warning arrangement for AU members. Specifically, the protocol establishing the PSC outlines its functional tasks, including: the promotion of peace, security and stability in Africa; peace building and post-conflict reconstruction; the development of a common defence policy; prevention and combating of international terrorism; and promotion of respect for the sanctity of human life and protection of human rights.[4] Indeed, the PSC seeks to promote peace and security in Africa through preventive diplomacy, conflict management, resolution and post-war reconstruction.

The PSC is advised by a Military Staff Committee composed of senior military officers from various African military establishments. In addition, the work of the PSC is supported by the Panel of the Wise, an early-warning system, a peace fund and an African Standby Force (ASF), which is supposed to be fully developed by the year 2010. The ASF is building on the military capabilities of the regional economic communities in Africa to develop the capacity to intervene militarily in African states for humanitarian purposes (African Union 2001). AU policymakers are counting on the support of advanced industrial societies to develop the various elements of the AU security regime. The establishment of AFRICOM, with its continent-wide security interests, begs the question of what kind of relationships exist between AFRICOM and AU security institutions.

Current views

Two main views have emerged in the literature. One suggests that the AFRICOM and AU security regime relationship is complementary. The second view is that AFRICOM and the AU security architecture have a conflictual relationship. I call the former the complementary view, and the latter the apocalyptic position.

The complementary view

The leadership of AFRICOM and some analysts, based primarily in the United States, claim that AFRICOM and the AU security apparatus complement each other because they share a common mission, vision and approach to solving problems in Africa. In the view of a leading US policymaker, AFRICOM 'complements the desires of ... the African Union' (Anyaso 2008). The official mission of AFRICOM and the AU security arrangement is to prevent, manage, and resolve conflicts on the African continent and advance Africa's development. In the words of President George W. Bush, AFRICOM will promote African 'efforts to bring peace and security to the people of Africa,' and promote the 'goals of development, health, education, democracy and economic growth' (Bush 2008).

The leadership of AFRICOM and the AU security apparatus contend that they envision an Africa that is secure, stable and developed, and that the goal is to use the two security institutions to contribute to the realization of that vision. In the words of the first commander of AFRICOM, 'in the years to come, people will see an Africa that is secure, stable and developed in ways meaningful to its people and our global society' (Ward 2008b). Similar to General Wade's assertion, the then chairperson of the AU, President Denis Sassou-Nguesso of the Republic of Congo, claims that the AU security regime will help 'African people ... conquer war and disease' (Maloka 2001). In the view of Liberian President Ellen Johnson Sirleaf, even though AFRICOM 'is undeniably about the projection of American interests ..., [it] does not mean that it is to the exclusion of African ones' (quoted in Reed 2007). She claims AFRICOM seeks to empower 'African partners to develop a healthy security environment through embracing good governance, building security capacity, and developing good civil-military relationships' (ibid.).

Publicly, the two security institutions have adopted similar approaches to resolving problems in Africa. AFRICOM officials appear to concur with the AU mantra that African solutions must be the first to be used to deal with African security and developmental problems. AFRICOM may intervene in a crisis when an African solution fails to resolve the problem. Thus, AFRICOM would not only first seek 'African solutions to African problems' (Ward 2008b), but, as Ryan Henry, a senior US defence official points out, it will be used primarily to support the 'indigenous leadership efforts that are currently going on' (Henry 2007).

Moreover, AFRICOM and the AU security structure have adopted the Three D (defence, diplomacy, development) approach to dealing with African challenges (Kfir 2008; Jaotody 2008). Three D is part of the 'transformational diplomacy' policy that was introduced by the then US Secretary of State Condoleezza Rice (Rice 2006; Kfir 2008), and emphasizes 'the growing strategic importance of Africa within the US spectrum of vital interests' (McFate 2008c). As part of the defence apparatus of Three D, AFRICOM has been established to improve the Department of Defense's (DoD) ability to support US government military-to-military activities and other programmes in Africa by harmonizing the three separate commands that dealt with African issues in the past. The integration of the three commands into one would make coordination of US military activities in Africa easy. On the diplomacy side, AFRICOM shows the willingness of US policymakers to treat African partners as equals, advance the US Secretary of State's diplomatic policies, and provide the opportunity for continuous dialogue between the US military and policymaking community and their African partners to develop a greater understanding of upcoming issues and to plan well. AFRICOM will advance the development objectives of the transformational foreign policy inasmuch as it is developed to 'prevent problems from turning into crises and crises from turning into conflicts.' In particular, the peace and stability that AFRICOM will help provide will, in turn, promote economic prosperity on the continent. Similarly, the thinking within the AU security establishment is that defence, diplomacy, and development are intertwined, and the 'hope [is] that AFRICOM would advance these interrelated policy objectives in Africa' (Jaotody 2008).

In the view of some of the analysts in the complementary camp, Africa has moved to centre stage in US policy thinking, in part because of its vast natural resources, youthful and growing population and untapped markets, and in part because the United States sees Africa as a potential breeding ground for terrorism (Kraxberge 2005; Carmody 2005). These factors, together with the absence of effective central governments capable of controlling vast areas in the Horn and in North and West Africa, have compelled the United States to establish AFRICOM as part of a broader strategy to give special attention to the African region (McFate 2008c).

Those who subscribe to the complementary view identify at least three areas in which they believe AFRICOM will have a positive impact on AU security. First, they claim that AFRICOM will strengthen the capacity of the AU security architecture, especially the African Standby Force (ASF), to prevent, manage and resolve conflicts on the continent (Hess 2007). Second, they assert that AFRICOM will provide training and technical support to AU counter-terrorism operations. Third, some of the supporters contend that AFRICOM will cooperate with the AU security regime 'to build and sustain democratic, well-governed states that will respond to the needs of their people and conduct themselves responsibly in the international system' (Rice 2006; Kfir 2008).

The apocalyptic position

The complementary camp's rosy picture is disputed by other groups of scholars, commentators and NGO activists. They see no synergy between the AU and AFRICOM. They think AFRICOM 'has no plans to cooperate with the AU's Peace and Security Council and … [will] undermine the Common Defense and Security Policy of AU' (Makinda 2008). They complain that US policymakers have failed to outline in a specific way how AFRICOM will enhance AU security institutions, in particular the PSC objectives. Those policymakers have been silent on AFRICOM's relationship with the AU security institutions, in part because they are aware that AFRICOM will undermine the AU's efforts to foster defence cooperation among African states, and in part because they have no plans to use AFRICOM to assist African states in their collective response to threats to continental African security.

Those who subscribe to the apocalyptic view do not make monolithic claims; rather, they make at least four slightly different claims. There are those who think that AFRICOM is just a continuation of a broader US strategy to militarize its foreign policy (Glover and Lee 2007). For those who make this claim, AFRICOM has nothing to do with African development. Rather, it was established to give the United States a firm military foothold on the continent. The claim is that the United States does not need AFRICOM to pursue her development agendas in Africa as it already has relatively effective development agencies for Africa. Wafula Okumu of South Africa's Institute for Security Studies got to the heart of the issue when he quipped, 'Why use the military? Why not use other effective methods, like USAID [United States Agency for International Development], or even the Peace Corps, who used to be very effective in winning the hearts and the minds of the African people?' (quoted in Reed 2007). A closely related claim is that AFRICOM was established to give the DoD the space and capacity to gather intelligence in Africa (Benton 2007). The strong opposition to AFRICOM by member states of the Southern African Development Community (SADC) group within the AU is based in large part on their belief that AFRICOM is an intelligence-gathering facility.

Others even believe that AFRICOM will undermine the AU's ability to engage in proactive intervention by using its military presence to determine African security priorities and areas where the ASF can deploy. The worry for some observers is that past experiences elsewhere in Africa show that Western states not only usually do not act even when they have troops stationed on the ground, but that the United States in particular often discourages and even deters others from intervening in areas in which it has a strong military presence (TransAfrica Forum 2008). Regional powers such as South Africa and Nigeria, who are obviously concerned that their ability to use AU security to police their backyards will be considerably reduced should the United States gain a firm military foothold in Africa, have used this argument effectively to mobilize opposition to AFRICOM within the AU.

There are also those who are opposed to the AU developing close relationships with AFRICOM because they feel it would inflame terrorist threats against AU member states. They draw on the widely held view that the 1998 al-Qaeda bombings of embassies in Kenya and Tanzania were driven by the relatively large numbers of US citizens in those countries. This leads them to think that similar attacks may become a regular occurrence in Africa should the AU develop a close working relationship with AFRICOM, as well as increasing the likelihood of al-Qaeda-related attacks against AU forces. Others are opposed to it because they believe that an increased US military presence in Africa would exacerbate local conflicts and encourage African governments to become dependent on US security, which would delay the development of a common African defence and security pact.

There is little doubt that AFRICOM seeks to promote and protect the United States' vital national interests in Africa, but US policymakers' pursuit of these interests does not have to mean a negative outcome for Africans. The zero-sum assumption underlying the apocalyptic position exaggerates the potential negative effects of AFRICOM, although the behaviour of some Western governments and citizens in Africa has meant that a sceptical stance is usually necessary when dealing with Western-initiated policies on the African continent. The sunny picture painted by defenders of AFRICOM, together with US policymakers'

Failed states?

penchant for hiding behind rhetorical language without providing clear assurances to allay genuine concerns of well-meaning sceptics, appears to strengthen the apocalyptic position.

The thinking behind AFRICOM is driven too much by the so-called failed-state hypothesis, and in particular, its sub-text. The failed-state crowd mistakenly assumed that, first, there is disorder or no governance in areas where African governments have not established a coercive presence and, second, that those areas are automatic breeding grounds for terrorists and hotbeds of terrorist activity. What the failed-state theorists fail to realize is that central government in Africa is just one of many governance structures and, in fact, over 60 per cent of territories in Africa are governed and ruled by non-governmental actors such as chiefs. The majority of areas in Africa in which central governments have not established a coercive presence are actually very peaceful.

The claim that failed states or failing states promote terrorism is speculative and grounded in logical reasoning rather than facts. Careful empirical studies and descriptive statistical work show that terrorist groups do not find the territories of so-called failed states to be safe havens or conducive to their work (Menkhaus 2003; von Hippel 2002; Hehir 2007). They are rather vulnerable in failed states because external powers and the international community find it easy to set aside the international norm of the territorial integrity of states when it comes to weak states. In addition, the presence of few foreigners in such states makes it easy for them to be exposed and targeted by local rulers.

Crucially, the partisan nature of the debate on AFRICOM has obscured our ability to gain a deeper understanding of the emerging security structures. In particular, it constrains our ability to not only comprehend the enormous challenges presented by the operation of the two security institutions in Africa, but also the opportunities they offer. We need a different analytical trope to help us understand the way the two security institutions impact upon each other and how they might affect African peace and security. The section below recasts and reconceptualizes the relationship between AFRICOM and AU security institutions.

Towards an alternative conceptualization

One way to examine the relationship between AFRICOM and AU security institutions is to categorize the various activities of the two into hard, soft and smart. Hard activities embedded in AFRICOM and the AU security architecture are direct military intervention, sanctions, counter-terrorism and military-to-military programmes. Soft activities are in the areas of mediation, consultation, communication, education, early warning, human security promotion and democracy promotion. Smart activities are intelligence sharing, joint military training, joint delivery of humanitarian assistance, joint provision of development assistance programmes and joint exchanges of personnel. AFRICOM and the AU security institutions have yet to develop their smart activities in a meaningful way. Besides capacity building, AFRICOM and the AU security institutions have had few dealings in the area of smart activities.

Hard activities

Hard activities of AFRICOM include military intervention, counter-terrorism programmes, proxy wars, threats and sanctions. The AU security institutions' hard activities revolve around humanitarian intervention, such as the AU's deployment of troops in Burundi in 2003 and in Sudan in 2005; sanctions, such as suspensions of member states; and its undeveloped counter-terrorism measures.

One of the hard activity areas in which AU security institutions and AFRICOM appear to converge is counter-terrorism. They seem to share a normative understanding of acts that constitute terrorism. The AU Plan of Action for the Prevention and Combating of Terrorism in Africa, adopted in July 2002, defines terrorism in ways similar to the understanding of terrorism by the DoD, the Federal Bureau of Investigation (FBI) and the State Department (Deegan 2009). Like the DoD and the State Department, whose programmes form the bedrock of AFRICOM, the AU considers terrorism as an act of violence designed to create fear, intimidate and coerce government and societies in pursuit of political, social and ideological goals (African Union 2002; Deegan 2009). The state-centric nature of the conception of terrorism by the AU dovetails with the position of US government, which sees terrorism as acts perpetrated not by governments but by sub-national groups.[5] Yet the United States' primary focus on global terrorists, specifically those who threaten American interests, and the AU's insistence that its meagre resources should be devoted to domestic terrorists and those trying to harm its member states mean that the anti-terrorism efforts of the two security institutions are hardly in sync. Each feels that the other's terrorists are not necessarily their own terrorists. A classic case in point is the United States' disagreements with Ethiopia on the Ogaden National Liberation Front (ONLF). The AU security institutions gave their tacit support to Ethiopia to pursue some members of the ONLF whom Ethiopia accused of killing 77 civilian Chinese and Ethiopian oil workers. Members of the US Congress, however, felt that Ethiopia's relentless pursuit of these individuals constituted human rights violations, and threatened to impose sanctions on Ethiopia (Dange 2008).

The failure by US policymakers to consult widely with AU officials on AFRICOM's counter-terrorism programmes has become another source of friction. The more elaborate US counter-terrorism programmes have operated on the basis of bilateral agreements, and the DoD kept AU officials in the dark about the way those programmes operated in Africa. Senior AU officials were never consulted on the deployment of key programmes, including Operation Enduring Freedom-TransSahara (OEF-TS)'s Trans-Sahara Counter-Terrorism Program (TSCTP), which was inherited by AFRICOM. The bilateral nature of the DoD's approach to counter-terrorism has created the unfortunate impression that the United States wants to undermine regional approaches. The perception within the AU system is that the United States adopted the bilateral approach because it was unwilling to work within AU rules and structures, thereby instilling a negative attitude towards AFRICOM among key AU members.

The prevention of international crime, such the narcotics trade, is another hard activity area where AU and AFRICOM interests should have converged. The AU leadership, especially in West Africa, has become increasingly concerned about the spread of drug trafficking networks there. They have been alarmed by the rapid pace at which West Africa has been seized by wealthy, well-armed and technologically advanced narcotics traffickers from Latin America, the Caribbean and South America. The UN estimates that at least 50 tonnes of cocaine are shipped through the West African region every year, and 99 per cent of all drugs seized in Africa since 2003 were found there (UNODC 2008). One-quarter of all cocaine consumed in Europe passes through West Africa. The European retail value of drugs trafficked through West Africa is estimated in the region of about \$10.8 billion, which is more than the national income of many West African states. The trafficking menace is a recent phenomenon; the total quantity of cocaine seized each year in Africa between 1998 and 2003 was around 600 kg, but by 2006 it had increased fivefold (Vulliamy 2008). While the security agencies in Nigeria, Guinea, Liberia and Ghana have made high-profile seizures of drugs passing through their airports to Europe, West African leaders are acutely aware that they do not have the capacity to effectively fight drug trafficking. They have therefore been pushing for the AU approach to combating the drugs trade and preventing West Africa becoming a hub of international crime.

Just as AU leaders want to use the new Pan-African security architecture to fight international organized crime, US policymakers appear willing to employ AFRICOM to fight international crime and drug trafficking on the West Coast of Africa. The synergetic interests of the two security institutions notwithstanding, there is little indication that AFRICOM will depart from the bilateral approach adopted by the United States' anti-drugs programme for Africa, such as the Counter Narcotics and Terrorism (CNT) programmes. Officials of AFRICOM, which has integrated CNT programmes into its work, have shown little appetite for a multilateral approach. They have shown no interest, at least in public, in coordinating their work with African regional organizations, including the AU. The focus of the AFRICOM counter-narcotics programme is to provide funding to militaries and police in individual African states to help them develop expertise and capabilities in fighting international crimes. There is virtually no multilateral component to the programme.

Military intervention is one of the hard activity instruments underlying the work of AU security institutions and AFRICOM. The AU security institutions have the right to intervene to prevent genocide, war crimes and crimes against humanity. The AU has used this instrument in Burundi, Comoros, Sudan and Somalia. The United States, of course, has the capability to intervene militarily in Africa, although it has traditionally been careful in deploying military troops into African territories. The United States has exercised restraint in the use of coercive instruments in Africa, besides the ill-fated Somalia intervention in the early 1990s, the naval patrols of African waters and the counter-terrorism activities in which US forces have directly been involved in combat activities, including the US bombing of Somalia in January 2007, which was meant to eradicate alleged Islamic extremists in the Horn of Africa. It has often preferred to use proxy African states, such as in the case of the recent Ethiopian incursions into Somalia, to pursue some of its military objectives in Africa. The use of key member states of the PSC as proxies has had a negative long-term effect on AU security. It is unlikely that AFRICOM will be able to serve US interests better by exercising considerable military muscle in Africa.

In the coming years, three issues will test the patience of the United States. The priority attention that counter-terrorism now enjoys in AFRICOM circles might increase the temptation to use direct military intervention in certain parts of Africa. In particular, the resolve of counter-terrorism programmes such as Operation Enduring Freedom (OEF), Combined Joint Task Force – Horn of Africa (CJTF-HOA) and the Trans-Sahara Counter-Terrorism Initiative (TSCTI) will be tested. Second, the United States' desire to protect vital natural resources from China's increasing hunger for African goods is likely to encourage AFRICOM to use covert coercive instruments in Africa. Third, the likelihood of using military force in Africa might increase if key AFRICOM officials buy into the claim that African governments' inability to govern vast territories under their jurisdiction has allowed terrorist organizations to breed.

Proxy wars are another hard activity instrument that have been used often by US policymakers, especially at the height of the Cold War. They helped the United States contain the Soviets in Africa, but as Glover and Lee (2007) point out, the proxy wars had a 'devastating impact on African democracy, peace and development.' They undermined African security, inflamed local conflicts, destabilized parts of Africa, created tyrants, led to the waste of billions of dollars, and created a bad image for the United States in Africa. They never made the United States popular within the circles of Pan-Africanists, and in large part explained the chilly relationship between the United States and the OAU. The proxy wars approach may appear attractive, in part because of competition from China, and in part because of the desire of US policymakers to fight the war on terrorism on the cheap. There is a strong view within the AU political leadership that these factors might encourage the United States to increase its proxy war activities should AFRICOM gain a foothold in Africa. Some key members of the AU feel that AFRICOM will take a lesson from the Cold War manual, and decide to use the proxy approach, which will have a negative impact on AU security. They fear that AFRICOM activities in this area will reignite the high level of disunity and distrust that the proxy wars of the Cold War era planted in the OAU, and undermine the Pan-African solidarity norm, which is the currency of the AU.

Soft activities

Soft activities that unite AFRICOM and the AU security architecture are in the areas of human security, democracy promotion, consultation and mediation. AFRICOM seeks to address human security issues such as human rights abuses, poverty alleviation, the building of health clinics and schools, and the digging of wells. Similarly, AU security institutions take a human-centred approach to dealing with economic, social and political challenges facing Africa, claiming that it seeks to create the conditions necessary for, first, sustainable development; second, the survival and dignity of the individual; third, respect for human rights and the protection of good governance; and fourth, each individual to attain his or her full development potential (African Union 2005).

Another soft activity area in which the two security institutions converge is democracy promotion, understood as any effort by external actors to encourage or facilitate the growth and consolidation of democratic institutions in states (Hawkins 2008). They approach democracy promotion in ways that are similar in at least three respects. First, both make democracy promotion an explicit purpose of their work. The Constitutive Act of the AU, the African Charter for Popular Participation in Development, the African Charter on Democracy, Elections, and Governance (the African Democracy Charter) and PSC Protocol made the promotion of representative democracy an explicit purpose of the AU security architecture. Democracy promotion is at the heart of US foreign policy towards Africa, and it is expected that AFRICOM will not only take a strong stand against undemocratic practices, but will provide assistance to pro-democracy movements. Second, both are grounded in a strong anti-coup norm. The PSC has made it clear that it will not be a forum for, or a friend of, new military rulers. Since its creation, the PSC has taken decisive action against military officers who have come to power. In a similar way, AFRICOM officials have not been shy about letting those who would listen know that they intend to use a mixture of diplomatic pressure, electoral assistance and civil society to drive militaries out of African politics. Third, both have strong sanctions against coup makers. Unconstitutional change of government in African states is usually followed immediately by the PSC's announcement that it has suspended the country in question from AU activities. The PSC usually gives the country six months to restore constitutional rule. It often follows this up with additional measures, such as the imposition of sanctions and freezing of assets of members of the junta, if the state fails to take those steps. Like the PSC, AFRICOM officials intend to continue the US policy of withdrawing military, economic and other support from African states that experience unconstitutional change of government. AFRICOM officials will use economic instruments, such as the disbursement of the Millennium Challenge Account (MCA), diplomatic pressure and naming-and-shaming to punish military juntas and create positive incentives for political liberalization.

Consultation is deemed by both AFRICOM and AU security officials to be an essential aspect of their work. Both parties appear interested in engaging in higher level consultations. The United States dispatched a series of high-level delegations led by General Ward to the AU headquarters in Addis Ababa in November 2007 to discuss the creation of AFRICOM and to seek the AU's support. Theresa Whelan, Deputy Assistant Secretary of Defense for African Affairs, seemed to take consultations with Africans seriously when she said, 'We must go out in a way never done before and consult with the nations affected. This manner of approaching partnership was not done with EUCOM, PACOM, or CENTCOM' (quoted in McFate 2008c:11). Yet the type of consultations on which US policymakers embarked prior to the announcement of the establishment of AFRICOM is not the kind of soft activity that will create genuine partnership between the two security institutions. Many senior AU officials felt they were brought into the process after Washington had finalized every detail of the creation of AFRICOM. They saw their meetings with US officials as information sessions, courtesy calls or, even, educational tours to inform them about the establishment of AFRICOM and what it intended to do. Neither was there any indication that the officials who visited the AU headquarters were interested in knowing the genuine opinions of the AU, nor were they interested in involving the key PSC officials in the operationalization of AFRICOM. Little wonder, then, that the position of key PSC members and senior AU officials on AFRICOM does not go beyond diplomatic niceties. They show qualified support for or outright indifference towards AFRICOM.

One area of soft activity where the United States has a genuine chance to work with the AU security regime is conflict mediation. This is not only because the United States has worked well with the Department of Peace and Security on conflict mediation in the past, but also because the AU is in the process of developing its mediation capacity, and AU officials are willing to develop partnerships with states that have a strong capacity in the field. The United States is certainly one of the leaders, if not the leader, in the field of conflict mediation, and its support would be very much welcome. Surprisingly, AFRICOM officials have said virtually nothing about the relationships they hope to build with the AU security regime in the area of mediation, and nothing substantive on mediation can be found in AFRICOM documents in the public domain. The absence of a strong mediation programme in AFRICOM is striking given that the United States has often provided technical and financial support for some of the most successful AU mediation work on the continent, and given that the United States has already established a programme on relationship building, called the State Partnership Program (SPP). AFRICOM officials could have built on this underdeveloped and under-resourced programme to develop a partnership with the AU security regime in the area of mediation.

Smart activities

The idea of smart activities draws on the concept of smart power, which brings together aspects of hard power and soft power in ways that are mutually reinforcing (Wilson 2008). Smart activities of AFRICOM and the AU security regime include education and capacity building, exchanges of personnel between the AU and the US military, intelligence sharing, joint training, joint delivery of humanitarian assistance, joint provision of development assistance programmes to Africans and meaningful consultations between US policymakers and their AU counterparts.

African leaders understand that education will be an important tool for fighting terror and one of the concrete actions the AU made to support the AU

Commission's counter-terrorism activities was to establish an African Centre for the Study and Research on Terrorism in Algeria. The centre hopes to provide centralized access to information on terrorism, commission studies and analysis of terrorist threats and groups, develop counter-terrorism training programmes for security agencies and develop the capacity of African institutions to combat and prevent acts of terrorism in Africa. The centre has opened the space for the AU security institutions and AFRICOM to develop joint capacity in the area of terrorism. Yet, there is little indication that AFRICOM officials are genuinely interested in harmonizing their counter-terrorism educational and research activities with the work of the AU. They have yet to move beyond the professional military education, which is one of the smart activities that seem to have generated meaningful cooperation between AFRICOM and the AU security institutions. AFRICOM has designed professional military education programmes for senior AU military officers. It draws on the experiences of the CJTF-HOA, which provided professional military education to a number of African states in the Horn of Africa in order to develop a continent-wide military training programme for member states of the AU.

Three US capacity building programs absorbed by AFRICOM would strengthen cooperation between AFRICOM and the AU security institutions in the area of professional military education. First, AFRICOM hopes to build on the experience of the State Department-funded programme, International Military Education and Training (IMET). Through IMET, the DoD has already built strong relations with military and civilian personnel from around 45 African states in the areas of expertise. Second, the two security institutions will be tapping into the reservoir of good working relationships developed between African militaries and their US counterpart through African Contingency Operations Training and Assistance (ACOTA). AU and AFRICOM officials will draw on the over 100,000 African military officers who have been trained under the ACOTA programme for UN and AU peace missions. Third, AFRICOM will avail itself of US military personnel who have acquired useful experience working with the AU in the areas of peacekeeping planning, training, intelligence gathering and logistics provision in Comoros, the DRC, Burundi, Darfur and Somalia. Thus, although AFRICOM is a new institution, the personnel it has on the ground have useful, if not extensive, African experience.

AFRICOM is building the capacity of the AU security regime in information technology. The DoD has provided advanced training on a satellite system called the Very Small Aperture Terminal (VSAT) to the AU Mission in Somalia (AMISOM). Lieutenant Brian Canuel of the DoD developed and supervised the VSAT training programme, which eight AU senior military officers have undergone. The trainees then built the capacity of AMISOM troops in installation procedures, proper communications component connection and locating and gaining the satellite signal. The training of AMISOM personnel allowed the AU to deploy the VSAT system to Mogadishu in support of the AMISOM. Doing so has facilitated high-speed data and voice transmission between the AMISOM force commander and the AU headquarters in Addis Ababa. Communication between the AU officials and forces on the ground has improved significantly, due largely to the VSAT training programme.

The rest of the smart activities embedded in AFRICOM and the AU security regime remain under-developed. There is little indication that AFRICOM or AU officials have had serious dialogue on them. The absence of serious movement on smart activities is perhaps surprising given that the concept of smart power, to some extent, inspired the creation of AFRICOM. It is neither a sheer accident that the creation of AFRICOM came a few months after the sustained discussions in the blogosphere (www.smartpowerblog.org) and those of the Commission on Smart Power about the utility of smart power for US foreign policy,[6] nor mere coincidence that US policymakers decided to combine the DoD and State Department African work to generate AFRICOM. The move was to ensure that the DoD's flexing of military muscle in Africa in pursuit of US national interests is coordinated with the charm offensive of the State Department.

US policy officials' reluctance to develop AFRICOM's relations in the area of smart activities appears to be driven by two considerations. First, US officials feel that AU bureaucrats and member governments do not take the issue of terrorism seriously enough. As a consequence, they think the AU is neither willing to nor capable of developing strong and reliable counter-terrorism programmes. Second, there is a concern that developing solid relations with the AU in the area of smart activities might give African governments access to vital and, perhaps, strategic security information. In private, some senior AFRICOM officials do not feel comfortable opening up to many AU member states. They feel either that the majority of them are failing states that are harbouring terrorist groups and contributing to the growth of terrorism, or that they have become recruitment grounds and places used by terrorists from which to launch attacks abroad. Thus, they see some AU members as part of the problem rather than as a solution to their main security concerns. In addition, they think some of the AU member governments cannot be trusted to handle the information properly, and there is a genuine concern that some of them might misuse it.

Conclusion

The United States established AFRICOM in 2007, ostensibly to harmonize and promote its security, defence and development objectives in Africa. The creation of AFRICOM occurred about the same time that African leaders were trying to develop the continental security capacity to resolve conflicts, maintain peace, protect and defend the continent. In the corridors of the AU, the emergence of AFRICOM has quite rightly raised questions about the impact it will have on AU security institutions. Some AU members suggest it will have a negative impact on AU security institutions and, as a result, they do not want the AU to have anything to do with it. In their view, AFRICOM does not fit into AU security priorities and its foothold on African oil will undercut the AU's ability to develop the capacity to police the African continent. Others fear AFRICOM will make the AU security institutions subservient and enable the United States to dictate African security priorities.

Supporters of AFRICOM, however, think it will complement the AU's peace and security activities by strengthening the capacity of the AU security architecture, especially the ASF, to prevent, manage and resolve conflicts on the continent, and by providing training and technical support to AU peacemaking, peacekeeping and counter-terrorism operations. Moreover, AFRICOM's objectives to build, sustain and create democratic and well-governed states in Africa dovetail nicely with the AU's conflict prevention goals. The complementary nature of AFRICOM and the AU security mission, vision and approach suggests that the activities of the two institutions will complement and enhance each other.

This chapter has argued that the partisan turn of the discussions on AFRICOM and the AU security architecture has undermined the ability of keen observers of African politics to explore and theorize the emerging security structures. In particular, it constrains our ability to not only comprehend the enormous challenges presented by the operation of the two security institutions in Africa, but also the opportunities they offer. It has claimed that a different analytical trope is needed to help us understand the way the two security institutions might impact upon each other, and how they might affect African peace and security. Using the conceptual lenses of soft, hard and smart powers, this chapter has recast, reconceptualized and explored the relationship between AFRICOM and AU security institutions, showing that US policymakers have neglected to develop areas of AFRICOM that have the greatest chance of enhancing the AU security regime and winning the support of key African states.

Notes

1 26 May 2001 is recognized as the official date that the AU came into existence because it was the date that the Constitutive Act of the African Union entered into force. It was exactly 30 days after the deposit of the instrument of ratification by two-thirds of the member states of the OAU, as provided for in Article 28 of the Constitutive Act.
2 The article has been amended to include intervention to 'restore peace and stability' and in response to 'a serious threat to legitimate order.'
3 Ten of the 15 are elected to serve for two years. The other five are elected to serve for three years.
4 See Article 2 of the Protocol relating to the establishment of the PSC of the AU. The Protocol is available online at www.iss.co.za/AF/RegOrg/unity_to_union (accessed 20 January 2004).
5 For details, see www.state.gov/s/ct/rls/crt/2007/103716.htm (accessed 2 December 2009).
6 The discussion was led by Joseph Nye of the Kennedy School of Government and Richard Armitage at the Center for Strategic and International Studies.

9   Into Africa – always something new

AFRICOM and a history of telling Africans what their problems are

David Chuter

It is a truism that the identification and analysis of the major security problems of the world are, for the most part, in the hands of Western interests. This dominance is not complete, and not unchallenged, and is starting to fray at the edges as new forces like China seek to shape the global agenda towards their own interests. But it remains true that the most discussed global security issues tend to be those which are important to Western governments, and which are analysed by Western think-tanks and Western media. These issues may, or may not, be truly the most important, and the solutions proposed may or may not be appropriate. Likewise, local elites may genuinely share the Western analysis or they may not. But in any event, there is usually only one game, with a dominant discourse, and those who wish to be players have to accept it.

There is nothing particularly sinister or unusual about this state of affairs. It has been normal for much of history; one thinks of the power of the discourse of the medieval Church in Europe, for example. But this domination has not been seriously challenged since the end of the Cold War, and it has been especially strong, and effectively unchallenged, in Africa.

We take it for granted that most books on Africa are written by non-Africans, and that, for example, the vast majority of the sources on the 1990–4 Rwandan crisis available to a researcher in Mali or Malawi will be written by whites, and often non-experts at that. While African intellectual capital is abundant, much of it has to go abroad if it is to make a living, and learn to express itself in a former colonial language if it is to have influence. Books by scholars of African origin are almost always published in the West, or by African institutions, themselves funded by Western donors. There are more researchers on African problems outside Africa than there are on the continent, just as there are probably more government officials working on African issues in the external world than there are African diplomats. It is only when we try to imagine, say, an international conference on the current American economic crisis held in Dar-es-Salaam, where the working language is Swahili, that we realise how strange this situation is.

The same is true at a more practical level. Western leaders attempt to solve African crises, rather than the reverse. It is regarded as normal that Western states form contact groups, and take the lead in finding solutions to problems in

Africa. When Africans try to do this among themselves, as recently in the Ivory Coast, the West feels hurt and excluded.

There is nothing new about this dominant/submissive relationship between the West and Africa, either in its substance or in the way it is reflected in academic and popular discourse. The perception of African security issues and the discussion of ways of dealing with them have been so firmly in the hands of the outside world for so long that it is legitimate to describe the situation as one of hegemony, in the intellectual sense of the term.

As defined by the Italian political philosopher Antonio Gramsci, hegemony refers to the ability of one group to impose a discourse (a way of thinking and speaking about the world) on other groups. Critically, this involves not only the use of coercion, but, more importantly, the spontaneous agreement of other groups that this discourse is correct.[1] An example from history would be the loyalty of many ordinary Europeans to a monarchy, even when a move to democracy would have benefited them. Gramsci was writing in a domestic political context, but of course the same idea can be usefully applied at the international level.

Western intellectual hegemony has a long history in Africa, and it began in the nineteenth century with the concept of a "continent without history". The lack of written records encouraged the idea that there was no civilisation in Africa, and never had been, and that, as a result, African experience itself was irrelevant. Thus, "nothing useful could develop without denying Africa's past ... and a slavish acceptance of models drawn from entirely different histories".[2] This was believed not simply by colonialists, but by Africans themselves. From the pioneers of African nationalism in the nineteenth century to the founding fathers of African independence, African intellectuals and leaders believed that they must reject the past entirely, and follow models imported from the West, if they were to become truly modern and part of the international community. There having been no states in Africa in the past, it was assumed, they had to be built through imitation of European models.[3]

African leaders did not want to borrow from the West alone, of course, and they frequently looked at Asian states, especially Japan, for inspiration. Yet Japanese modernisation (like that of Korea, Singapore and others later) was not based on a rejection of the past, but rather its use as a firm base from which to select only those foreign ideas which seemed interesting and useful. Moreover, Japan was not colonised, and was free to choose between different sources of advice – the British to train the Navy, the Germans to train the Army, etc. This was a model subsequently followed by other Asian nations. African nations not only lacked the well-organised and effective states that had developed organically in Asia, but tended to be overwhelmed after independence by the influence of the former colonial power.[4]

The natural result of all this was a lack of African self-confidence in defining African problems and solutions, and the growth of a deracinated African elite, educated abroad, speaking a colonial language, and with a pre-emptive cultural cringe towards foreign experts, whether they were missionaries or Marxist-

Leninist political commissars. Nowhere was this more obvious that in the definition of Africa's security problems, and AFRICOM, with its stated objectives of bolstering security, preventing and responding to humanitarian crises, encouraging African unity and preventing conflict, fits very much into this historical paradigm.

During the colonial era, the problem of African security could be defined simply as the preservation of colonial rule. Security forces were largely recruited from indigenous peoples, and were geared to maintaining internal order rather than protecting borders. They would have been much too small for the latter task, and anyway, apart from a few skirmishes in the margins of the First and Second World Wars, the imperial powers did not fight over their African territories: it simply wasn't worth it. Meanwhile, the first stirrings of nationalism in the 1930s attracted the interest of the colonial police authorities, who assumed that the nationalists were Communist agitators, or at least were manipulated by them.[5] Africans were not consulted about such issues.

There was a distinction, certainly, between the majority of colonies, where independence arrived quickly, and those with large settler populations, like Rhodesia, Mozambique, Angola and, of course, South Africa, where the colonial or settler governments resisted independence violently. The African security problem in the 1960s was defined as preventing the takeover of white settler colonies by Moscow-financed terrorist groups. African leaders like Patrice Lumumba (the Osama bin Laden of the 1960s) were regarded with horror and terror by Western political leaders, fearful that Africa would collapse into bloody chaos if they were to take power. Lumumba's murder in 1961 was greeted with relief by right-thinking people everywhere.[6]

By the 1970s the African security problem was seen as countering the policies of the Soviet Union and, to an extent, China by financing more or less anyone (UNITA, RENAMO) opposed to a government which enjoyed Soviet or Chinese backing, and supporting moderate African political leaders in states which were still settler-run. In Rhodesia this meant backing the deservedly forgotten Abel Muzorewa and Ndabanige Sithole (both, conveniently, churchmen) who favoured accommodation with the white regime, over Joshua Nkomo and Robert Mugabe, collectively the Osama bin Laden of the 1970s. Africans were generally not consulted, but where they were, as in the 1972 Pearce Commission on the future of Rhodesia, they turned out to have very different views from those of the West.[7] The "trans-national terrorism" element of AFRICOM's mandate is essentially a continuation of this policy of countering attempts by non-Western actors to become influential in Africa.

By the 1980s, the security problem in Africa was seen as the sustainment of the white regime in South Africa, as the West's one reliable anti-communist ally, but without being too obvious about it. African leaders like Hastings Banda of Malawi, who advocated accommodation with the Apartheid regime, were praised for their realism. Those like Kenneth Kaunda of Zambia, who supported the African National Congress (its headquarters was in Lusaka), were criticised for supporting terrorism. Africans were not consulted unless, like Chief Mangosutu

Buthelezi, they were prepared to ally themselves with the Apartheid regime. Above all, the West was concerned that any transition of power to the black majority should be to leaders like Buthelezi, rather than the terrorist Nelson Mandela, the Osama bin Laden of the 1980s.

By the time of the unexpected end of the Cold War, the tradition of foreign definition of Africa's security needs was well established. Subsequently, the weakness of many African economies has meant that this domination has been extended to actual influence, and even control, over the security sector itself. The debts the West had persuaded African countries to take on to finance export-oriented growth became impossible to repay when that same export growth led to a huge surplus of raw materials and a corresponding fall in prices and export earnings. African economies were thus delivered largely into the hands of Western economic institutions, and their governments and security sectors soon followed. As a result, the security sectors of many African countries have been extensively remodelled in recent years, often by different actors at the same time, and not infrequently in ways that are inconsistent with each other. But this is, in fact, merely a continuation of former colonial practice.

The colonial effort was always confused and divided, and never limited to the formal European authorities. Especially in colonies where "indirect rule" was practised, these authorities did not intervene very much in the lives of the ordinary people. Few colonies were rich (Cecil Rhodes' British South Africa Company never paid a dividend in all its decades of operation) and there was little appetite in colonial capitals for expensive health and education schemes. Their priorities were internal peace and economic benefits to the homeland. Finance ministries were always complaining about the costs involved, and infrastructure projects were largely limited to constructing ports and railways to assist exports. Some colonies, indeed (like Rhodesia), were private businesses with their own mercenary armies: the Congo was initially a personal economic possession of King Leopold of the Belgians. A surprising amount of African colonisation came about when governments – often reluctantly – took over territories originally acquired by private businessmen looking for a quick profit.

Much of the white man's burden, in Africa at least, was therefore taken up by voluntary societies, especially missionary organisations like the large and influential London Missionary Society, founded in 1795. While practice varied among denominations, missionaries naturally tended to be active and evangelical, as well as highly dedicated. In the British tradition, they applied the logic of their domestic missions – saving souls and reforming morals – to the African population. They aimed at nothing less than the complete transformation of African society and the production, through the schools they ran, of young Christian gentlemen (and later women) essentially like themselves. (Joseph Conrad's International Society for the Suppression of Savage Customs in *The Heart of Darkness* was not entirely a joke.) Their ambitious objectives and high moral tone have been inherited by many of the NGOs who work in Africa today.

Africa remains the only continent still receiving large amounts of development aid (more than half of all IMF loans go to African states), and the only one where the West still has a real ability to influence internal political and economic developments. Unsurprisingly, therefore, nations, international organisations and NGOs compete with each other to define Africa's problems as ones that they have the answer to, and this is nowhere more obvious than in the security sector.

As a result, there is no single Western discourse about African security, but rather a complex set of competing ones, with a rather different mix in different countries, and sometimes overlapping and conflicting efforts even in the same country. It is thus arguments among Westerners, rather than debates among Africans, which determine what Africa's security priorities are seen to be. One can follow, for example, the evolution in the thinking of the development community from the 1960s to the present day, from hostility to wary acceptance of the security sector, and from indifference to deep involvement in its transformation.[8] There are signs that international financial organisations may be moving gently in the same direction; again, the interlocutors remain the same, but the message changes subtly over the years. Even within governments, the balance of power between ministries can shift over time; the UK's Department for International Development, created in 1997, rapidly became an actor in a field hitherto dominated by others. Elsewhere, development ministries have become involved in the African security sector to an unprecedented degree, and in some countries – Germany for example – they are the most powerful actors in making security policy towards Africa. But development ministries, for all their expertise elsewhere, do not have automatic credibility with professionals from the security sector. Some of them resort to arm's-length financing to secure influence indirectly, others to seeking to expand the definition of the security sector to include elements – like parliaments – where they believe that their involvement will have more credibility. It is no surprise that Africans are often confused by the variable geometry in which the West appears.

The same is true of NGOs. Like missionaries of different sects a century ago, they are in competition with each other in the market of ideas, and have to attract funding by offering to work in areas which are attractive to donors, even if they are not necessarily the most important areas as seen by Africans. Moreover, almost all NGOs in Africa are ultimately funded by governments in some form, and they are often resented by locals as mechanisms for indirect Western influence. It is also true that, when NGOs employ local talent, they frequently hire the good people from government and the security forces, because they pay better and offer more reliable salaries.

For more than a century, therefore, Africa's problems have largely been identified and analysed by different groups of foreigners, who have then set out to solve them, often in competition with each other. Whether this analysis and these solutions have been correct or not is not really the issue. The missionaries have won, and it is simply impossible to know whether, despite their best endeavours, Africans are actually articulating their own security needs, or unconsciously rehearsing what they have learned from us. All of this makes the current – laudable – desire for African "ownership" of security issues rather problematic.

Often unconsciously, the West has been able to impose a series of under-standings about security issues on Africa, and, often unconsciously, Africans have accepted this imposition. At the highest level, the West's international security agenda of non-proliferation and "terrorism" has generally been accepted by Africans as applying to their own continent as well.[9] More importantly, Africans have largely come to accept the West's characterisation of their own problems – corruption, poor leadership, ethnic rivalries, war, atrocity, even child soldiers – as well as the West's proposed solutions, even as the latter have changed over time. Now some of these are real problems, even though there is little comparative evidence that corruption has any real influence one way or the other on economic growth.[10] But even if Africa could somehow benefit from the stellar level of political leadership we take for granted in the West, it is not clear that all its problems would thereby be solved. The *real* problems in Africa are those of hunger and malnutrition, poverty, infant mortality, and avoidable deaths from communicable diseases and polluted drinking water, as well as an undeveloped infrastructure, and states which were hustled into the world without the necessary economic underpinning. The common factors among these problems are that they are rarely photogenic, often structural and difficult to resolve, and take time before results are visible. It is not necessary to accuse the West of hypocrisy or callousness in preferring to address, say, child soldiers rather than infant mortality; politicians, like NGOs or the media, have to mobilise public opinion and money, and some causes are easier than others. But it does mean that Africa's problems tend to be defined as those which the West thinks it understands and can do something about.

Obviously, these two sets of problems are not wholly distinct from each other. In particular, there is a recognised link between security and development – the one is essential for the other, although it does not guarantee it. But the human security problems listed above are not necessarily the result of wars, nor does peace necessarily make them better. Indeed war, or even "armed conflict", is not really the fundamental problem in Africa. Studies suggest that for ordinary people it is the insecurity of daily life, the exposure to petty crime and violence without a capable state to protect them, which is more the problem.[11] Even during African wars, most casualties are not directly from violence, but from second- and third-order effects. Estimation of deaths in African conflicts is always problematic, and most figures quoted are simply wild guesses. But even if we accept that the orders of magnitude of deaths in recent conflicts are roughly correct (several million in the Congo, several hundred thousand in Darfur) nine out of ten such deaths are likely to be from hunger and disease rather than violence, and this kind of suffering does not necessarily stop when the fighting does.

One way in which the West has traditionally tried to understand Africa is through the relentless ethnicisation of its problems and conflicts. Europeans arriving in Africa, armed with the racialist ideology of the time, expected to find tribes (as they were then called) and tribes they duly found. So the assumption that the political conflict in Rwanda (and neighbouring Burundi) was essentially one of racial struggle and hatred led to an ethnic interpretation of the 1990–4 crisis, and its accompanying discourse of "genocide", which Africans themselves had to accept if they wanted to be taken seriously. Ironically, "such is the instru-mentalisation of conflict today that the actors involved spontaneously give an ethnic explanation for it".[12] Once more, the missionaries have won. In turn, this interpretation leads to Western-sponsored "reconciliation" processes among ethnic groups, or alternatively trials of alleged "ethnic entrepreneurs", or some-times both at the same time. The West is therefore puzzled to find that apparent bitter ethnic enemies are capable of cooperating and negotiating with each other for their mutual political benefit, as in the Ivory Coast.

The situation is very similar with attempts to rebuild states after a conflict. Planning and execution of post-conflict reconstruction is largely in the hands of Western organisations, to the point that if the African Union (AU), for example, did prepare a plan for rebuilding a country, "international aid agencies would probably ignore it". But it remains true that even if Africans want "ownership of reconstruction processes", few, if any, African governments are doing anything to challenge the factors that perpetuate the "donor domination of the develop-ment agenda".[13]

Armed with these understandings, then, the contemporary Western response to Africa's security problems, as it perceives them, has been to suggest, once more, that African states become more like the West. The African response has generally been to agree. A series of initiatives has aimed at reinforcing African military capabilities through Western-sponsored training programmes. The Brit-ish Military Advisory and Training Teams (BMATT), the French RECAMP[14] programme and the US African Crisis Response Initiative (ACRI) have all been intended, in the words of the official description of the ACRI concept, to "enhance the capacity of African nations to better perform peacekeeping and relief tasks and thus encourage regional self-reliance".[15] AFRICOM is essen-tially the latest bilateral initiative. The culmination of these ideas is the planned African Standby Force (ASF), intended to be operational in 2010. AFRICOM is intended to support the ASF, as now is the French RECAMP initiative (since taken over by the European Union). Bilaterally, the French have also reconfig-ured the command of their stationed forces in Africa to match the ASF regions.

The ASF, established under Article 13 of the Protocol Relating to the Estab-lishment of the Peace and Security Council of the African Union, agreed at the 2002 Durban summit, is intended to carry out "a multiplicity of peace support operations" including "preventative deployment, peacekeeping, peace building, post conflict disarmament, demobilisation and humanitarian assistance".[16] It is intended to consist of five regional brigades, each of some 4,300 personnel, including four infantry battalions, with signals, engineer and logistic support. Reasonable progress is being made towards this capability, though with consid-erable variations between the regions.

It is always useful in a situation of this kind to reverse-engineer the proposed solution, and to ask what the problem must be for the proposed solution to be appropriate: in other words, if the ASF is the answer, what must the African security problem be? Continuing in the line of the Western initiatives of the 1990s, the ASF implicitly defines the problem primarily as the incapacity of Africans to perform the kind of peacekeeping and post-conflict reconstruction tasks which were carried out by the UN in countries such as Sierra Leone and Liberia. This incapacity is not really disputed; what is less clear is that it is the main factor in Africa's security problem.

Depending on the scenario, a brigade should generally be capable of deployment within 30 days, less (14 days) for intervention operations. To keep a multinational force available at that degree of notice means that its components cannot do much else, nor can they be kept at that level of preparedness forever. When a brigade is deployed, there is also a limit to how long it can be expected to remain before being relieved. At the moment, it is assumed that an ASF brigade would be relieved by a UN force – and that may not always be a safe assumption.

The purpose of this argument is not to criticise the ASF, or any of the schemes which preceded it. It is rather to point out that the ASF only makes sense under certain defined circumstances, and if certain analyses of Africa's problems are broadly correct. The ASF is fundamentally a Western-style concept, and it is thus not surprising that, in several regions, "officers seconded from donor countries [are] rapidly outnumbering their African counterparts". Moreover, these advisors have access to funds and influence beyond anything the locals can muster, and so "[i]t is not uncommon to find middle ranking expatriate officers from European countries effectively in control of ASF preparations, and exerting considerable influence on the concepts, standards and decisions taken at every level."[17] A cynic might wonder whether, a century after they were first raised, the King's African Rifles are not staging a return.

It is also assumed that the ASF could be deployed as an intervention force to "pre-empt or bring to halt a genocide, crimes against humanity and war crimes".[18] This is not only another reflection of the Western obsession with ethnicising African conflict, but also an instance of the recurrent Western fantasy that a well-timed cavalry charge can bring the ungodly to justice and resolve a political crisis. The idea that African conflicts are *not* the result of deep-seated and complex issues, but rather manufactured by ethnic entrepreneurs who can be picked up in a Special Forces raid, is fundamental to this kind of thinking, and of course it is false. There are cases where individual political ambitions have kept conflict going in Africa – Jonas Savimbi and Charles Taylor come to mind. But these were unusual circumstances and, in any event, both leaders were able to appeal to legitimate grievances and did draw genuine support from parts of the population. A more typical case would be Sierra Leone, where the Revolutionary United Front, for all its lurid reputation, was more than just a bunch of thuggish limb-choppers, and more than just a vehicle for the personal ambitions of Foday Sankoh. It reflected and benefited from very real anger and disgust at the corruption, incompetence and cynicism of successive governments since independence. The British intervention in 2001 – the model which stands silently behind much of this literature – dealt the final blow to the rebels militarily, but by definition could not address the wider problems of the country.[19] There is little sign that they are being adequately addressed even today, and so it is not clear whether the current peace will endure.

It also reflects the traditional Western obsession, which has varied only in detail since the nineteenth century, with turning complex African problems into brightly coloured moral lessons, like those in missionary school books, with clearly distinguished Good Guys and Bad Guys. It's not clear that this reductionism actually has ever helped the resolution of African security problems in the past, or will in the future.

Sierra Leone was not an ethnic war, and violence was used as a tool to terrorise populations that could not be controlled otherwise. The same holds true for many other African conflicts. Nonetheless, Western ethnicisation of African conflicts shows no signs of coming under control, and continues to influence thinking about African security issues. In particular, the shadow of Rwanda in 1994 falls heavily over all recent attempts to develop more capable African forces; so it is worth looking for a moment at what a hypothetical ASF brigade deployed in, say, early 1994 would actually have encountered. At that date, a brutal war between the invading Rwandan Patriotic Front/Army (RPA) and the government Forces Armées Rwandaises (FAR) had been in suspension for some months. An ASF brigade would have been deployed into a country where the two sides fielded perhaps ten times as many men, battle-hardened, better armed and probably better trained. Moreover, the mass killing of the French-speaking indigenous Tutsi was carried out less by the FAR – who were fighting and losing to the RPA – than by police and civil society groups, including thousands of women and children, using machetes and, in some cases, vehicles to kill their victims. Few of these groups had uniforms or were distinguishable from their Tutsi neighbours. It is hard to imagine what, in practical terms, an ASF brigade might have accomplished. Securing a point of entry and separating the combatants – two missions which have been proposed as part of an intervention operation – would clearly have been difficult.

The ASF itself is part of a wider background – the progressive establishment, over the last few years of the African Peace and Security Architecture (APSA).[20] Some progress is being made in putting this architecture together, and it is not my purpose here to evaluate it. Rather, it is interesting to put it into its historical context, and to ask, once more, what factors would have to be true for it to be effective.

First, the concept itself is based on a European example. The idea of a peace and security council, of a common defence and security policy, and of a mutual security guarantee, are all taken from the history of the development of the European Union. Logically, therefore, the security situation in Africa today must be sufficiently close to that of Europe after 1945 for these experiences to be relevant and transferable. It is not clear that this is this case. In particular, Europe had a long history of wars between powerful nation-states disputing territory which was economically developed and heavily populated. The European integration process was seen as the only escape from nationalist conflict, and was built on a common linguistic and cultural heritage. The security problems of

Europe had historically been those of inter-state wars and the competition for dominance between Germany and France. None of this is to be found in the history of Africa.

Second is the assumption that a strong organisation can be created on the basis of weak states. The states which formed the European Union in 1992 were strong and wealthy, and capable of providing their citizens with security in their daily lives. Yet while it is true that an international organisation is more than the sum of its parts, it is also less. International organisations like the European Union have more resources than individual states, and they may also have more political legitimacy in certain cases. But they also have difficulties of coordination and consensus, and the larger the organisations are, the bigger the problems. The European Union, for all its virtues, is necessarily often less effective overall than the average European state, because of the problems of reconciling the different views of 27 nations. It is not clear that Africa can escape this problem.

Third, the APSA also assumes a surplus (or at least no deficit) of capable and experienced diplomats, military officers and civilian specialists who can be seconded from national governments to work in the more complex and demanding environment of the AU and the sub-regional organisations. The success of these bodies will mainly depend on the quality of their staff. As everyone who has worked in an international organisation knows, getting capable staff is never easy. Some governments play the game and send their best people; others are mainly interested in the political benefits of securing this or that post; still others send people they want to get rid of. It is unlikely that the APSA bodies can escape these problems entirely, and it begins from a situation where most African governments have too few trained and experienced people in the first place.

It may be, of course, that the European model will be smoothly transferable to Africa, and that the APSA will attract the good-quality people it needs to make it work. One must hope so. And it would not be fair to treat the APSA simply as a carbon copy of its European original. The Panel of the Wise, for example, is an interesting idea that owes nothing to any European model. But it is faithfully, in the long line of imported Western schemes, based on the European nation-state concept, and is in many ways a logical development of the acceptance by African nations on independence of the nation-state model for their continent.

Nation-states need armies, and in the peaceful transitions, the departing colonial powers turned over their internal security forces as the nucleus of the armies of the new states. These forces were, of course, organised on the European model, and some of the European officers who had commanded them stayed on for several years after independence. The organisation and structure of these new armies only really made sense if one believed that the security problems of Africa after independence would be approximately those of Europe in the middle of the last century, and so needed to be dealt with similarly. This assumption was demonstrated in African constitutions (essentially written by Europeans), which defined the principal task of the new armies as the defence of the nation, according to the classical European model. This is what we find in Chapter XVII of the Constitution of Ghana, for example, and we would therefore expect to see the Ghanaian military frequently practising defensive tactics against a possible foreign invader. In fact, of course, the main *actual* role of the Ghanaian Army (formed after independence from the Gold Coast Regiment of the Royal West African Frontier Force) has been UN peacekeeping, at which it has performed very well.

Part of the assumption of the "continent without a history" was that there had been no proper wars and no organised armies before Europeans came. Like everything else, the military could be organised from scratch along European lines. We know better now, but we also know that traditions of warfare in Africa were very different from those in Europe. In particular, given the very low population density, capture of territory has always been pointless, not least because of the impossibility of garrisoning it. The objectives of traditional African warfare were "to take women, cattle and slaves". The latter, in particular, "should be seen as part of the process by which African states grew: by capturing people rather than by gaining control over territory".[21]

States were therefore formed in Africa not through territorial conquest, but by assimilation and forcing other groups to pay tribute. As a result, African political history, before and after the colonial period, has almost nothing in common with general concepts of state formation (which tend to be based specifically on the European experience), or for that matter on standard international relations theory.[22] In the post-colonial period, wars of territorial aggression have been very rare because there has been little point in fighting them. Tanzania invaded Uganda in 1979 to oust the Amin government, not to take over the country. Rwanda and Uganda invaded what was then Zaire in 1996 to install a puppet ruler in Kinshasa, and re-invaded several years later when that puppet refused to behave. Subsequently, the two nations looted the east of the country in traditional style, before falling out and fighting each other through surrogates, again in traditional style.

The historical style of African warfare produced very different military organisations from those in Africa today, even though the strategic fundamentals have not changed that much in the last few centuries. Although we must be careful not to over-generalise, it seems that pre-colonial Africa had little experience of professional armies. A rudimentary aristocratic officer class existed in some parts of the continent – as it did in Europe at the time – and some kingdoms used a form of conscription for war. But in many cases, going to war was just part of life for young men, who might otherwise be herders or cultivators of crops (the same was true in other parts of the world also). The military systems of Africa in those days developed naturally from the organisation of societies and do therefore seem to have been well suited to the needs of the time.

If the above appears critical, it is no more than to say that there is an apparent mismatch between the reality of Africa's contemporary security problems on the one hand, and the assumptions that obviously lie behind recent initiatives by the West to address them, on the other. This is not deliberate – it is not that either side positively wishes to address the wrong problems. But both Westerners and

Africans are to some extent prisoners of history, and of historical patterns of intellectual dominance and subservience. Africans have no history of collectively being able to impose ideas on the West, or resist the imposition of Western ideas upon them. If anything, Africans have been more open to Western influence and less confident of their own judgement than any other civilisation the West has ever encountered. Westerners, for their part, have commendably begun to ask Africans what they want, and to promote African "ownership" of security issues. But the historical legacy of Western intellectual domination in Africa is such that Africans tend to articulate ideas which – whatever their intrinsic merit – often resemble those of the West. Like a priest conducting a catechism, the West can therefore find itself effectively talking to itself. Moreover, the difficulties of coordination in a large and diverse continent of weak governments are such that answers to Western enquiries do not always come quickly. In the interests of making progress, the West suggests, perhaps, that *this* may be a good idea, and the historical pattern of domination and subservience is renewed. Is there another option?

One way to address the problem is to ask what would happen if we took, as an experiment, some of the objective factors about African security which have been reviewed above, and tried to construct a security paradigm based on them. To begin with, we could take the fundamental difference between *defence of* territory and *control over* territory. The former is seldom necessary in Africa; the latter is essential.

If this is indeed the problem, then it would be logical to suggest that one solution would be to increase the *size* of African security forces, since ability to control territory is partly a function of numbers. This does not necessarily mean that existing armies must become bigger, though. An alternative would be to have larger but lighter forces, organised predominantly on a part-time basis, or through compulsory military service. In effect, these would be militias. It is interesting that militias appear almost immediately in African conflicts. The Western professional military model, which has no roots in Africa, often breaks down during conflict, as communities turn to protect themselves in the face of the government's inability to do so. Conventionally, the militias are seen as a bad thing, and large disarmament, demobilisation and reintegration (DDR) exercises have been mounted to break up militias after a conflict and disarm the members. DDR can have a useful role to play, but it is increasingly clear that the problem in Africa is not the number of weapons as such, but control of those weapons. A militia with a cadre of professional officers and NCOs would be a way of extending and maintaining control over territory in a way which is not currently possible. It would also be closer to African traditions than the current model.

In the end, the problem is not that the West is consciously and deliberately trying to dominate thinking about security in Africa, nor is it that Africans are failing to take the intellectual lead when they should be doing so. It would be much simpler if that were the case. The problem is really the absence of an indigenous modern African tradition of security analysis which does not take Western ideas and experiences as a starting point. Who controls the past controls the future, said George Orwell in *1984*, and who controls the present controls the past. The West controls Africa's present, as it has controlled its past, even if neither Westerners nor Africans quite understand why or how. But whether the efforts of foreign military trainers today will be any more productive and enduring than the efforts of missionaries and colonial administrators a century ago is very open to question.

Notes

1　These terms come from Gramsci's essay, "The Intellectuals", reprinted in Hoare and Smith 1972.
2　Davidson 1992: 42.
3　Ade Ajayi 2000.
4　For the different experiences of African and Asian states, see Chang 2007.
5　See Davidson 1992: 170 for one example.
6　de Witte 2000, is based on contemporary Belgian and other records.
7　Pearce 1972.
8　See, for example, Brozoska 2003.
9　Although African governments have often been reluctant to join the "war on terror" in any tangible form, African officials say privately – and sometimes publicly – that they have no desire for their countries to get mixed up in violent conflicts between the United States and those who oppose its Middle East policies.
10　The disgust of many ordinary Africans with the corruption of their political elites is, of course, understandable and entirely justified, but is rather a different issue.
11　See, for example, the pioneering World Bank study *Voices of the Poor*, available at web.worldbank.org.
12　Neuman and Trani 2006: 144. Neuman and Trani quote an astonishing article from *Le Monde*, dated as late as 1990, talking of "Nilotic" Tutsi and "Bantu" Hutu. Perhaps it is the exalted racial status of the Tutsi during the colonial period that accounts for the extreme – almost hysterical – Western reaction to the 1994 Rwanda crisis. The Tutsi were seen, then and subsequently, as not really Africans at all, and basically as whites. The slaughter in 1994 was therefore an acting out of the white settler nightmares of the colonial period, where the brutish Africans (here represented by the Hutu) would rise up and slaughter their colonial masters.
13　Gueli 2008: 89.
14　Renforcement des capacités africaines maintien de la paix. See www.diplomatie.gouv. fr/fr/pays-zones-geo_833/afrique_1063/renforcement-capacites-africaines-maintien-paix-recamp_335/programme-du-recamp_8886.html
15　At http://usinfo.state.gov/regional/af/acri.
16　Cilliers 2008: 1.
17　Ibid.: 18.
18　Policy Framework for the establishment of the African Standby Force and the Military Staff Committee. Assembly of the African Union, Third Ordinary Session, Addis Ababa, Ethiopia, 6–8 July, p. 17.
19　On the background to the fighting see Richards 1996.
20　On the APSA see, for example, Kingebiel 2005.
21　Herbst 2000.
22　See, for example, Malaquias 2001: 13.

10 Geo-politics beyond Washington

Africa's alternative security and development partnerships

Josephine Osikena

With little fanfare, the US government launched Africa Command (AFRICOM) on 1 October 2008. Ironically, this twenty-first-century defence arrangement has been relegated to reside in Stuttgart, Germany, as there is little (with the exception of Liberia), if any, appetite in Africa for it to be relocated to the continent. How relevant is AFRICOM for Africans and Africa? To what extent is Africa's response to AFRICOM, and broader US strategic interests, influenced and challenged by Africa's alliances with new global centres of power beyond Washington who have competing motives and approaches to development and security? What are the implications of all this for US policymakers in a new administration?

This chapter explores the challenges associated with AFRICOM's predominant focus on the militarisation of African security, by surveying examples of African partnerships with non-OECD (Organisation for Economic Cooperation and Development) actors. In an emerging world order with a shifting global balance of power, the chapter provides an illustrative analysis of African attempts to identify and address their broader strategic security interests. It examines the geo-political alliances that Africa has attracted in the areas of: aid, investment and trade, as well as development cooperation and the opportunities and challenges this poses for US engagement across the continent. The first section explores Brazil–Africa collaboration in the sphere of social development. It demonstrates how Brazil has ostensibly been able to set aside its own short-term gains and national commercial interests to promote long-term sustainable development, by sharing and exchanging examples of its own development experience. This section also discusses what lessons this form of engagement provides which could be the basis for developing better US Africa relations. The second section examines Africa's diplomacy and power partnerships with India, which have helped to secure greater self-determination and underpin Africa's (and India's) sense of sovereignty and improve integration and cooperation, both amongst African states and throughout the developing world, as well as advance efforts to make global governance institutions more representative. This section identifies that this political assertiveness does not always produce a convergence of interests between Africa and India, and discusses the implications that this dynamic might bring to bear on US Africa relations. The third section explores the continent's expanding relations with the People's Republic of China (PRC) and the impact this has had on Africa's own economic growth agenda, particularly in the areas of commodities and infrastructural development. It demonstrates that China's significant presence in Africa represents a sizable challenge for both American and African strategic interests, and unless the United States is able to provide a coherent and informed response to this challenge, there is a risk that US interests may become increasingly marginalised in Africa. The final section examines the emerging role that Africa has begun to play regarding food security in the Middle East. It examines how Africa can exploit its comparative advantage in abundant arable land and surplus labour to ensure its own food security and agricultural development needs are met, as well as meeting regional and global demand. The section also discusses the challenges Africa faces in employing agriculture as a platform for industrialisation and the implications of this for US Africa engagement. In closing, the chapter raises a number of questions for US policymakers to consider: how, in a changing world with the rise of new centres of power, might US Africa policy better connect with African people and African governments? How might a more informed and coherent US approach better serve Africa's own development and security agendas, as well as secure strategic US interests on the continent? Indeed, it asks if this is even possible.

AFRICOM

AFRICOM now coordinates US peacekeeping activities, humanitarian aid missions and military partnership operations with African countries, as well as offering defence support in non-military operations such as the Millennium Challenge Account (MCA) (which awards grants to countries who meet good governance criteria); the President's Emergency Plan for AIDS Relief (PEPFAR – an initiative to combat global HIV/AIDS); the Africa Education Initiative (expanding education to the world's poorest children); the Water for the Poor Act (a strategy to provide affordable and reliable access to safe water and sanitation); and the African Growth and Opportunity Act (AGOA – an initiative which allows nearly 40 economies in sub-Saharan Africa to export specific goods duty- and quota-free into US markets) (US Africa Command 2008a). AFRICOM thus coordinates US military support by bringing the humanitarian work of the State Department, the US Agency for International Development (USAID) and other US government agencies engaged with Africa, under the direction of the US Department of Defense (DoD) (Volman 2008).

The creation of this new US hybrid civil–military headquarters devoted to Africa (ibid.) was ostensibly designed to support Africans in building greater capacity to deliver their own security (US Africa Command 2008b). Yet many argue that this military-centred strategy only very narrowly filters the realities of security challenges across the continent through a military prism. As such, the initiative assumes that counter-terrorism (Tuckey 2008) and safeguarding US supplies of fossil fuels, minerals and other natural resources (particularly in the context of China's growing presence in Africa) are among the main priorities and challenges confronting Africa (Kidane 2008). This is perhaps illustrated by the level of US military sales, financing and training expenditure devoted to just eight African countries, which are regarded as particularly strategic for what was once described (under the George Bush II administration) as the 'war on terror.' In fact, expenditure has increased from approximately US$40 million between 1997 and 2001, to over US$130 million between 2002 and 2006 (LeMalle 2008).

Africa defining its own security interests

The military thrust of AFRICOM too narrowly defines the security interests of Africans and Africa. In 2001 the African Union (AU) established the New Partnership for African Development (NEPAD). NEPAD represents a vision and a strategic framework for Africa's renewal. The framework produced an action plan which identifies four broad African priorities: peace and security, democracy and governance, regional cooperation and integration, and capacity building. In addition, the framework highlights eight sectoral priorities, including: agriculture, human development, infrastructure, intra-African trade market access and the environment (New Partnership for African Development 2001). Thus, economic and political development and cooperation are regarded as important tools for the continent's transformation. Yet, how can US Africa policy in general and AFRICOM in particular adequately recognise the importance of the priorities and challenges identified by Africa, when the US initiative's emphasis is focused on 'conducting security engagement through military-to-military programs, military-sponsored activities, and other military operations in support of U.S. foreign policy' (US Africa Command, 2008b)?

A rapidly changing world

AFRICOM's ongoing development needs to be situated against the backdrop of a dynamic and emerging new world order which is shaping Africa's future and US influence across the continent. There are the cyclical contexts of a global economy in the throes of an unprecedented global financial crisis, deep economic recession coupled with the fact that Africa is by no means the principal priority preoccupying the new US administration. Developing a more effective strategy in Afghanistan, potential engagement with Iran, preparation for a withdrawal in Iraq and stabilising Pakistan, as well as a long-awaited workable peace process for the State of Israel and the Palestinian Authority, all appear to be much higher political priorities.

More significantly, however, as the global balance of power shifts from a unipolar to an increasingly multipolar system, new global powers are competing for influence and resources. Thus the United States is becoming less dominant, with limited strength and leverage (US National Intelligence Council 2008).

The rise of China, India and other emerging economies exemplifies this transition. Notwithstanding this, however, the changes in today's international distribution of power have yet to take real shape and continue to undergo a process of evolution that has so far been neither accurately defined nor confidently articulated. For example, in 1973 China, India, Brazil and South Africa's collective share of world income was just over 10 per cent, but by 2001 this had risen to 21 per cent. Furthermore, in 2000 their combined GDP was less than 15 per cent of the total GDP of the United States, Japan, Germany, the United Kingdom, France and Italy (G6). By 2050, however, it is predicted that only the United States and Japan will remain amongst the six largest global economies (Nayyar 2008). Ironically, however, recent data compiled by the UN Food and Agricultural Organisation (FAO) on the state of global food insecurity, estimates that of the 907 million undernourished people living in the world today (2008), 65 per cent live in only seven developing countries. China, India and Indonesia represent three of these seven (FAO 2008). In spite of the economic ascent of many of these emerging economies and the impact of this for the global economic landscape, these countries continue to confront severe developmental challenges. Therefore, what role does and can Africa play in this rapidly changing world, and what implications does this transition have for US influence across the continent?

Today, Africa has once again become a strategic priority for sovereign states and regional entities outside the continent. A simple illustration of this is the plethora of new summits and fora which the AU has established with regions such as the European Union and South America, and with countries such as China, India, Japan and Turkey. Why is Africa being courted by these new centres of power and what impact might this have for United States–Africa relations?

For the most part, the partnerships established by African states with non-OECD[1] partners (both governments and non-state actors, such as private companies) in Asia, the Middle East and Latin America are far from new, but the level of engagement with respect to scale and scope is unprecedented. This is particularly pertinent as notions of security have undergone a process of transformation. It is important, therefore, to view Africa's non-OECD partnerships as beyond merely trade, investment flows and instruments of development cooperation. In fact, this age of greater engagement is part of a wider package of economic and political strategic cooperation which affects African nations, regions and social groups in diverse ways. More importantly for the United States, however, this transformation will greatly influence and ultimately shape US strategic interests across the continent and, in turn, the future of AFRICOM itself.

Brazil's Africa policy: a platform for social development?

At first sight, the scale of Brazil's engagement with Africa does not appear to challenge US strategic interests, or indeed the future of AFRICOM. For example, between 1998 and 2004, Brazilian government data suggests that US$15 million was made available in development aid. In 2003 Lusophone Africa received 34 per cent of Brazil's ODA (overseas development aid), the majority of which went to Angola and São Tomé and Príncipe. This compares to mammoth levels of US development programme funding in Africa. In 2007 US$575 million was provided to Africa in trade-related assistance, an increase of 66 per cent compared to 2005. Since 2003 a staggering US$18.8 billion has been committed to fighting HIV/AIDS worldwide, with a particular focus on 12 African countries (US Africa Command 2008a).

Therefore, while the quantity and scope of Brazilian cooperation across Africa is modest compared with other partners on the continent, Brazil's history and development experience suggest that its influence across Africa should by no means be underestimated, and might be used to inform future US engagement across Africa (Schläger 2007).

Between 2002 and 2006 Brazilian trade with African economies tripled to approximately US$13 billion. Behind China and Kuwait, Brazil is the third largest emerging market creditor to least developed countries (LDCs). During his two terms in office, President Luiz Inácio Lula da Silva has made several official visits to Africa, visiting over 17 countries. Since 2003 more than ten Brazilian embassies have opened or been re-established across the continent (ibid.).

In 2006, on the initiative of the Brazilian president, the first Africa–South America Summit (ASA) was convened in Nigeria with the aim of developing greater South–South cooperation between the two continents. The terms and principles of the partnership agreed at the summit include commitments to exchange information on successful experiences for combating hunger and poverty. On health, the two sides agreed to facilitate greater accessibility to antiretroviral drugs, as well as preventive and curative drugs for communicable diseases such as tuberculosis. Furthermore, the two sides agreed to cooperate on joint research on vaccines, care and treatment of cross-border and neglected diseases. On education, there was an agreement to develop cooperation across all levels of schooling and the exchange of best-practice strategies for combating illiteracy. The summit also created the Africa–South America Cooperative Forum (ASACOF). Coordinated jointly by Brazil and Nigeria, forum activities are focused on agriculture, trade, investment, energy, technology, water resource management and tourism, many of which are represented in the NEPAD sectoral priorities for Africa previously highlighted.

Partnerships free from commercial interests and short-term economic or political gains?

Brazil does not share the global economic dominance that other emerging markets can boast. Yet it has made good progress in economic and social development. It is ranked significantly higher than India and China in the UN Human Development Index (HDI),[2] but receives much less aid from the international donor community; 0.023 per cent of its GDP compared to 0.075 per cent for China and 0.109 per cent for India (ibid.). For example, in the case of China, almost 20 per cent of the world's poor live in this rapidly growing economy (World Bank 2007) and income inequality – the relative income distribution gap between the rich and the poor – has risen from 28 per cent in 1981 to its current level of 41 per cent, representing the largest income inequality gap in Asia (McGregorin 2007).

Globally, Brazil is juxtaposed between the industrialised world and the developing world. On the one hand, it is the world's second largest food exporter and Companhia Vale do Rio Doce (CVRD – formerly a state-owned enterprise) is the world's second largest mining multinational (CVRD invested US$2 billion in the construction of a coal mine in Mozambique in 2006). On the other hand, Brazil continues to confront a number of significant development challenges. For example, in 2006, the UNDP estimated that 45 per cent of the country's wealth is controlled by 10 per cent of the population, and over 20 per cent of Brazilians live on less than US$2 per day.

In spite of this, Brazil has built substantial expertise of its own, both in terms of improving living standards and livelihoods by reducing poverty, and fostering more inclusive economic growth to promote social development (Schläger 2007). Brazil's expertise thus provides a good base from which to help Africa meet its own social development challenges.

The Brazilian government regards its development policy in Africa as a critical part of its foreign policy outreach. In fact, the Brazilian Agency for Development Cooperation (Agencia Brasileira de Cooperação (ABC)), originally established in 1987 to coordinate development assistance from international donors into Brazil, has transformed itself into an international donor agency. In stark contrast to the OECD and other emerging market donors, Brazil's assistance to Africa appears to be free from national commercial interests and conditionalities. This places little, if any, priority on short-term economic or political gain. It promotes partnerships where economic and social development play an integral role in building international security and peace, as well as cooperation and collaboration between developing countries to exchange know-how and technical expertise and build capacity through strengthening institutions (de Sousa 2007). How might Brazil's approach to its Africa policy influence US interests in Africa and AFRICOM?

Brazil's development cooperation is focused on the long-term development of human capital across the continent. In 2005, of the 54 bilateral technical cooperation projects undertaken by ABC, 35 were across the Portuguese-speaking countries of Africa. In Angola, Guinea-Bissau and Mozambique, vocational training programmes focused on peace building were provided to reintegrate former combatants into their local communities and wider society. Brazil is also supporting efforts in Mozambique, São Tomé and Príncipe and Angola to develop local agricultural research capacity. São Tomé and Príncipe, Namibia and Guinea-Bissau have partnered with Brazil to develop plant cultivation technology. In addition, across Lusophone Africa, as well as Botswana, Burundi and Burkina Faso, HIV/AIDS programmes to improve universal access to treatment, support and care are being replicated following their success in Brazil. In 2010, Brazil is set to launch an anti-retroviral manufacturing plant in Mozambique. Furthermore, there are education, literacy, renewable energy and environment programmes (with Brazil having pioneered ethanol production), all of which enjoy an enviable international reputation.

In the area of social protection, Brazil has worked with OECD donors to advance welfare programmes in Africa. For example, supported by the United Kingdom's Department for International Development and the Inter-American Development Bank (IADB), the 'Livelihood Empowerment against Poverty' (LEAP) (International Poverty Centre 2008) programme in Ghana replicates the Brazilian government's *Bolsa Famillia* programme, providing conditional cash transfers to poor families. This provides a direct incentive for poor parents to invest in their children's education and health, as cash transfers are only received if parents meet criteria related to enrolling children at primary school. The programme also ensures children receive regular vaccinations and encourages expectant mothers to avail themselves of full pre-natal care. Other African nations have expressed interest in the scheme, including Zambia, South Africa, Nigeria, Mozambique and Guinea-Bissau. This is particularly relevant as the global economic downturn threatens much of the recent progress achieved in reducing poverty across Africa.

While Brazilian development cooperation could be criticised for its strong focus on the Lusophone countries and a lack of public information regarding technical assistance, funding volumes and assistance-awarding criteria, the nature of partnerships with Brazil appear to appeal to African states because of the long-term collaborative nature and lack of conditionality involved. So, while Brazil's approach is by no means in direct competition with US programmes in terms of scale and scope, the popular nature of the partnerships offered implies that US policymakers might be wise to consider how best to balance short-term self-interest with more long-term strategic priorities in order to improve engagement across the continent.

Power and diplomacy: Indo-Africa relations

What impact might India's growing political importance on the world stage, as well as her expanding engagement across Africa, have for the future of AFRICOM? An important part of the answer to this question lies in the declaration and framework for cooperation established at the inaugural Africa–India New Delhi Summit that took place in April 2008. In the area of political cooperation, the framework agreed to develop a joint platform for the discussion of global political and economic issues in order to enable greater leverage on the global stage for both Africa and India (African Union 2008a). In addition, the Delhi Declaration recognised that Africa–India partnerships would be based on a number of fundamental principles, including the right to self-determination and sovereignty (African Union 2008b). Thus, in 2006/7, India pledged US$200 million to support the NEPAD process in Africa (Schläger 2007).

Since Indian independence was declared in 1947, and in the wake of her unwavering support for the nationalist independence struggles across Africa in the aftermath of the Second World War, India has sought to position herself as a global political driver on the international stage. India not only regards herself as a voice for the developing world in global fora and a facilitator for greater South–South solidarity and self-determination, but, more importantly, India is keen to advance her own global political ambitions (Mawdsley 2007). Thus, during Cold War hostilities, India played a pivotal role in the Non-Aligned Movement (NAM)[3] and the G77.[4] In 1998 India undertook her first nuclear weapons test, and according to the industrialised economies of the G7, has demonstrated her responsibility as a nuclear power by not promoting nuclear proliferation (Bava 2007). India, along with the other members of the Group of Four (Germany, Japan and Brazil), continues to campaign tirelessly for reform of the UN Security Council (UNSC) and for the establishment of additional permanent seats. She has successfully secured support from African countries for her own UNSC ambitions. India's political significance is further demonstrated by her participation as a member of the 'outreach group' at G8 summits and ministerial. Furthermore, in 2003 India, together with Brazil and South Africa (collectively known as IBSA), established the IBSA Dialogue Forum, an initiative committed to poverty reduction, democratic values and greater multilateralism in global governance institutions (Schläger 2007). India is a principal stakeholder in the Bretton Woods Institutions (along with Brazil, China and South Africa), and assumes a seat as a permanent executive board member. In addition, India (along with Brazil) has also long been a vocal advocate for the developing world in the World Trade Organization (WTO). She is also a member of the principle WTO institutional mechanism for resolving disputes, the Quad, alongside Brazil, the United States and the European Union.

For Africa, India's growing geo-political influence has the potential to develop a greater voice for multilateralism, which promotes the coordination and cooperation essential for latecomers to develop. On one hand, this has the potential to provide the opportunities needed to reshape the current global, rule-based order and create policy space for African countries to define and prioritise their own development trajectories (Nayyar 2008). Nonetheless, India's foreign policy stance and the partnerships she seeks in African contexts are, by her own admission, regarded as instruments to advance her national political and economic interests (Bava 2007). Therefore, to a large extent, India's agenda can often compete directly with Africa's interests. For example, freer trade between the European Union and the United States has favoured India at the expense of preferences once enjoyed by African agriculturalists and manufacturers (Mawdsley 2007). As it stands, India could be one of the biggest beneficiaries of an ambitious settlement of the Doha multilateral trade round.

With respect to self-determination, in 2003 India further underlined her keenness to independently pursue her own national interests by suspending bilateral development programmes with 22 donors (excluding the United States, United Kingdom, Japan, Germany and the European Union). As such, where possible, India accesses multilateral aid to minimise administration and transaction costs. For example, until very recently India remained the World Bank's largest single borrower. In 2006, she received loans totalling US$2.9 billion, more than double the amount lent in 2004 (World Bank 2008). Yet, almost in contradiction to the principle of recipient country autonomy, India ties the distribution of its ODA to the consumption of Indian goods and services (Jobelius 2007). In addition, India never acts solely as a donor in a partner country. Indian aid must be accompanied by investment, trade, political alliances or a combination of these elements. For example, with respect to financial aid in 2006/7, a credit line of US$500 million was made available to develop India's relations with resource-rich West African countries. Sudan receives one of the largest volumes of Indian aid outside South Asia, and also receives significant amounts of Indian foreign direct investment (FDI). In 2003 the Indian state-owned oil company ONGC Videsh invested US$1 billion in the Sudanese oil sector (Embassy of India, Khartoum 2003). In Senegal, the Indian car manufacturer Tata benefited from internal reform which restructured the national public transport system. India has become one of the top destinations for Senegalese exports, as well as one of the country's largest donors (Jobelius 2007).

While India is more overt about the geo-political agenda it pursues through development assistance, this presents challenges as well as opportunities for Africa. So what does all this mean for AFRICOM? US policymakers might consider giving greater priority to Africa's desire to exercise greater self-determination and autonomy, but how can AFRICOM help to achieve this (Kidane 2008)? Moreover, while India enjoys growing international influence and an ability to galvanise those in the developing world (particularly in Africa) around the principles of solidarity and common interest, its own national strategic interests always take priority. This often conflicts with the international image India attempts to project and can be to the detriment of partnerships with African states. The way that the United States chooses to respond to this shortcoming may prove an effective entry point for more meaningful and relevant engagement in Africa with Africans, which also helps to highlight some of the limitations of AFRICOM as it stands today.

Riding the dragon: China and growth in Africa?[5]

Can economic expansion in China provide a new catalyst for growth in Africa and what significance will this have for United States–Africa relations and AFRICOM?

In November 2006 Beijing hosted the third Forum on China–Africa Cooperation (FOCAC). The Beijing Action Plan it produced outlined a number of important areas of partnership. In the area of economic cooperation there was an agreement to retain infrastructure development as a key area of cooperation. The Chinese government also committed to continuing to encourage its private sector to participate in Africa's infrastructure development. African leaders pledged to support and facilitate such investment through reform programmes that would liberalise relevant sectors. In addition, Beijing would promote investment expansion in Africa by supporting Chinese banks through the establishment of a China–Africa Development Fund, whose total resources would gradually reach

US$5 billion and would contribute to the development of local technology and employment opportunities. Furthermore, both sides would continue to work to create favourable conditions for more equitable growth in China–Africa trade. To support this, China pledged to further open up its markets to African LDCs – those with which it already enjoys good diplomatic relations – thus increasing the number of export items that qualify for zero-tariff treatment from 190 to over 440. In the areas of energy and resource cooperation, China and Africa agreed to continue to exploit their energy and resource complementarities for mutual benefit and common development. China also agreed to help Africa to convert its rich endowment in energy and mineral resources into a catalyst for greater sustainable economic development, while promoting environmental sustainability.

Until 1993 China's oil and abundant coal reserves meant that it could self-supply a significant proportion of its energy needs, but by 2003 China became the second largest global consumer of oil, and by 2004 the third largest importer of oil. While oil imports currently meet approximately 50 per cent of its demands, imports are predicted to meet a staggering 80 per cent of China's oil needs by 2020 (Downs 2006). What is significant about these figures is the extent to which the security of energy supplies is driving China's foreign policy across Africa and how this interplays with US dependency on fossil fuels.

Apart from oil, China is also the world's leading importer of plastic materials, metal ores, oil seeds, textile fibres, pulp and paper. For Africa, the major non-energy commodities are metal ores. China is the number-one importer of iron ore, manganese, lead and chromium, with shares of world imports ranging from 32 per cent to 54 per cent. In addition, China accounts for 19 per cent of world copper ore imports, coming second only to Japan (Trinh *et al.* 2006).

A significant share of China's manganese imports come from Africa, where Gabon, South Africa and Ghana are among China's top-five manganese suppliers, together accounting for 37 per cent of China's total manganese imports. Several African countries possess large reserves of cobalt and the continent is China's main supplier, with 85 per cent of imports coming from only three countries: the Republic of Congo, the Democratic Republic of Congo (DRC) and South Africa (Foreign Policy Centre *et al.* 2008).

China boosts demand for Africa's primary commodities because of its significant population, despite the fact that its levels of per capita consumption of primary commodities are still relatively low. Increased demand raises commodity prices and improves terms of trade for primary commodity exporters in Africa. Moreover, China has become the workshop of the world, being the world's primary exporter of manufactured goods (Nayyar 2008). That China and Africa's trade in commodities has increased is beyond doubt. Bilateral trade exploded from US$2 billion in 1999 to US$39.7 billion by 2005 (Hofmann 2006), and by 2006 trade volumes exceeded US$55 billion – a 40 per cent increase compared to the previous year (*People's Daily* 2007).

China has emerged as Africa's largest trading partner after the United States. The state-run China National Offshore Oil Corporation (CNOOC) is the biggest foreign investor in Sudan. It claimed to have provided 4,000 local jobs and built hospitals and schools (Sheridan 2007).

Nevertheless, Chinese engagement in Africa continues to draw bitter criticism. It is perceived as consistently using its diplomatic influence at the UNSC to protect the Sudanese regime which, some would argue, helps to perpetuate the crisis in Darfur. In the oil-producing region of the Upper Nile area of Sudan, Chinese investment stands accused of displacing Dinka and Nuer villages and destroying their communities (Askouri 2007). In the Zambezia province of Mozambique, Chinese timber merchants in partnership with local business and the national government's forest services are blamed for over-exploiting precious slow-growing tropical hardwoods, the trade in which could see this resource depleted over the next 5–10 years (Lemos and Ribeiro 2007). The proposed US$2.3 billion Mpanda Nkuwa dam in the Zambezi, backed by China's overseas lending arm Ex-Im Bank, is another often-cited example of Chinese investment overlooking human rights and social issues, as well as environmental concerns raised by local and international civil society groups.

The growth of Sino-African trade has risen even more rapidly than Chinese trade with the rest of the world. In 2006 China's exports to Africa were worth US$26.7 billion, an increase of 43 per cent from the previous year, and African imports to China were worth US$28.8 billion, an increase of 37 per cent. Over the ten-year period leading up to 2004, China provided over US$5 billion in loans to Africa. From 2006 China pledged to double Africa's development aid in loans and investment credits to US$5 billion (Hofmann 2006). Currently China is one of the continent's main lenders, rivalling the World Bank (Third World Network 2006). The lion's share of this is dedicated to aid programmes for infrastructure, a NEPAD priority sector which OECD donors, including the United States, for a long time showed very little interest in supporting.

To assume that China's investment is directed solely toward the extractive industries such as oil and mining would be incorrect. Investments have also extended to apparel, food processing, retail ventures, fisheries, seafood farming, commercial real estate, transport, construction, tourism, power plants, banking (and financial services) and telecommunications, amongst other sectors (Hofmann 2006). The telecommunications company Zhongxing Communications, which began investing in Africa in 1995, has ploughed in more than GB£3 billion, and in 2008 employed 1,100 people across the continent. In agriculture, the Chinese have secured deals from Zimbabwe to Zambia and Kenya. The China Agricultural Cultivation Group claims to have transformed grain production in Zambia and saved the country a fortune in transport costs by reducing the need to import grain from South Africa. In 2007 the Industrial and Commercial Bank of China (ICBC) agreed to pay GB£2.7 billion for a 20 per cent stake in Africa's largest bank, Standard Bank, based in Johannesburg. This provides ICBC with an interest in a continent-wide banking network with more than 200 branches in 18 African states (Sheridan 2007). In addition, the China Development Bank entered into a partnership with United Bank for Africa (UBA), one of Nigeria's biggest banks (Anderlini and Green 2007). The deal is expected to expand the

Chinese bank's ability to finance infrastructural projects in Africa. Moreover, Chinese levels of investment in these areas have been far from insignificant. In 2007 China struck a US$5 billion deal with the DRC government to acquire mineral resources in exchange for infrastructure finance for development. This is currently either non-existent or in a state of severe disrepair (Wallis 2008).

China: threat or opportunity?

An overview of China's links with sub-Saharan Africa distinguishes different channels of impact transmission. As this discussion has already explored, there are a number of prominent channels, including trade, investment flows (FDI and portfolio investments) and aid. Within each of these channels is a combination of both complementary and competitive impacts. For example, with regard to trade, China may provide both cheap inputs and consumer goods, and act as a market for sub-Saharan Africa exports. On the other hand, imports from China can readily displace local African producers. The key element demonstrated by these interactions is that impacts both within countries (between social groups and regions) and between countries vary (Kaplinsky 2008).

The complementary–competitive dynamic of China's impact on Africa is readily understood and widely recognised. Less well explored, however, is the distinction between direct and indirect impacts. This is, in part, because indirect impacts are difficult to measure. Indirect impacts occur in third-country markets and institutions. For example, China's trade with the United States may open up or crowd out opportunities for sub-Saharan Africa economies to export into that market. Again, the effects of these impacts vary (ibid.).

To what extent is China's bilateral engagement with economies in Africa inducing growth through structural transformation, and does this present risks or opportunities for US strategic interests? China is a huge source of labour-intensive manufactured goods, while other emerging markets such as Brazil are more important sources of manufactured goods made from natural resources. China has a significant pool of surplus low-wage rural and urban labour. Therefore, it is reasonable to assume that China competes with African economies for export opportunities to the industrialised world, as well as the developing world. This could reinforce the dependence of African countries on exports of primary commodities and severely limit opportunities to develop manufacturing industries (through adding value to exports). In short, African economies need to move from a complementary to a more competitive pattern of trade with China in order to generate trade specialisations between their economic sectors and industries (ibid.). How US policymakers are able to work with African governments and Africans across the continent to respond to the challenge might provide some clues as to how the US government might engage with Africa to meet its own strategic interests more successfully.

A second concern regarding Africa's complementary trading pattern with China is that, arguably, China could displace and redirect FDI opportunities. From 2001 to 2005 China, India, Brazil and South Africa absorbed 37 per cent of inward FDI to the developing world (11 per cent of global FDI inward flows). In 2005 China accounted for 50 per cent of inward investment stock (but only 27 per cent of outward investment stocks). While investment stocks and flows in and out of China are modest relative to the wider trend globally, China is more of a competitor for investment flows into Africa than an investment source for Africa (Nayyar 2008). Again, US policymakers might explore ways they could work with Africa to overcome this challenge effectively, helping to reinforce US leverage and interests across the continent.

This analysis demonstrates the significance of Sino-African engagement for US Africa policy and suggests that, despite the potential risks associated with Chinese partnerships, economic development is a huge priority for Africa and the sacrifices the continent is willing to make to secure this are evident. In addition, it demonstrates that US Africa policy needs to broaden its understanding of security in the African context and engage with the issues that matter to Africa and Africans. For example, China's focus on the infrastructure deficit has resonance across the continent. Finally, the scale and scope of China's engagement across Africa suggests that US strategic interests may be best served by complementing China's interests rather than competing with her. There are a number of unmet African development challenges, such as environmental sustainability and civil society participation, which China as yet appears unable to adequately respond to. Therefore, US strategic interest may be best served by focusing on some of these deficits as entry points to address their own security and strategic demands.

The global food crisis: Africa – the breadbasket for Gulf States?

The NEPAD Action Plan prioritises agriculture-led development as an engine for economic growth. The plan identifies a number of targets, which include increasing food supplies and reducing poverty by contracting the level of food imports through accelerated domestic production, increased rural agricultural productivity and sustainability through increased spending on agricultural research and extension services across Africa over a ten-year period (2001/2–2011/12) (New Partnership for African Development 2001). Yet, the reality of the current state of African agriculture could not be further from NEPAD's aspirations.

In many African economies, agriculture constitutes a significant share of GDP. Between 2003 and 2005 agriculture represented a sizable percentage of GDP in Niger (39.9 per cent), Rwanda (41.6 per cent), Sierra Leone (46.2 per cent), Sudan (36.1 per cent) and Tanzania (45.8 per cent). Almost 80 per cent of Africans reside in rural areas and 60 per cent of the rural working population are smallholder farmers. These producers depend on food production (through farming or the rearing of livestock) to sustain their lives and livelihoods (Le Roux 2007). Ironically, despite the fact that agriculture is the mainstay of many African economies, food insecurity on the continent is commonplace. In 2007 236 million people, or one in three Africans, were chronically hungry. Those living in the DRC were the most undernourished as the widespread and intractable conflict there caused the number of hungry people to rise from 11 million to 43 million between 2003 and 2005. The proportion of undernourished people rose from 29 per cent to 76.5 per cent of the total population in the same period. Overall, however, sub-Saharan Africa (particularly Congo, Nigeria, Mozambique and Malawi) has made some progress in reducing levels of chronic hunger, falling from 34 per cent between 1995 and 1997 to 30 per cent between 2003 and 2005 (FAO 2008). Yet the current global economic crisis is set to threaten this progress.

The continent's food security vulnerability is further demonstrated by the fact that many countries import a significant amount of staple foods such as rice. The rate of demand for rice is currently double that of the growth of the African population itself, and it has outstripped the growth in consumption of all other major staple foods. The surge in demand for rice has been accompanied by stagnating levels of production. The self-sufficiency ratio (rice production relative to consumption) fell from 112 per cent in 1961 to 61 per cent in 2006 (Africa Rice Centre 2007).

In early 2007 the World Food Programme (WFP) appealed to the international donor community to help plug an emergency funding shortfall in its budget created by what, at the time, had been escalating food and fuel prices. US$960 million was pledged by 32 countries, of which over 50 per cent (US$500 million) came from Saudi Arabia (Sands 2008). This represented a staggering climb for Saudi Arabia from being placed as twenty-seventh in the league of donor contributions in 2007 (providing just over US$6.5 million), to being the second largest contributor in 2008 (behind the United States which, until 2008, contributed just under US$617 million) (World Food Programme 2008). On the one hand, as the world's largest oil producer, Saudi Arabia had been blamed for providing an inadequate response to oil supply constraints that had led to rising fuel costs, which only served to increase agricultural input prices and which, when compounded by disappointing harvests in some areas, worsened the food crisis by squeezing food stocks. Even with the recent fall in commodity prices, for many countries in Africa, the relative costs of fuel and food remain high due to weak local currencies relative to the US dollar. On the other hand, and more strategically, many Gulf States (including Saudi Arabia) are heavily dependent on food imports. Seeking advice from the World Bank (England and Blas 2008), Saudi Arabia and other Middle Eastern governments and their private sector companies are looking to Africa to provide a solution to their food security challenges. For example, Qatar is keen to lease farmland in Kenya, and Saudi Arabia is keen to secure farmland in Ethiopia, Sudan and Senegal. Abu Dhabi – the largest of the seven emirate states of the United Arab Emirates (UAE) – is preparing to launch a large-scale agricultural project in Northern Sudan to develop more than 70,000 acres of land as part of its efforts to secure food supplies. The project is being led by the Abu Dhabi Fund for Development. Sudan is keen to attract both funding and technology for its agriculture sector, and as such is willing to provide land free of charge to investors for such projects.

African agricultural growth and job creation

Growing concerns regarding the weak state of many African agricultural sectors led African leaders to call for foreign investment in African agriculture to replace food aid during the 2008 UN General Assembly annual summit (UN News Centre 2008). What impact might agricultural partnerships between African countries and economies in the Middle East have for the future of AFRICOM and broader US strategic interests across the continent? The potential prospect of Obama's Add Value to Agriculture (AVTA) initiative – a presidential campaign pledge to facilitate research and innovation to promote an agricultural revolution in Africa (Obama/Biden 2008 Presidential Campaign) – would seem to be mere rhetoric, if the US Farm Bill continues to allow US taxpayer money to heavily subsidise US farmers at the expense of African smallholder farmers. Agricultural growth in Africa has the potential to generate employment in local industry and services in rural areas, working to significantly reduce poverty levels.

The International Labour Organisation (ILO) suggests that Africa needs 15 million jobs a year to absorb the growth in its labour force (Africa Commission 2008). Joblessness poses one of the greatest security risks on the continent today due to the dangerously high and rising levels of unemployment and underemployment, particularly amongst the youth. Unlocking African agricultural development capacity has the potential to absorb Africa's excess low-skilled labour. In addition, agricultural growth though technological advancement induced by increased investment, as well as a reduction in agricultural input costs, could help to raise domestic savings and increases in household incomes. The latter also translate into demand for non-farm and non-tradable goods, which stimulates job creation. If African governments are supported to put the right policies in place, this could help to stimulate the development of local manufacturing industries and local services (as infrastructural investment in roads, transportation and logistics, as well as irrigation and grain storage facilities are developed), and help to work towards achieving broad-based inclusive economic growth. Empirical research has shown that in low-income economies, every US$1 of agricultural spending generates US$2.75 demand for non-agricultural inputs and services. In the case of Burkina Faso, additional income was US$1.88, in Zambia it was US$1.48 and in Niger it was US$0.96 (UNCTAD 2007).

The benefits which stem from agricultural growth can in turn be magnified by integration with global markets through export opportunities. If Africa plays the role of breadbasket to economies in the Middle East and beyond, there is the potential to achieve this kind of growth, but such steps do not come without risks.

The risks of FDI in African agriculture

The Director-General of the FAO, Jacques Diouf, is cautious about the Gulf States' farmland investment in Africa. He has described the relationship as perpetuating dependency and reintroducing neo-colonialist relationships with Africa. Early Gulf State projects in Sudan demonstrated only limited benefits to local populations as projects extracted the benefits from arable land and water supplies and failed to source specialist labour and farming inputs locally, as well as providing very few opportunities for smallholder farmers to access capital, agricultural know-how or improve their market access. Yet, agricultural development across Africa could provide a lifeline to improve food self-sufficiency, create employment and provide a launch pad for industrial development. Is AFRICOM able to work with Africa to meet this challenge?

The emerging role that Africa has begun to play in responding to increasing concerns about food security in the Middle East demonstrates how Africa can exploit its comparative advantage and how agricultural development could help to create a much-needed platform for industrial development. The risks associated with this strategy might enable US policymakers to consider options that could help to secure American national interests while also enabling African economies to transform their economic base through agricultural development.

Conclusion

In conclusion, this chapter raises a number of issues for US policymakers to consider how, in a changing world, with the rise of new centres of power, might US Africa policy better connect with African people and African governments? In addition, how might this approach help to inform and improve America's understanding of Africa's own agenda of priorities, in order to help secure US strategic interests?

This analysis has perhaps raised many more questions than it has addressed. This is principally because the contours of the interplay between AFRICOM, Africa and non-OECD countries are in a continuous process of evolution, and as such, mapping out the issues and questions in this way is a useful exercise in illuminating current understanding.

So, how might US Africa policy better connect with African people and African governments?

First, Africa's partnership with Brazil involves the sharing and exchanging of experiences focused on social development transformation. This provides lessons about the forms of engagement that can deliver long-term results. Second, Africa's diplomacy and power partnerships with India underpin the importance of African autonomy and self-determination in a world where there is a growing number of centres of new power with divergent interests. The implication for US policymakers is to identify opportunities for a more effective US Africa policy that allows Africa to demonstrate greater political assertiveness on the international stage without compromising either Africa's or its own strategic interests.

Third, China's significant presence in Africa represents an unprecedented challenge for both American and African strategic interests, albeit in very different ways. Africa may wish to explore how to develop a more competitive relationship with China in order to avoid commodity dependence, while the United States may wish to examine how it can begin to coherently complement China and minimise the risk of tensions with an emerging global power and perhaps becoming increasingly marginalised across the African continent. Finally, responding to food insecurity in the Middle East by achieving food security in Africa and agriculture-led industrialisation implies that US policymakers might consider ways in which a transformation in the economic base of African economies might help the United States better pursue its own strategic interests on the continent.

The second challenge posed at the outset of this article was, how might a more informed and coherent US approach help better identify Africa's own priority agenda, as well as secure US strategic interests on the continent? With the arrival of President Obama in the White House, US policymakers may wish to seize the opportunity to consider innovative ways of listening and negotiating with Africa to pursue their strategic interests, recognising that their dominance, leverage and strength has becoming increasingly relatively (but not absolutely) challenged by new centres of power with different models and approaches to African development and security.

Notes

1 Those countries not members of the group of 30 member states committed to democratic government and the market economy. The OECD provides a forum where governments can compare and exchange policy experiences, identify good practices and promote decisions and recommendations. *OECD Annual Report 2008* www.oecd.org/dataoecd/39/19/40556222.pdf.

2 HDI measures development by combining indicators of life expectancy, educational attainment and income into a composite Human Development Index. United Nations Development Programme, http://hdr.undp.org/en/statistics/indices/hdi.

3 The NAM is made up of 118 developing countries and aims to represent the political, economic and cultural interests of the developing world. *BBC News* 'Profile: Non-Aligned Movement', http://news.bbc.co.uk/1/hi/2798187.stm.

4 The G77 is the largest intergovernmental organisation of developing states in the UN. It provides a platform for the countries of the South to articulate and promote their collective economic interests and enhance their joint negotiating capacity on all major international economic issues within the UN system and promote South–South cooperation for development. www.g77.org/doc.

5 See Wambu 2007.

Conclusion

AFRICOM and the future of United States–Africa relations

David J. Francis

What will be the future of United States–Africa relations? Continuity or change? Given the increasing strategic significance of Africa to US national interests and the global security environment, America is forced to engage or 'do business' with the continent, sometimes, not on its own terms, even as the world's only superpower. As this edited volume has illustrated, most of the US vital strategic foreign and security policy priorities are present or at play in Africa. Notwithstanding, US strategy and future engagement in Africa will continue to be based on reactive, selective strategic interests and moral impulses around issues of poverty, humanitarian disasters, wars, governance and human rights, with AFRICOM as the main structural framework for achieving these priorities. The debate is how AFRICOM will change the historic pattern of United States–Africa relations, or whether it will be business as usual, marked by a half-hearted change of policy approach to the continent, largely driven by US strategic interests, whereby African security predicaments and challenges are neglected or subjected to secondary consideration by current and future US governments. For a start, and as pointed out by Daniel Volman in Chapter 3, there does not seem to be a significant policy departure on AFRICOM by the new US President, Barack Obama.[1] Though President Obama has used every available opportunity to stress the significance of Africa to US national security and global peace and security, and in particular, the commitment of his administration to non-military security concerns in Africa by committing to a US$3.5 billion food security initiative for the continent, he is also on record confirming the imperative for military interventions in Africa in the pursuit of the Global War on Terror (GWOT).[2] In addition, much has been made of the fact that AFRICOM is 'primarily an internal bureaucratic shift', a cost-effective institutional re-structuring and, in particular, a much needed framework to enhance consistency of policy focus on Africa and to centralise a better coordination and harmonisation of operational activities by all the previous three separate government departments and military commands with responsibility for the continent. In other words, a straightforward strategy to ensure an 'efficient and sensible way of organising US military relations with Africa' in the implementation of its non-military foreign policy engagement and operational activities in Africa.[3] Perhaps, the litmus test of not only the eventual success of AFRICOM to win the hearts and minds of people and critical stakeholders in Africa, but also the credibility and perception of President Obama on the continent, is the use to which his administration will put AFRI-COM in the coming years. While the use of US Marines to free the captain of a US ship held by Somali pirates in April 2009 was roundly applauded in Africa, use of the military dimensions of AFRICOM to prop up friendly dictators or effect regime change, even against internationally recognised repressive regimes such as Mugabe's Zimbabwe, will be met with continent-wide opposition by African states, regional organisations and civil society organisations and people, for the simple fact that any such use of AFRICOM will create a palpable fear and powerful precedent that could potentially end up unifying opposition to the United States in Africa.

There are indications that the United States and, in particular, the Obama administration, is concerned about the global anti-Americanism and the perception of America as a capricious and bullying hegemonic power in the conduct of its relations with rest of the world and, in particular, developing regions such as Africa and the Middle East. In his seminal speech to the Muslim world in Cairo on 4 June 2009, President Obama called for 'a new beginning with mutual interest and mutual trust between America and the Muslim world' and not only confirmed that the United States will never be at war with Islam, but also encouraged long-term partnerships to help fight violent extremism; resolve the Israeli–Palestinian dispute; reduce nuclear weapons; and promote democracy, religious freedom, rights of women and economic development. Based on this, it is reasonable to assume that the Obama administration, given the burden of history on Obama's shoulders because of his African descent, will be mindful of the potential negative impact of AFRICOM in the pursuit of US foreign and security policies. But this perception is challenged by the fact that President Obama's view of Africa as a tragic continent in perpetual need of international charity is largely informed by the dominant Western-centric explanations and interpretations of why Africa is the poorest continent on earth. Critiques point to the fact that President Obama, during his first visit to sub-Saharan Africa, trivialised the devastating impact of colonialism and the disadvantageous manner in which the continent had been incorporated into the international division of labour and power, stating that 'the West is not responsible for the destruction of the Zimbabwean economy over the last decade'.[4]

Nevertheless, the real test will be how the Obama administration responds to the inevitable conflict of interests that will emerge between the pursuit of US strategic interests and the delivery of non-security and humanitarian programmes in Africa that consistently focus on conflict prevention and peace building, rather than the traditional military/security considerations that have framed and informed United States–Africa relations.

A major concern expressed by some African governments, civil society advocacy groups and security organisations is that if there will be no large US military garrison or base in Africa, and given the reluctance of the United States towards US military deployments in African conflict zones due to the 'Somalia Syndrome' and the restrictions imposed by the Presidential Decision Directive

25, who will do the military job of AFRICOM? The plausible explanation is that AFRICOM will train African militaries and security agencies to undertake its military and traditional security-related activities in Africa. This explanation is strengthened by the fact that a core mandate of the unified command is to increase and strengthen African capabilities through training and partnership operations with African regional organisations and states as a strategy to complement the ongoing peace and security efforts on the continent. However, the United States is strategically overstretched, given its current global military commitments in pursuit of the GWOT and war fighting in Iraq and Afghanistan. There is, therefore, the potential to privatise AFRICOM's military activities and deployments to private military companies (PMCs) and private security companies by outsourcing its operational activities to private security contractors, a phenomenon increasingly used in the US wars in Iraq and Afghanistan. The evidence, according to McFate, is that EUCOM has been outsourcing its African military and security operations to PMCs.[5] The concern in Africa is that the prospect of outsourcing future AFRICOM military and security activities to PMCs and security companies and contractors will only further compound the increasing privatisation of security and military activities in Africa. These companies often operate without regulation and independent defence and security oversight of their operations, lacking in accountability for gross violations of human rights. Most of the time they undermine the sovereignty of African states, especially those PMCs and private security companies involved in civil wars and armed conflicts in the continent's troubled regions.

What is more, and as the chapters in this book have illustrated, military security alone will not bring durable peace, long-term stability and sustainable development to Africa, nor will it secure and guarantee US strategic national interests on the continent. That is why some critiques dispute the link between poverty and terrorism in Africa and, as Alex de Waal and Abdel Salam argue,

> the link between poverty and international terrorism is spurious. North-East Africa is where terrorism and militant jihadism should have the best chance of combining. To date, they do not. There is plenty of good reason both humanitarian and self-interested, for the Western powers including America to be concerned with Africa's plight. But fear of terrorism born of poverty should not figure high on the list.[6]

While this may be the case in the specific context of northeast African regions, the recent violence orchestrated by the Boko Haram militant Islamic sect in northern Nigeria demonstrates the link between poverty and terrorist activities. In July 2009 Boko Haram radical Islamic sect – opposed to all forms of Western education and 'civilisation' – sparked a violent and bloody military confrontation with the security forces that led to more than 100 civilian casualties. The militants, branded as terrorists by the Nigerian government, are recruited from amongst the poor and marginalised youth, young men and women as well as unemployed graduates. Even the Nigerian Information Minister, Dora Akunyili, alluded to conditions of extreme poverty and widespread youth unemployment as the driving force for the radicalisation and recruitment of the Boko Haram sect. Similarly, the origins and recruitment base of the 1980s Marwa Maitasine militant Islamic sect also lay in widespread and extreme poverty and unemployment. This West Africa example illustrates that, in some situations and contexts, there is link between poverty and terrorist activities, though not conceived in terms of automatic or deterministic relationships. If this is the case, the challenge for AFRICOM is how to implement both the traditional military security interventions in the pursuit of the GWOT and at the same time facilitate the delivery of non-military security programmes on poverty, empowerment and participation, development and humanitarian relief, and democracy and human rights – all in the strategic effort to assist African partners to address the root causes of terrorism.

Notwithstanding, there has been increasing opposition to AFRICOM from within the US political and defence establishments. The House of Representatives Appropriation Committee stressed that traditional US military operations are not an appropriate response to most of the security and development challenges facing Africa, and therefore used this as a justification to demand a substantial cut in AFRICOM's requested budget for FY 2008/9, with Congress allocating only US$266 million of the US$390 million requested.[7] Even Defense Secretary Robert Gates has been critical of the ambitious mandate of AFRICOM (i.e. military, security, development and humanitarian relief) as well as the nature of the partnership with Africa, stating:

> I think in some respects we probably didn't do as good a job as we should have when we rolled out AFRICOM. I don't think we should push African governments to a place they don't really want to go in terms of relationships.[8]

This muted criticism of AFRICOM from within the US military and political establishments demonstrates that the controversies and debates around the purpose, motivations and long-term commitment of AFRICOM to Africa-centred security challenges and predicaments will, no doubt, continue. The contributors to this edited volume have highlighted the core debates and arguments around the establishment of AFRICOM, the problems and potential opportunities for a new beginning in United States–Africa relations and long-term strategic partnerships focusing on peace, security and development on the continent, which would be mutually beneficial to America's national interest and its global foreign and security policy agendas.

Notes

1 See also, Volman and Minter 2008.
2 President Barack Obama, Speech delivered during his first visit to sub-Saharan Africa to the Ghanaian Parliament on 11 July 2009, at: www.bbc.co.uk/Africannews. Presid-

ent Obama also used this key policy speech to confirm the strategic significance of the continent, stating that 'I see Africa as a fundamental part of our interconnected world – as partners with America on behalf of the future that we want for all our children.'

3 Mills *et al.* 2007, p. 1.
4 Quoted in *New African Magazine* 2009, p. 14.
5 McFate 2008b.
6 de Waal 2004, p. 233. See also, Pipes 2001/2.
7 Summary of 2009 Defence Appropriations. Washington DC: House of Representatives Committee on Appropriations, 22 September 2008. For more details, see Appendix of Chapter 3.
8 Quoted in De Young 2008, p. 18.

Bibliography

Abraham, K. (2006) *The Bin Laden Connection and the Terror Factor in Africa*, Addis Ababa: EIIPD.

Abrahamsen, R. (2005) 'Blair's Africa: The Politics of Securitisation and Fear', *Alternatives* 30: 55–80.

Addis Ababa (2003) Report of the Meeting of Experts to Consider Modalities for the Implementation of the AU Plan of Action on the Prevention and Combating of Terrorism in Africa.

Addis Ababa (2005). Declaration of the Heads of State and Government of the African Union on the Fourth Ordinary Session of African Union.

Ade Ajayi, J.F. (2000) 'The Continuity of African Institutions Under Colonial Rule' in *Tradition and Change in Africa: The Essays of JF Ade Ajayi*, edited by Toyin Falola, Trenton, NJ, Africa World Press.

Africa Commission (2008) '15 Million Jobs a Year Please!', Ministry of Foreign Affairs of Denmark. At: www.africacommission.um.dk/en/menu/Background/Youth+and+Employment/15+million+jobs+a+year+please.

Africa Rice Centre (2007) 'Overview of Recent Developments in the sub-Saharan African Rice Sector', Africa Rice Trends brief. At: www.warda.org/publications/Rice%20Trend%2023-10-07.pdf.

Africa–South America Summit (2006) 'Abuja Action Plan'. At: www.mce.gov.ma/ASAMinCom/EN/downloads/AbujaPlanofAction.pdf.

African Union (2001) 'The New Partnership for Africa's Development (NEPAD)', Main Document.

African Union (2002) 'Reports of the first High-Level Intergovernmental Meeting on the Prevention and Combating of Terrorism in Africa Algiers', Algeria, 11–14 September.

African Union (2005) 'Declaration of the Heads of State and Government of the African Union on the Fourth Ordinary Session of African Union', Addis Ababa.

African Union (2008a) 'India–Africa Forum Summit 2008: Africa India Framework for Cooperation'. At: www.africaunion.org/root/UA/Conferences/2008/avril/BCP/India%20Summit%2004-09avr/INDE%20-%20AFRIQUE%20SITE/AFRICA-INDIA%20FRAMEWORK%20FOR%20COOPERATION%20ENGLISH%20-%20FINAL%20VERSION.doc pp. 1–12.

African Union (2008b) 'India–Africa Forum Summit 2008: Delhi Declaration'. At: www.africaunion.org/root/UA/Conferences/2008/avril/BCP/India%20Summit%2004–09avr/INDE%20-%20AFRIQUE%20SITE/DELHI%20DECLARATION%20%20-%20ENGLISH%20-%20FINAL%20VERSION.doc.

Ahmed, Nafeez Mosaddeq (2009) 'Our Terrorists', *New Internationalist*, October: 17–20.

Ake, Claude (2006) *Democracy and Development in Africa*, Washington, DC: The Brookings Institute.

Al-khiyal (2007) 'U.S. Department of Defense behind www.magharebia.com'. At: www. algeria.com/forums/computer-internet/20556-u-s-department-defense-behind-www-magharebia-com.html.

Amnesty International (2007) 'Niger: Extrajudicial Executions and Population Displacement in the North of the Country'. At: www.amnesty.org/en/for-media/press-releases/ niger-extrajudicial-executions-and-population-displacement-north-country.

Anderlini, J. and Green, M. (2007) 'China's CDB seals Nigerian Deal', *Financial Times.* At: http://us.ft.com/ftgateway/superpage.ft?news_id=fto103020071819291104.

Anyaso, C. (2008) 'AFRICOM is Historic Step in U.S.–Africa Relationship'. At: www. america.gov/st/peacesecenglish/2008/April/20080423140127wcyeroc0.177273.html.

Arkin, William M. (2002) 'The Secret War: Frustrated by Intelligence Failures, the Defense Department is Dramatically Expanding its "Black World" of Covert Operations', *Los Angeles Times*, 27 October 27. At: http://web.archive.org/web/ 20021031092436/www.latimes.com/la-op-arkin27oct27001451,0,7355676.story.

Askouri, A. (2007) 'China's Investment in Sudan: Displacing Villages and Destroying Communities', in Manji, F. and Marks, S. (eds), *African Perspectives on China in Africa*, Oxford, UK: Fahamu, pp. 71–86.

Ayoob, M. (1995) *The Third World Security Predicament: State Making, Regional Conflict and the International System*, Boulder, CO: Lynne Rienner.

Azzam al-Ansari, A. (2006) 'Al-Qaeda is Moving to Africa', *Sada al Jihad* 7 (June): 27–30. At: www.sada.aljihad.ca.tc.

Bacevich, A. (2002) *American Empire*, Cambridge, MA: Harvard University Press.

Barnett, Thomas P.M. (2007a) 'Africa Command: Inside the Mission', *Esquire*, 19 June. At: www.esquire.com/features (accessed 3 May 2008).

Barnett, Thomas P.M. (2007b) 'The Americans Have Landed', *Esquire*, 27 June. At: www.esquire.com/features (accessed 3 May 2008).

Bava, U.S. (2007) 'New Powers for Global Change? India's Role in the Emerging World Order', Briefing Paper 15. Friedrich Ebert Stiftung (FES), Berlin, pp. 2–7. At: http:// library.fes.de/pdf-files/iez/global/04372.pdf.

Benton, Shaun (2007) 'Location of US Command in Africa to be Announced', 20 September. At: www.buanews.gov.za/view.php?ID=07092009451001&coll=buanew07.

Blair, T. (2001). Speech to the Labour Party Conference.

Bowman, Marion E. (Spike) (2002) Statement to Senate Select Committee on Intelligence, 31 July 2002. At: www.fas.org/irp/congress/2002_hr/073102bowman.html.

Broadman, H.G. (2006) 'Africa's Silk Road: China and India's New Economic Frontier'. At: http://siteresources.worldbank.org/AFRICAEXT/Resources/Africa_Silk_Road.pdf.

Brozoska, Michael (2003) 'Development Donors and the Concept of Security Sector Reform', Occasional Paper 4, Geneva, Centre for the Democratic Control of Armed Forces.

Burnley, Terry (2005) 'Emory S. Land Completes Gulf of Guinea Deployment', *Navy Newsstand* (22 March). At: www.navy.mil/search/display.asp?story_id=17600.

Bush, G. (2008) 'Transcript of President Bush's comments on U.S. Africa Command (AFRICOM)', Council of Foreign Relations. At: www.cfr.org/publication/13255.

Buur, L., Jensen, S. and Stepputat, F. (eds) (2007) *The Security–Development Nexus: Expressions of Sovereignty and Securitisation in Southern Africa*, Cape Town: HSRC Press.

Buzan, B., Wæver, B.O. and de Wilde, J. (1997). *Security: A New Framework for Analysis*, Boulder, CO: Lynne Rienner.

Cabinet Office (2008) 'The National Security Strategy of the United Kingdom: Security in an Interdependent World'. At: http://interactive.cabinetoffice.gov.uk/documents/security/national_security_strategy.pdf.

Campbell, Kurt and O'Hanlon, M. (2006) *Hard Power: The New Politics of National Security*, New York, NY: Basic Books.

Canney, Donald L. (2006) *Africa Squadron: The U.S. Navy and the Slave Trade, 1821–1861*, Dulles, VA: Potomac Books.

Carmody, P. (2005) 'Transforming Globalization and Security: Africa and America Post-9/11', *Africa Today* 52 (1): 97–120.

Cedoz, Frederick, Heiler, Robert E., Lewis, William E., King Meadows, Tyson and Michael Wihbey, Paul (2005) *Breaking the Oil Syndrome: Responsible Hydrocarbon Development in West Africa*, Washington: Congressional Black Caucus Foundation.

CENTCOM (2007) 'Combined Joint Task Force-Horn of Africa (CJTF-HOA), Factsheet'. At: www.hoa.centcom.mil/factsheet.asp.

Chandler, D. (2007) 'The Security–Development Nexus and the Rise of "Anti-Foreign Policy"', *Journal of International Relations and Development* 10: 362.

Chang, Ha-Joon (2007) *Bad Samaritans: Rich Nations, Poor Policies and the Threat to the Developing World*, New York, NY: Random House.

Chimutengwende, C. (2003) 'Making the African Union Succeed: The Greatest Issue in Africa from Now to 2010 Will Be the African Union's Consolidation and Development or Its Failure to Do So', *New African* 12. At: www.thefreelibrary.com/Making+the+African+Union+succeed%3a+the+greatest+issue+in+Africa+from...-a0102695606

Cilliers, J. (2003a) 'Terrorism and Africa', *African Security Review* 12 (4): 100.

Cilliers, J. (2003b) 'A Summary of Outcomes from the 2002 OAU/AU Summits in Durban', Institute for Security Studies Occasional Paper 76. At: www.iss.co.za/pubs/Papers/60/Paper60.html.

Cilliers, J. (2008) 'The African Standby Force: An Update on Progress', ISS Paper 160, p. 1.

Cilliers, J. and Sturman, K. (2002) 'The Right Intervention: Enforcement Challenges for the African Union', *African Security Review* 11: 3. At: www.iss.co.za/PUBS/ASR/11NO3.

Cisse, Almahady (2007) 'Gunmen Hit U.S. Military Plane in Mali', *Washington Post*, 13 September. At: www.washingtonpost.com (accessed 14 September 2007).

CJTF-HOA (2008) 'Defense, Diplomacy and Development in the Horn of Africa', *CHIPS*, 1 April.

Clays, M.M. (2003) 'The Interagency Process and America's Second Front in the Global War on Terrorism', Defense Technical Information Center, April, Accession No: ADA424995.

Cline, Steve (2008) 'Across Kenya, U.S. Forces Share Knowledge, Assistance', CENTCOM news release, 2 May. At: www.hoa.cencom.mil (accessed 7 May 2008).

Cockburn, Andrew (2008) 'Secret Bush "Finding" Widens War on Iran', *Counterpunch* 2 May. At: www.counterpunch.org/andrew05022008.html.

Collier, P. and Hoeffle, A. (2004) 'Greed and Grievance in Civil War', *Oxford Economic Papers* 56: 563–95.

Collier, P., Elliot, L., Hegre, H., Hoeffler, A., Reyan-Querol, M. and Sambanis, N. (2003) *Breaking the Conflict Trap*, New York, NY: World Bank and Oxford University Press.

Commission on Human Security (2003) *Human Security Now*, New York, NY: United Nations. At: www.humansecuritychs.org/finalreport/English/FinalReport.

Dange, B. (2008) 'The Rejection of Africom'. At: http://forums.csis.org/africa/?p=72.

Davidson, Basil (1992) *The Black Man's Burden: Africa and the Curse of the Nation State*, Oxford: James Currey.

Davis, John (2007) 'Africa's Road to the War on Terror', in Davis, John (ed.), *Africa and the War on Terrorism*, Burlington, VT: Ashgate, pp. 1–14.

Deegan, H. (2009) *Africa Today: Culture, Economics, Religion and Security*, New York, NY: Routledge.

Defense Science Board (2002) 'DSB Summer Study on Special Operations and Joint Forces in Support of Countering Terrorism', US Department of Defense, Final Outbrief, 16 August; 78 pages (in PowerPoint format). At: www.fas.org/irp/agency/dod/dsbbrief.ppt.

Department for International Development (2008) 'Reducing Poverty Through Cash Transfers'. At: www.dfid.gov.uk/casestudies/files/south-america/brazil/brazil-bolsa2.asp.

Diallo, Tiemoko (2007) 'U.S. Plane Hit by Gunfire on Resupply Flight in Mali', *Washington Post*, 13 September. At: www.washingtonpost.com (accessed 14 September 2007).

Dixon, B. (2008) 'America's Military Foot in Africa's Doorway'. At: http://74.125.95.132/search?q=cache:KfTwqWrVeV4J:www.peuplesawa.com/downloads/288.pdf+africom+filetype:pdf&hl=en&ct=clnk&cd=21&gl=ca.

Dorn, Walter (1998) 'Regional Peacekeeping is not the Way', *Peacekeeping and International Relations* 27 (2): 1.

Downs, E. (2006) 'China', The Energy Security Series, Brooking Foreign Policy Studies, Brookings Institute. At: www3.brookings.edu/fp/research/energy/2006china.pdf.

Duffield, M. (2008) *Development, Security and Unending War: Governing the World of Peoples*, Cambridge: Polity.

Dufour, J. (2007) 'The Worldwide Network of US Military Bases: The Global Deployment of Military Personnel', *Global Research*, July. At: www.globalresearch.ca/index.

Economist, The (2009) 'Building on the B in BRIC'. At: www.economist.com/theworldin/displayStory.cfm?story_id=12494572.

Ellis, Stephen (2004) 'Briefing: The Pan-Sahel Initiative', *African Affairs* 103 (412): 459–64.

Embassy of India, Khartoum (2003) 'India and Sudan Partners in Development'. At: www.indembsdn.com/eng/india_sdn_partners.html.

Empowerment Against Poverty (LEAP) 'Brazil & Africa Newsletter'. At: www.undp-povertycentre.org/ipc/PageAfrica-Brazil.do?id=11#leap.

England, A. and Blas, J. (2008) 'Abu Dhabi Looks to Sudan to Secure Food Supply', *Financial Times*. At: www.ft.com/cms/s/0/4bbd1ecc-319c-11dd-b77c-0000779fd2ac.html.

Erlanger, S. (2001) 'In Europe, Some Say the Attacks Stemmed from American Failings', *New York Times*, 22 September.

EUCOM (2005) 'Exercise Flintlock 05 Under Way in Africa', 9 June. At: www.eucom.mil/english/FullStory.asp?art=565.

Evans, M. (1984) 'The Frontline States, South Africa and Southern African Security', *Zambezia* 5 (12): 1–19.

Fisher-Thompson, Jim (2004) 'US–African Partnership Helps Counter Terrorists in Sahel Region: New Maghreb Co-operation Central to Pan-Sahel Initiative', Washington File, US Department of State Information Service, 23 March 2004.

Floyd, Chris (2002) 'Into the Dark: The Pentagon Plan to Promote Terrorist Attacks', *Counterpunch*, 1 November. At: www.counterpunch.org/floyd1101.html.

Food and Agriculture Organisation of the United Nations (2008) 'The State of Food Insecurity in the World 2008; High Food Prices and Food Security – Threats and Opportunities'. At: ftp.fao.org/docrep/fao/011/i0291e/i0291e00.pdf.

Foreign Policy Centre *et al.* (2008) 'Going for Growth; Can Commodities Transform Development in Africa and China?', London conference. At: http://fpc.org.uk/fsblob/996.pdf.

Forum On China–Africa Cooperation (2006) 'Beijing Action Plan'. At: www.fmprc.gov.cn/zflt/eng/zyzl/hywj/t280369.htm.

Francis, D. (2006) *Uniting Africa: Building Regional Peace and Security*. Aldershot: Ashgate.

Franke, Benedikt (2007) 'Enabling a Continent to Help Itself: U.S. Military Capacity Building and Africa's Emerging Security Architecture', *Strategic Insights* 6 (1): 1–13.

Furet, F. (2001) 'From Narrative History to Problem-Oriented History', in Roberts, G. (ed.), *The History and Narrative Reader*, London: Routledge.

G8 Africa Action Plan (2005) *Progress Report by the G8: African Personal Representatives on the Implementation of the African Action Plan*, London: G8. At: www.dfid.gov.uk/pubs/files/98-africa-progress-report-pdf.

Gerth, J. (2005) 'Military's Information War is Vast and Often Secretive', *New York Times*, 11 December.

Gèze, F. and Mellah, S. (2007) '"Al-Qaida au Maghreb", ou la très étrange histoire du GSPC', *Algeria-Watch*, 22 september. At: www.algeria-watch.org/fr/aw/gspc_etrange_histoire.htm

Ghebremeskel, A. (2002) 'Regional Approach to Conflict Management Revisited: The Somali Experience', *Online Journal of Peace and Conflict Resolution* 4 (2): 9–29.

Gilmore, Gerry (2007) 'U.S. Naval Forces Europe Prepares for AFRICOM Stand Up', American Forces Press Service, 1 June. At: www.defenselink.mil (accessed 4 September 2007).

Glasius Marlies, (2009) 'Human Security from Paradigm Shift to Operationalization', *Security Dialogue* 39 (1): 31–54.

Glover, Danny and Lee, Nicole C. (2007) 'Say No to Africom', *The Nation. At:* www.thenation.com/doc/20071119/glover_lee (accessed 10 November 2009).

Goldwyn, D. (2004) Testimony before the U.S. Senate Committee on Foreign Relations, Subcommittee on International Economic Policy, Export and Trade Promotion.

Goldwyn, D. and Morrison, S. (2004) 'Promoting Transparency in the African Oil Sector', report of the CSIS Task Force on Rising US Energy Stakes in Africa. At: www.CSIS.org/africa/goldwynAfricanoilsector.pdf.

Goldwyn, D. and Morrison, S. (2005) 'A Strategic US Approach to Governance and Security in the Gulf of Guinea', report of the CSIS Task Force on Gulf of Guinea Security. At: http://csis.org/files/media/csis/pubs/0507_gulfofguinea.pdf.

Gueli, Richard (2008) 'South Africa: A Future Research Agenda for Post-Conflict Reconstruction', *African Security Review* 17 (1): 89.

Haddad, L. (2008) 'US Development Policy in 2009: Maverick or Audacious', Dangerous Ideas seminar series, Institute of Development Studies, UK; held at the House of Commons, London. At: www.tmnside.org.sg/title2//finance/twninfofinance010.htm.

Han, Yuna (2008). 'A More Perfect Union: The AU's Failures and Future', *Harvard International Review* 30 (1): 8.

Hansen, E. (ed.) (1987) *African Perspectives on Peace and Development*, London: Zed Books.

Hawkins, D. (2008) 'Protecting Democracy in Europe and the Americas', *International Organization* 62 (3): 373–403.

Hehir, A. (2007) 'The Myth of the Failed State and the War on Terror: A Challenge to the Conventional Wisdom', *Journal of Intervention and State Building* 1 (3): 307–32.

Henry, Ryan (2007) 'DoD News Briefing with Principal Deputy Under Secretary Henry from the Pentagon', Department of Defense News. At: www.defenselink.mil/tran-scripts/transcript.aspx?transcriptid=3942.

Herbst, J. (2000) *States and Power in Africa: Comparative Lessons in Authority and Control*, Princeton, NJ: Princeton University Press.

Herd, G. (2006) *Soft Security Threats and European Security*, London: Routledge.

Hess, E. Michael (2007) Testimony before the U.S. Senate Committee on Foreign Rela-tions, 1 August. At: http://foreign.senate.gov/testimony/2007/HessTestimony070801.pdf.

Hess, Pamela (2002) 'Panel wants $7bn elite counter-terror unit', *United Press Interna-tional*, 26 September. At: http://bailey83221.livejournal.com/107138.html.

Hoare, Quintin and Smith, Geoffrey Noel (eds) (1972) *Selections from the Prison Note-books*, New York, NY: International Publishers.

Hofmann, K. (2006), 'New Powers for Global Change? Challenges for International Development Cooperation: The Example of China', Dialogue on Globalization, Brief-ing Paper 15. Friedrich Ebert Stiftung, Berlin. At: http://library.fes.de/pdf-files/iez/global/04663.pdf.

Howe, H. (2001) *Ambiguous Order: Military Forces in African States*, Boulder, CO: Lynne Rienner.

Human Rights News (2007) 'Niger: Warring Sides Must End Abuses of Civilians: Com-batants Engaged in Executions, Rape, and Theft', Human Rights Watch, Dakar, 19 December. At: http://hrw.org/english/docs/2007/12/19/niger17623.htm.

Humphreys, M. and Varshney, A. (2004) Violent Conflict and the Millennium Develop-ment Goals: Diagnosis and Recommendations'. At: www.columbia.edu/~mh2245/papers1/HV.pdf.

Huntington, S. (1999) 'The Lonely Superpower', *Foreign Affairs* 78 (2): 35–49.

Ikenberry, G.J. (2001) 'American Power and the Empire of Capitalist Democracy', *Review of International Studies* 27: 191.

International Poverty Centre (2008) 'Social Protection in Ghana: the Livelihood', *Inter-national Review* 30 (1): 8.

Isenberg, David (2002) ' "P2OG" Allows Pentagon to Fight Dirty', *Asia Times Online*, 5 November. At: www.atimes.com/atimes/Middle_East/DK05Ak02.html.

Isike, C., Okeke-Uzodike, U. and Gilbert, L. (2008) 'The United States Africa Command: Enhancing American Security or Fostering African Development?', *African Security Review* 17 (1): 22.

Jackson, R. (2000) 'The Dangers of Regionalising International Conflict Management: The African Experience', *Political Science* 52 (1): 41–60.

Jane's Defence Weekly (2004) 'US to Bolster Counter-terrorism Assistance to Africa', 6 October. At: www.jiaa.janes.com (accessed 24 October 2004).

Jane's Islamic Affairs Analyst (2004) 'US Deploys Further Forces in Africa', 4 August. At: www.jiaa.janes.com (accessed 24 October 2004).

Jobelius, M. (2007) 'New Powers for Global Change? Challenges for International Devel-opment Cooperation – The Case of India', Dialogue on Globalization, Briefing Paper 3, Friedrich Ebert Stiftung, Berlin. At: www.basas.org.uk/projects/Jobelius.pdf.

Johnson, C. (2000) *Blowback: The Costs and Consequences of American Empire*, New York, NY: Metropolitan Books.

Kaldor, M., Martin, M. and Sabine, S. (2007) 'Human Security: A New Strategic Narrative for Europe', *International Affairs* 83 (2): 273–88.

Kaplinsky, R. (2008) 'What Does the Rise of China do for Industrialization in Sub-Saharan Africa?', *Review of African Political Economy* 115: 7–22.

Keenan, J. (2006) 'Military Bases, Construction Contracts and Hydrocarbons in North Africa', *Revue of African Political Economy* (ROAPE) 33 (109): 601–8.

Keenan, J. (2007) 'Niger: Tuareg Unrest, Its Recent Background and Potential Regional Implications', Writenet Report commissioned by the United Nations High Commissioner for Refugees, Emergency and Technical Support Service.

Keenan, J. (2009) *The Dark Sahara: America's War on Terror in Africa*, London: Pluto.

Keenan, J. (2010). *The Dying Sahara: US Imperialism and Terror in Africa*, London: Pluto.

Kfir, I. (2008) 'The Challenge That Is U.S. AFRICOM', *Joint Force Quarterly* 49: 110–13.

Kidane, N. (2008) 'AFRICOM: Militarization, and Resource Control: A Civilian-Military Partnership?', Pambazuka News. At: www.pambazuka.org/en/category/comment/51201.

Kingebiel, S. (2005) 'African's New Peace and Security Architecture: Converging the Roles of External actors and African Interests', *African Security Review* 14 (2). At: www.iss.co.za/pubs/ASR/14No2/FKlingebiel.htm.

Kioko, B. (2003) 'The Right of Intervention Under the African Union's Constitutive Act: Non-interference to Non-intervention', *International Review of the Red Cross* 85: 807–25.

Klare, Michael and Volman, Daniel (2006) 'The African "Oil Rush" and U.S. National Security', *Third World Quarterly* 27 (4): 619.

Knorr, K. (1973) *Power and Wealth: The Political Economy of International Power*, New York, NY: Basic Books.

Kraxberger, M.B. (2005) 'The United States and Africa: Shifting Geopolitics in an "Age of Terror"', *Africa Today* 52 (1): 47–68.

Laski, H.J. (1947) 'America-1947', *Nation* 165.

Last, Alex (2007) 'Nigeria Makes "al-Qaeda" Arrests', *BBC News*, 12 November. At: http://news.bbc.co.uk/2/hi/africa/7090642.stm

Le Malle, G. (2008) 'Africa Outlook 2008', Foreign Policy In Focus, Institute for Policy Studies. At: www.fpif.org/pdf/reports/0802africaoutlook.pdf.

Le Roux, M. (2007), 'Annan Leads Drive to Reverse African Farming', *Terra Daily*. At: www.terradaily.com/reports/Annan_Leads_Drive_To_Reverse_African_Farming_Decline_999.html.

Lemos, A. and Ribeiro, D. (2007) 'Taking Ownership or Just Changing Owners?', in Manji, F. and Marks, S. (eds), *African Perspectives on China in Africa*, Oxford: Fahamu, pp. 63–70.

Liotta, Peter (2002) 'Boomerang Effect: The Convergence of National and Human Security', *Security Dialogue* 33 (4): 473–88.

Lutz, C. (ed.) (2008) *The Bases of Empire: The Global Struggle Against US Military Posts*, London: Pluto Press.

Lyman, P.N. (2006) 'A Strategic Approach to Terrorism', in Rothchild, Donald and Keller, Edmond J. (eds), *Africa–U.S. Relations: Strategic Encounters*, Boulder, CO: Lynne Rienner.

McCrae, C. (2008) *The Final Betrayal*, film produced and directed by Callum McCrae.

An Outsider Television production for Al Jazeera (English). First transmitted 19 August 2008.

McFate, S. (2008a) 'U.S. Africa Command: A New Strategic Paradigm', *Military Review*  88 (1): 10.

McFate, S. (2008b) 'Outsourcing the Making of Militaries: DynCorp International as Sovereign Agent', *Review of African Political Economy* 35 (118): 645–55.

McFate, S. (2008c) 'US Africa Command: Next Step or Next Stumble?' *African Affairs* 107: 426.

McGregorin, R. (2007) 'China's Prosperity Brings Income Gaps', *Financial Times*. At: www.ft.com/cms/s/9ebb585a-4610–11dc-b359–0000779fd2ac.html.

McIntire, M. (2009) Testimony given before the House Sub-committee on National Security and Foreign Affairs, Committee on Oversight and Government Reform.

McIntire, M. and Gettleman, J. (2009) 'A Chaotic Kenya Vote and a Secret U.S. Exit Poll', New York Times, 31 January. At: www.nytimes.com/2009/01/31/world/africa/31kenya.html.

Magdoff, H., Foster, J.B., McChesney, R. and Sweezy, P. (2002) 'US Military Bases and Empire', *Monthly Review* 53 (10): 1. At: www.monthlyreview.org/0302editr.htm.

Magyar, K. (ed.) (2000), *United States Interests and Policies in Africa: Transition to a New Era*, London: Macmillan.

Makinda, S. (2008) 'Why AFRICOM Has Not Won Over Africans'. At: http://csis.org/blog/why-africom-has-not-won-over-africans.

Malan, Mark (2002) *New Tools in the Box? Towards A Standby Force for the African Union*, Johannesburg: Institute of Security Studies.

Malan, M. (2008a) 'U.S. Civil Military Imbalance for Global Engagement: Lessons from the Operational Level in Africa', *Refugees International*. At: www.refugeesinternational.org/sites/default/files/RI_CivMil_imbalance.pdf

Malan, M. (2008b) 'Africom: Joined-up Geographical Command or Federal Business Opportunity?' Testimony given before the House Subcommittee on National Security and Foreign Affairs, Committee on Oversight and Government Reform. Washington, DC, 23 July.

Mandela, Nelson (1994). Speech to Assembly of OAU Heads of State and Government at the 30th Ordinary Session of the Organization of African Unity. At: www.anc.org.za/ancdocs/history/mandela/1998/sp980608.html.

Malan, M. (2001) *New Tools in the Box? Towards a Standby Force for the African Union*, Johannesburg: Institute of Security Studies.

Malan, M. (2008a) *U.S. Civil Military Imbalance for Global Engagement: Lessons from the Operational Level in Africa*, Washington, DC: Refugees International.

Malan, M. (2008b) Africom: Joined-up Geographical Command or Federal Business Opportunity? Testimony given before the House Subcommittee on National Security and Foreign Affairs, Committee on Oversight and Government Reform. Washington, DC.

Malaquias, Assis (2001) 'Reformulating International Relations Theory: African Insights and Challenges', in Dun, Kevin C. and Shaw, Timothy M. (eds), *Africa's Challenge to International Relations Theory*, Basingstoke: Palgrave, p. 13.

Maloka, E. (2001) *A United States of Africa*, Pretoria: African Institute of South Africa.

Mawdsley, E. (2007) 'Changing Global Geographies of Power and Development: Contemporary Indian–East Africa Relations', The British Association for South Asian Studies, pp. 2–10. At: www.basas.org.uk/projects/BASIS-application.pdf.

Menkhaus, K. (2003) 'Quasi-States, Nation-Building and Terrorist Safe Havens', *Journal of Conflict Studies* 23 (2): 7–23.

Menkhaus, K. (2004) 'Vicious Circles and the Security Development Nexus', *Conflict Security & Development* 4 (2): 150–65.

Miguel, E., Satyanath, S. and Sergenti, E. (2004) 'Economic Shocks and Civil Conflict: An Instrumental Variables Approach', *Journal of Political Economy* 112 (41): 723–53.

Miles, Donna (2004) 'US Must Confront Terrorism in Africa, General Says', US American Forces Press Service, US Department of Defense, Washington, DC, 16 June.

Miles, Donna (2005) 'New Counterterrorism Initiative to Focus on Saharan Africa', American Forces Press Service, 16 May. At: www.defenselink.mil/news/newsarticle.aspx?id=31643.

Mills, Greg, McNamee, Terence and De Lorenzo, Mauro (2007) 'AFRICOM and African Security: The Globalization of Security or the Militarization of Globalization?', Brenthurst Discussion Paper 4, Johannesburg, Brenthurst Foundation.

Mlambo, N. (2006) 'Evolution of peace and Security Council of the African Union and the African Standby Force', *Africa Insight* 36 (3/4): 41–56.

Moeller, Vice Admiral Robert (2008) 'United States Africa Command: Partnership, Security, and Stability', presentation at the Conference on Transforming National Security: Africom – An Emerging Command, organized by the Office of the Under Secretary of Defense for Forces Transformation and Resources and by the Center for Technology and National Security Policy at the National Defense University, Fort McNair, Washington, DC, 18 February.

Mohamed Salih, M.A. (1989) 'The Europeanization of War in Africa: From Traditional to Modern Warfare', *Current Research on Peace and Violence* 12 (1): 27–37.

Mohamed Salih, M.A. (1990) 'Savagery and Neo-Savagery: An African Perspective on Peace', in Harle, Vilho (ed.), *European Values in International Relations*, London and New York: Pinters Publishers, pp. 110–25.

Mohamed Salih, M.A. (2001) *African Democracies and African Politics*, London: Pluto Press.

Mohamed Salih, M.A. (2008a) 'Poverty and Human Security: The Liberal Peace Debate', in Francis, David (ed.), *Peace and Conflict in Africa*, London: Zed Books, pp. 174–84.

Mohamed Salih, M. A. (2008b) *Greater Horn of Africa Horizon: Study of Africa's New Regional Security Structure*, Djibouti: Greater Horn of Africa Initiative.

Morris, Daniel (2006) 'The Chance to Go Deep: U.S. Energy Interests in West Africa', *American Foreign Policy Interests* 28 (3): 225–38.

Mwagiru, M. (2004) *African Regional Security in the Age of Globalization*, Nairobi: Heinrich Böll Foundation.

Navy Newsstand (2005) 'Coast Guard Cutter *Bear* Kicks off 6th Fleet Deployment', 7 June. At: www.navy.mil/search/display.asp?story_id=18620.

Nayyar, D. (2008) 'China, India, Brazil and South Africa in the World Economy Engines of Growth?', Discussion Paper 2008/05, United Nations University, World Institute for Development Economic Research.

Neethling, T. (2005a) 'Shaping the African Standby Force: Developments, Challenges, and Prospects', *Military Review*, 1 May: 65–71.

Neethling, T. (2005b) 'Realizing the African Standby Force as a Pan-African Deal: Progress, Prospects, and Challenges', *Journal of Military and Strategic Studies* 8 (1): 1–25.

Neuman, Michael and Trani, Jean-François (2006) 'Le Tribalisme Explique tous les Conflits', in Courade, Georges (ed.), *L'Afrique des Idées Reçues*, Paris: Belin, p. 144.

New African Magazine (2009) 'Obama: Do Something Before You Go', *New African Magazine* 487: 14.

New Partnership for African Development (2001) 'A Summary of NEPAD Action Plans'. At: www.nepad.org/2005/files/documents/41.pdf.

New Partnership for African Development (2002) 'Final Report: Workshop on Implementation of NEPAD'.

Norman, M. (2006). 'Evolution of Peace and Security Council of the African Union and the African Standby Force', *Africa Insight* 36 (3/4): 41–56.

Nye Jr, S.J. (2004) *Soft Power: The Means to Success in World Politics*, New York, NY: Public Affairs.

Obama/Biden (2008) Presidential Campaign 'Strengthening our Common Security by Investing in our Common Humanity'. At: www.barackobama.com/pdf/issues/Fact_Sheet_Foreign_Policy_Democratizationand_Development_FINAL.pdf.

Office of Logistics Management, Department of State (2008) 'AFRICAP Program Re-Compete', 21 February. At: www.fbo.gov (accessed 5 March 2008).

Oliver, R. (2006) 'Human Security and the Liberal Peace: Tensions and Contradictions', paper presented in 2006 for EKEM Workshop on International Peacekeeping and Peacemaking: Global and Regional Perspectives.

Organization of African Unity (1999) Convention on the Prevention and Combating of Terrorism (adopted 14 July 1999), Art. 1 §3 (a). At: www.africa-union.org/Official_documents/Treaties_%20Conventions_%20Protocols/Algiers_convention%20on%20Terrorism.pdf#search=%22african%20unity%20convention%20terrorism%22.

Paz, R. and Terdman, M. (2006) 'Africa: The Goldmine of Al-Qaeda and Global Jihad', Prism Occasional Paper 4, No. 2, June, pp. 1–6.

Pearce, E.H. (1972) *Rhodesia: Report of the Commission on Rhodesian Opinion under the Chairmanship of the Right Honourable Lord Pearce*, London: HMSO.

People's Daily (2007) 'China–Africa trade hits US$55.5 billion'. At: http://english.peopledaily.com.cn/200701/30/eng20070130_346085.html.

Peter Pham, J. (2007a) 'Next Front? Evolving U.S.–African Strategic Relations in the "War on Terrorism" and Beyond', *Comparative Strategy* 26 (1): 39–54.

Peter Pham, J. (2007b) 'The Battle for Nigeria', *The National Interest* 88: 97–100.

Pipes, D. (2001/2) 'God and Mammon: Does Poverty cause Militant Islam?', *The National Interest* 66: 14–21.

Powell, S.M. (2004) 'Swamp of Terror in the Sahara', *Air Force Magazine* 87 (11): 50–5.

Project for the New American Century (1997) 'Statement of Principles'. At: www.newamericancentury.org.

Putman, R. (2008) 'US Foreign Policy in Africa', in Cox, M. and Stokes, D. (eds), *US Foreign Policy*, Oxford: Oxford University Press, p. 316.

Pyne, David (2002) 'The New Second Front in the War Against Terrorism'. At: www.american-partisan.com/cols/2002/pyne/qtr4/1219.htm.

Ramcharan, B.G. (2002) *Human Rights and Human Security*, The Hague: M. Nijhoff.

Reed, Valerie (2007) 'A Big Image Problem Down There: Prospects for an African Headquarters for AFRICOM'. At: www.cdi.org/pdfs/reedAFRICOM.pdf.

Reno, William (2004) 'The Roots of Sectarian Violence, and Its Cure', in Rotberg, Robert I. (ed.), *Crafting the New Nigeria: Confronting the Challenges*, Boulder, CO: Lynne Rienner, p. 236.

Rice, C. (2006) *Transformational Diplomacy*, Washington, DC: Georgetown University.

Richards, Paul (1996) *Fighting for the Rain Forest: War, Youth and Resources in Sierra Leone*, Oxford: James Currey.

Rodman, P. (2000) 'The World's Resentment: Anti-Americanism as a Global Phenomenon', *The National Interest* 60: 33–41.

Rotberg, R.I. (2005) *Terrorism in the Horn of Africa*, Washington: Brookings Institution Press.

Rothchild, D. and Keller, E. (eds) (2006) *Africa–US Relations: Strategic Encounters*, Boulder, CO: Lynne Rienner.

Rothschild, E. (1995) 'What Is Security?', *Daedalus – Journal of the American Association for the Advancement of Science* 124 (3): 53–98.

Sachs, J. and Warner, A. (2001) 'The Curse of Natural Resources', *European Economic Review* 45: 827–38.

SADC-PF (1995) Constitution of the SADC Parliamentary Forum.

SADC-PF (2000) 'Strategic Plan: Development Community Parliamentary Forum'. At: www.sadcpf.org/documents/sadcpf_strategicplan_2000_2005.pdf.

Sahara Focus (2009) Subscription-based quarterly political risk analysis. Volume 4 (accessed at www.menas.co.uk).

Salim A.S. (1990). *The Political and Socio-Economic Situation in Africa and the Fundamental Changes Taking Place in the World*, Addis Ababa: Organization of African Unity.

Salim, A.S. (1995) *The Report of the Secretary General to the Special Session of the Council of Ministers on Economic and Social Issues in African Development*, Addis Ababa: Organization of African Unity.

Sands, D.R. (2008) 'Saudi Aid Bails out U.N. Food Agency', *Washington Times*, 24 May. At: www.washingtontimes.com/news/2008/may/24/saudi-aid-bails-out-un-food-agency.

Satyanath, M.E.S. and Sergenti, E. (2004) 'Economic Shocks and Civil Conflict: An Instrumental Variables Approach', *Journal of Political Economy* 112 (41): 725–53.

Schermerhorn, Lange (2005) 'Djibouti: A Special Role in the War on Terrorism', in Rotberg, Robert I. (ed.), *Battling Terrorism in the Horn of Africa*, Washington, DC: Brookings Institution Press, p. 57.

Schläger, C. (2007) 'New Powers for Global Change? Challenges for International Development Cooperation: The Case of Brasil', Dialogue on Globalization, Briefing Paper 3, Friedrich Ebert Stiftung, Berlin.

Schneidman, Whitney W. (2008) 'Obama's Three Objectives for Continent', online guest column for AllAfrica.Com, 29 September. At: www.allafrica.com (accessed 10 November 2008).

Schoeman, M. (2003) 'The African Union after the Durban 2002 Summit', Centre of Development. Organization of African Unity. Addis Ababa. At: www.teol.ku.dk/cas/nyhomepage/mapper/Occasional%20Papers/Schoeman_intenetversion.doc.

Schraeder, P. (1994) *United States Foreign Policy Towards Africa: Incrementalism, Crisis and Change*, Cambridge: Cambridge University Press.

Shakleina, T. (2007) 'Security Problems in the 21st Century: Soft vs. Hard Power. Russia's Approach', paper presented at the annual meeting of the International Studies Association 48th Annual Convention, Chicago, February 28.

Shaun, B (2007) 'Location of US Command in Africa to be Announced'. At: www.buanews.gov.za/view.php?ID=07092009451001&coll=buanew07.

Shay, S. (2008) *Somalia: Between Jihad and Restoration*, New Brunswick, NJ: Transaction.

Sheridan, M. (2007), 'China Builds Africa Empire: The Giant's Rush to Secure Resources', *Sunday Times*. At: http://business.timesonline.co.uk/tol/business markets/china/ article2889489.ece.

Smith, Craig S. (2004) 'U.S. Training African Forces to Uproot Terrorists', *New York Times*, 11 May. At: www.nytimes.com (accessed 14 May 2004).

Smith, Craig S. (2006) 'Qaeda-Linked Group Claims Algerian Attack', *New York Times*, 13 December. At: www.nytimes.com (accessed 13 December 2006).

Soft, H.G. (2006) *Security Threats and European Security*, London: Routledge.

de Sousa, J. (2007) 'Brazil as a New International Development Actor, South–South Cooperation and the IBSA Initiative', Fundación para las Relaciones Internacionales y el Diálogo Exterior. At: www.nsi-ins.ca/english/events/DAW/2_de%20Sousa.pdf.

Suhrke, A. (1999) 'Human Security and the Interests of States', *Security Dialogue* 30 (3): 265–76.

Summary Defense Appropriations (2009) 'Washington DC: House of Representatives. Committee on Appropriations Warfare', *Journal of Current Research on Peace and Violence* 10 (1): 27–37.

Sweezy, P. (1989) 'US Imperialism in the 1990s', *Monthly Review* 41: 1–17.

Tate, Deborah (2007) 'US Officials Brief Congress on New Military Command for Africa', *Voice of America*, 1 August. At: www.voanew.com (accessed 30 August 2007).

Terdman, Moshe (2007) 'The Movement for the Emancipation of the Niger Delta (MEND): Al-Qaeda's Unlikely Ally in Nigeria', *Islam in Africa Newsletter* 2 (1): 29.

Third World Network (2006) 'China: doubles aid and investment to Africa'. At: www. twnside.org.sg/title2/finance/twninfofinance010.htm.

Tisdall, Simon (2007) 'Africa United in Rejecting U.S. Request for Military HQ', *Guardian*, 26 June. At: www.guardian.co.uk (accessed 30 August 2007).

Toynbee, A. (1962) *America and World Revolution*, New York, NY: Oxford University Press.

Trinh, T. *et al.* (2006) 'China's Commodity Hunger: Implications for Africa and Latin America', Deutsche Bank Research, Deutsche Bank. At: www.dbresearch.com/PROD/DBR_INTERNET_DE-PROD/PROD0000000000199956.pdf

Tuckey, B. (2008) 'Obama, US–Africa policy and AFRICOM', Pambazuka News. At: www.pambazuka.org/en/category/comment/51787.

Thomas, C. (1987) *In Search of Security: The Third World in International Relations*, Boulder, CO: Lynne Rienner.

Thomas, C. (1999) 'Introduction', in Caroline Thomas and Peter Wilkin (eds), *Globalization, Human Security, and the African Experience*, Boulder, CO: Lynne Rienner Publishers, Inc, pp. 1–23.

Thomas, C. (2001) 'Global Governance, Development and Human Security: Exploring the Links', *Third World Quarterly* 22 (2): 159–75.

Thomas, C. and Wilkin, P. (1999) *Globalization, Human Security and the African Experience*, Boulder, CO: Lynne Rienner.

TransAfrica Forum (2008) 'AFRICOM: The Militarization of U.S. Diplomacy and ForeignAid'. At: www.transafricaforum.org/files/AFRICOMThe%20Militarization%20of%20US%20Diplomacy%20and%20Foreign%20Aid.pdf.

UNCTAD (2005) *Statistical Profiles of the Least Developed Countries*, Geneva: United Nations Conference on Trade and Development.

UNCTAD (2007) Least Developed Countries (LDCs) Report 2007; Knowledge, Technical Learning and Innovation for Development'. United Nations Conference on Trade and Development.

United Nations (2008) *Millennium Development Report 2007*, New York, NY: United Nations.

United Nations Development Programme (1994) *Human Development Report 1994*, New York, NY: Oxford University Press.

United Nations Development Programme (2004) *Human Development Report 2004*, New York, NY: Oxford University Press.

United Nations Development Programme (2006) *Human Development Index*, New York, NY: United Nations Development Programme.

United Nations Development Programme (2007) *Human Development Report 2007/2008*, New York, NY: Oxford University Press.

United Nations News Centre (2008) 'African Leaders at UN Call for Agricultural Investment to Replace Food Aid'. At: www.un.org/apps/news/story.asp?NewsID=28221&Cr=general+assembly&Cr1=debate.

United Nations Office on Drugs and Crime (2008) *Cocaine Trafficking in West Africa: The Threat to Stability and Development*, New York, NY: United Nations Organization.

US Africa Command (2008a) 'The United States and Africa: Partnering for Growth and Development'. At: www.africom.mil/getArticle.asp?art=2102.

US Africa Command (2008b) 'U.S. Africa Command FAQs'. At: www.africom.mil/AboutAFRICOM.asp.

US Department of Defense, Office of the Assistant Secretary of Defense (Public Affairs) (2007) 'Terror Suspect Transferred to Guantanamo', 6 June. At: www.defenselink.mil/releases/release.aspx?releaseid=10976.

US Department of Energy, Energy Information Administration (2007) 'U.S. Imports by Country of Origin'. At: http://tonto.eia.doe.gov/dnav/pet/pet_move_impcus_a2_nus_ep00_im0_mbblpd_a.htm.

US Department of Energy, Energy Information Administration (2008) 'U.S. Total Crude Oil and Products Imports', 25 March. At: http://tonto.eia.doe.gov/dnav/pet/pet_move_impcus_a2_nus_ep00_im0_mbbl_m.htm.

US Department of State (2008) 'Country Reports on Terrorism 2007', 30 April. At: www.state.gov/s/ct/rls/crt/2007.

US Joint Chiefs of Staff, 'Justification for US Military Intervention in Cuba (Top Secret)', US Department of Defense, 13 March 1962.

US National Intelligence Council (2008) 'Global Trends 2025: A Transformed World'. At: http://image.guardian.co.uk/sys-files/Guardian/documents/2008/11/20/GlobalTrends 2025_FINAL.pdf.

Voice of America (2008) 'Bush Comments Spark Debate on AFRICOM in Liberia'. At: http://voanews.com/english/archive/2008–02/2008–02–20-voa27. cfm? CFID=80900233 &CFTOKEN=28387469.

Volman, D. (2003) 'The Bush Administration & African Oil: The Security Implications of US Energy Policy', *Review of African Political Economy* 30 (98): 573–84.

Volman, D. (2008) 'Africom: From Bush to Obama', *Monthly Review*, 7 December.

Volman, D. (2009) 'Africom to continue under Obama', *Pambazuka* 437, 11 June 2009. At: http://pambazuka.org/en/category/features/56855.

Volman, D. and Minter, W. (2008) 'Making Peace or Fueling War in Africa', Foreign Policy in Focus. At: www.fpif.org.

Von Hippel, K. (2002) 'The Roots of Terrorism: Probing the Myths', *The Political Quarterly* 73 (25): 1–39.

Vulliamy, E. (2008) 'How a Tiny West African Country became the World's First Narcostate', *Guardian*, 9 March. At: www.guardian.co.uk/world/2008/mar/09/drugstrade.

de Waal, A. (ed.) (2004) *Islamism and Its Enemies in the Horn of Africa*, London: Hurst.

Wæver, B.O. and de Wilde, J. (1997) *Security: A New Framework for Analysis*. Boulder, CO: Lynne Rienner.

Wallace, W. (1999) 'Europe after the Cold War: Interstate Order or Post-Sovereign Regional System?' *Review of International Studies* 25: 201–23.

Wallis, W. (2008) 'China to invest US$5 bn in Congo', *Financial Times*. At: www.ft.com/cms/s/0/dcecec18–6642–11dc-9fbb-0000779fd2ac.html.

Walsh, David C. (2007) 'Africom: Stabilizing a Region in Chaos', *Serviam* 3 (2): 6–12.

Walter, D. (1998) 'Regional Peacekeeping is not the Way', *Peacekeeping and International Relations* 27 (2). At: www.africom.mil/fetchBinary.asp?pdfID.

Wambu, O. (2007) 'Riding the Dragon: African Leadership and China's Rise', in *Under the Tree of Talking: Leadership for Change in Africa*, London: Counterpoint.

Ward, W. (2008a). Testimony before the Armed Services Committee, U.S. House of Representatives. At: http://armedservices.house.gov/pdfs/FC031308/Ward_Testimony 031308.pdf.

Ward, W. (2008b). 'United States Africa Command: Partnering for Security and Stability'. At: www.africom.mil/getArticle.asp?art=2143.

Weiss, T.G. (2004) 'The Sunset of Humanitarian Intervention? The Responsibility to Protect in a Unipolar Era', *Security Dialogue* 35 (2): 135–53.

Whelan, T. (2007a) Testimony Before the US Senate Foreign Relations Committee, Subcommittee on African Affairs, Washington, DC, 1 August. At: www.loc.gov (accessed 6 August 2007).

Whelan, T. (2007b) Testimony before the Subcommittee on Africa and Global Health, Committee on Foreign Affairs, US House of Representatives, 2 August. At: http://foreignaffairs.house.gov/110/whe080207.htm.

White House (2002) 'National Security Strategy of the United States of America', 17 September.

White House, Office of the Press Secretary (2007) 'President Bush Creates a Department of Defense Unified Combatant Command for Africa', 6 February. At: www.whitehouse.gov/news/releases/2007/02/20070206–3.html.

Whitlock, Craig (2007) 'North Africa Reluctant to Host U.S. Command', *Washington Post*, 24 June. At: www.washingtonpost.com (accessed 24 June 2007).

Whitney W.S. (2008) 'Obama's Three Objectives for Continent', online guest column, www.allafrica.com.

Willett, S. (2005) 'New Barbarians at the Gate: Losing the Liberal Peace in Africa', *Review of African Political Economy* 106: 569–70.

William, R. (2004) 'The Roots of Sectarian Violence, and Its Cure', in Rotberg, Robert I. (ed.), *Crafting the New Nigeria: Confronting the Challenges*, Boulder, CO: Lynne Rienner.

Wilson, J. Ernest. III (2008) 'Hard Power, Soft Power, Smart Power', *The Annals of the American Academy of Political and Social Science* 616 (1): 110–24.

de Witte, Ludo (2000) *L'Assassinat de Lumumba*, Paris: Karthala.

World Bank (2007a) 'World Development Report 2008: Agriculture for Development'. At: http://siteresources.worldbank.org/INTWDR2008/Resources/2795087–1192112387976/WDR08_24_SWDI.pdf .

World Bank (2007b) 'China Quick Facts'. At: http://web.worldbank.org/WBSITE/EXTERNAL/COUNTRIES/EASTASIAPACIFICEXT/CHINAEXTN/0,,contentMDK:20680895~menuPK:318976~pagePK:1497618~piPK:217854~theSitePK:318950,00.html.

World Bank (2008) 'Ten things Worth Knowing about the World Bank in India'. At: www.worldbank.org.in/WBSITE/EXTERNAL/COUNTRIES/SOUTHASIAEXT/INDIAEXTN/0,,contentMDK:20158985~menuPK:295589~pagePK:1497618~piPK:217854~theSitePK:295584,00.html.

World Food Programme (n.d.) 'WFP Donor's Index'. At: www.wfp.org/appeals/Wfp_donors/index.asp?section=3&sub_section=4.

de Young, Karen (2008) 'U.S. Africa Command Trims Its Aspirations', *Washington Post*, 1 June: 1. At: www.washingtonpost.com (accessed 20 June 2008).

Youngs, R. (2007) 'Fusing Security and Development: Just another Euro-platitude?' FRIDE Working Paper 43.

Zakaria, F. (1999) 'The Empire Strikes Out', *New York Times*, 18 April: 99.

Index

eBooks – at www.eBookstore.tandf.co.uk

A library at your fingertips!

eBooks are electronic versions of printed books. You can store them on your PC/laptop or browse them online.

They have advantages for anyone needing rapid access to a wide variety of published, copyright information.

eBooks can help your research by enabling you to bookmark chapters, annotate text and use instant searches to find specific words or phrases. Several eBook files would fit on even a small laptop or PDA.

NEW: Save money by eSubscribing: cheap, online access to any eBook for as long as you need it.

Annual subscription packages

We now offer special low-cost bulk subscriptions to packages of eBooks in certain subject areas. These are available to libraries or to individuals.

For more information please contact webmaster.ebooks@tandf.co.uk

We're continually developing the eBook concept, so keep up to date by visiting the website.

www.eBookstore.tandf.co.uk

Printed by Publishers' Graphics Kentucky